The Guide to FRANCHISING

5th Edition

To Sue

with best wishes for a long happy and healthy career. You have been a valued member of our team and we are sorry you are leaving us

31.7.98

Martin Mendelsohn

CASSELL

TO PHYLLIS, PAUL and DAVID

Cassell

Villiers House	387 Park Avenue South
41/47 Strand	New York, NY 10016-8810
London WC2N 5JE	USA

First published 1970

Fifth edition 1992
This paperback edition first published 1993, reprinted 1994
Previous editions published by Pergamon Press

British Library Cataloguing-in-Publication Data
A catalogue record for this book is available from the British Library.

ISBN 0-304-32814-6

Typeset by Fakenham Photosetting Limited, Fakenham, Norfolk

Printed in Great Britain by Redwood Books, Trowbridge, Wiltshire

Contents

Foreword

It has been almost twenty-two years since the first edition of this book was published. This latest edition is a most welcome and valuable addition to the bibliography on franchising currently available in the United Kingdom. The author, Martin Mendelsohn, is well known in franchising not only in the United Kingdom but also abroad. The importance of this book should not be underestimated in that it is of value to those involved in franchising not only in the UK, but also overseas, because many of the principles enunciated have equal application and value to those in franchising elsewhere. Business format franchising as a marketing method has gained increasing currency throughout the countries where free enterprise is practised. Indeed, I am conscious of the fact that the newly emerging free economies of Eastern Europe are also expressing a keen and healthy interest in franchising as an efficient and controlled way in which they can develop their marketing and distribution networks.

As boundaries become more flexible in economic and marketing terms, so international franchising becomes increasingly important. It is for this reason that the latest edition contains case studies of international franchisors.

The *Guide to Franchising* is now well established and continues to be an authoritative book on the subject for all who have an interest in business format franchising. The author has a wealth of experience and knowledge on the subject and the reader is given the benefit of such experience and knowledge with practical examples.

I can strongly recommend this new edition to business people, their professional advisers, and to students of franchising. Martin Mendelsohn is to be congratulated on keeping this important work up to date.

DEREK EZRA
PRESIDENT, BRITISH FRANCHISE ASSOCIATION

Introduction

The first edition of this book was written in 1969 and published in 1970; it comprised only 84 pages of text. It is interesting to look back at some of the features dealt with in that edition for their relevance today.

The case for pilot operations was clearly stated:

> It is essential for the franchisor to set up his own operation, invest his own money in it and test it thoroughly in practice. It may be necessary and advisable for him to test the operation in a number of different locations so that the widest possible experience under varying conditions can be obtained before a franchise is sold.

There were four case studies: Budget Rent-a-Car; Five Minute Car Wash; Wimpy; and Dyno-Rod. Budget is also featured in this edition, Wimpy still operates in the table service format with a few counter service format restaurants remaining; Dyno-Rod now has a Dyno-stable of franchises. Only Five Minute Car Wash has not survived.

There was a plea for the establishment of a trade organization:

> There is a clear need in the UK for a trade organisation to be set up by the franchise companies. ... This organisation is what is needed in the UK to help raise standards of franchising and to afford protection to the public. In addition to protection for the public such an organisation can provide a very valuable information service for them. In addition, it will enable the industry to speak with one authoritative voice on all matters concerning the interests of the industry. Franchising in the UK is, on the

whole, developing along the right lines. If the industry will properly organise itself it will undoubtedly make rapid strides toward achieving respectability in the eyes of the public.

By the time the fourth edition was published in 1985 the text had grown to 211 pages followed by 102 pages of Appendices. Franchising has developed so considerably over the last 21 years since that first edition and the 27 years in which I have been involved with it that it is not surprising to see this development reflected by the growth in size of the text.

This edition has involved a complete review of the work: some features have been eliminated and some new chapters added; every chapter has been substantially rewritten and much new material introduced. Some of the material has been developed from articles which first appeared in *Franchise World* and some has been developed from the work which I have done in preparing for the many lectures which I give and seminars in which I participate in many parts of the world.

Chapter 6 uses as its foundation the series of articles which I prepared with David Achison for *Franchise World* and which were brought together into the booklet *How to Franchise Your Business*.

I have in the past had the pleasure of meeting a number of franchisors and franchisees who have expressed their thanks for the guidance which they obtained from previous editions of this book. I hope that this edition will prove to be useful, not only to those who wish to learn about franchising for the first time, but also to those who are already involved in whatever capacity. The book is based upon my practical experience in a number of roles in franchising over the last 27 years and there is little in it that cannot be backed by actual events.

There are many to whom I must extend my thanks for their assistance; to those who gave their time to enable me to prepare the case studies. In most cases the time made available was quite considerable. I particularly thank James Watson and Gill Turner of Apollo; Mike Moyle and Bob Taylor of Autela; Virginia Stourton of Colour Counsellors; Ian Johnson of Fastframe; Rodney Deslandes of Hometune; Derek Mottershead of Prontaprint; Richard Sneed and Tim Johnson of Burger King; Tony Alexander and Neil Summerville of Budget; Bob Rosenberg (who first introduced franchising and me to each other); and Peter Harwood of Dunkin' Donuts and Michael McGhee of ServiceMaster.

Brian Smart, the Director of the BFA, was most helpful in giving of his time to assist with the information relating to the BFA, as was Bob Riding in relation to the Franchise Consultants' Association. My thanks go to Michael Power for the information which forms the basis for Appendix A, and to my wife Phyllis who assisted me greatly in the tedious work of detail for which I am grateful. I am also greatly indebted to my secretary Eva Whitehead and to Angela Hensley for her word processing skills.

Lastly and certainly not least, my thanks are due to Derek Ezra for the honour that he has bestowed upon me by the foreword which he has so kindly and graciously contributed to this edition. It is not widely known that Derek, who is the President of the British Franchise Association, was a powerful influence in developing the interest which has been taken in franchising by the City University Business School and other academic institutions in England.

Martin Mendelsohn

Chapter 1

The meaning of 'franchise' and 'franchising'

Franchising as a legal or marketing concept is not new. Nevertheless, it is a concept which remains misunderstood by many. Franchising is not an industry; it is a method of marketing goods and services which knows almost no boundaries in terms of business categories. Franchising has proved over the last 15 or so years in the UK as well as in the rest of the developed world and in many developing countries, even through periods of economic slump, that it is a viable method of distributing goods and services which can have a positive influence on economic development. The advances made by the membership of the British Franchise Association in the 13 years of its existence are quite impressive (Chapter 7). There has been a steady increase in interest from many business sectors within the last 5 years which is gaining in momentum resulting in a rapidly expanding use of this marketing method.

This interest has resulted in large UK companies acquiring established franchise businesses. The acquisition by Grand Metropolitan plc of the Burger King Corporation with 6330 worldwide outlets quickly followed by its acquisition of the UK Wimpy franchise network demonstrates a recognition by leading companies of the strength of franchised businesses. This was followed by the acquisition by Allied Lyons of the US franchise companies Dunkin' Donuts Inc. and Mister Donut with a combined number of well over 2500 outlets worldwide.

The history of franchising is discussed in Chapter 2 from which it will be seen that franchising has evolved out of a number of business transactions, methods, and practices which have been common and popularly known for many years. Among the basic features of these business transactions, methods and practices are to be found the following.

1. The ownership by one person of a trademark, service mark, an idea, a secret process, a patent, or a specialized piece of equipment and the goodwill and know-how associated with it.
2. The grant of a licence by that person to another permitting the exploitation of such trademark, service mark, idea, process, patent or equipment and the goodwill and know-how associated with it.
3. The inclusion in the agreement granting the licence of regulations and controls relating to the operation of the business in the conduct of which the licensee exploits his rights.
4. The payment by the licensee of a royalty or some other consideration in the nature of a continuing fee for the rights which are obtained and for any services with which the licensor will provide the licensee.

These transactions are usually referred to as licensing arrangements and their features, as will be seen, among others, are also found in franchise transactions.

How then did franchising develop into what it is now? To put franchising into its proper perspective it is helpful to consider these well-known business arrangements which have been with us for so many years and then to compare franchising with them. It is evident, with the benefit of hindsight, that franchising has grown or, one may say, evolved as a consequence of the natural development of those arrangements. If this basic point is understood at this stage it will be considerably easier properly to understand the meaning of franchising.

One of the most common of these licensing arrangements arises out of the invention of some new machinery. The inventor will wish to ensure that he enjoys the fruits of his invention to the full and will, as a first step, secure his exclusive rights by obtaining a patent. He may not have the financial resources or the knowledge to achieve the maximum nationwide or, indeed, worldwide exploitation which his invention merits. He may overcome this problem by entering into agreements with others who do have the financial resources and the business acumen to take the best possible advantage of the invention. He will therefore enter into an agreement granting a licence to the other party permitting the manufacture, sale or perhaps merely the right to use the invention in return for a capital sum, a royalty or both. This arrangement makes the maximum use of the inventor's skills and know-how, on the one hand, and the financial resources, manufacturing, marketing and other abilities of the licensee, on the other hand.

Another of these arrangements arises out of the development of a trademark in relation to certain goods. The owner of the trademark, for reasons similar to those which motivate the inventor with his patent, will grant a right to others permitting them to manufacture the goods which are identified by the trademark. The technical name of the agreement employed in such a case is a 'registered user agreement', or, if the trademark is not registered, a 'licence'. A trademark user agreement contains provisions which regulate the standards to be observed in relation to manufacture, preparation, presentation, marketing, sale, and the quality of the goods. These provisions are necessary to preserve the standards of quality and the reputation associated with the trademark. So many of the elements of a franchise transaction are found in such an agreement that many franchise agreements incorporate its elements and registered user agreements are commonly found where the franchisor has registered a trademark or service mark.

On a slightly different level are those now very common arrangements whereby the use of a famous name in entertainment, sports, or even a cartoon strip character is licensed. This type of arrangement is referred to as 'character merchandising'. In each of these cases, by entering into licence agreements the owners of the names and their licensees are both obtaining benefits which would otherwise not be available to either.

There are other kinds of transaction designed to benefit licensor and licensee which are worthy of mention: the appointment of a dealer by a motor-car manufacturer (this frequently is a business format franchise which is explained below); the appointment of exclusive sales distributors; the licensing of the use of the name of a large oil company on a garage. In the latter case everyone is familiar with the Shell, Esso or BP station, but no one would think that all garages bearing an oil company's name are necessarily owned and operated by that company.

In many cases transactions involving licensing or other forms of grant of rights are commonly called franchises by business people.

What, then, is new? First, there is the wider use of the name 'franchising' to describe generically 'licence-type' transactions. Secondly, there is the 'business format' concept whereby a person develops a complete system for the setting up and licensing of a business under an identified brand which may be a trademark, service mark or trade name and licences (or franchises) others to trade utilizing the particular system and the branding associated with it.

Clearly, there are many types of transactions entered into, all described as a 'franchise', each having a different application. The differences will be apparent after the main type of franchise has been defined. To avoid confusion the main type of franchise (i.e. the total business concept) will be referred to as a 'business format' franchise, which is the name by which it is commonly known. It is the business format franchise which has been responsible for the rapid escalation in the franchised marketing method and for the wider public knowledge of its existence.

The business format franchise involves the exploitation, not merely of goods identified by a trademark or services identified by a service mark, but the preparation of the 'blueprint' of a successful way of carrying on a business in all its aspects. The blueprint must have been so carefully prepared as to minimize the risks inherent in opening any new business. Examples of the necessary preparations are given below.

- Criteria will be established by which the suitability of sites available for the positioning of the business will be judged. In the case of a mobile franchise (e.g. Service Master, Hometune), criteria will be established by reference to the availability of potential customers within a given marketing area.
- Facilities will have been established so that franchisees can be trained in the system and business methods which the franchisor has developed.
- The training provided will include, as may be appropriate, any special methods of manufacture, or processes to be applied to goods, or (as with fast food operations) secret recipes, methods of preparation and the manner of providing services.
- Training will also be provided in the methods of marketing and merchandising which are calculated to exploit the merits of the business to the full and, one hopes, to avoid the pitfalls.
- Following training, assistance will be given in getting the business ready to open for trading.
- The right to use the description (i.e. the brand image, which may include a trademark or service mark) by which the business is to be distinguished from other similar competing businesses will be granted while at the same time the business is recognized by the consumer as a part of the larger organization which comprises him and his fellow franchisees. Indeed it could be said that franchising comprises, for the customer, the benefits of a multiple network in multiple ownership resulting in the customer dealing with the owner rather than the manager of the business.
- In order that the person who is granting the licence can be sure that the standards associated with the branding and the system can be maintained there will need to be restrictions and controls introduced into the relationship which will be established.

The seller of the blueprint (the franchisor) will have prepared and smoothed the way for a person (the franchisee), who has probably never owned or operated a business before, to open up a business of his own, not only with a predetermined and established format, but with the backing of an organization which would not otherwise be available to him at a price he could afford, i.e. the backing of an organization characteristic of the head office of a large company without many of the disadvantages. For the acquisition of the franchise and the continuing services which the franchisee will obtain (see below) there will, of course, be a fee payable.

What we have then is something fairly close to the four basic features mentioned on p. 2.

1. The ownership by one person (the franchisor) of a trademark, service mark, trade name, an idea, a secret process, or a piece of equipment and the goodwill and know-how associated with it.
2. The grant of a licence (franchise) by the franchisor to another (the franchisee) permitting the exploitation of such trademark, service mark, trade name, idea, process, or equipment and the goodwill and know-how associated with it.
3. The inclusion in the licence (franchise) agreement of regulations and controls relating to the operation of the business in which the franchisee exploits the rights granted.
4. The payment by the franchisee of a fee or other consideration for the rights which are obtained and the services which the franchisor will continue to provide to the franchisee.

But, in addition and fundamentally, there will always be a continuing relationship which should provide the franchisee with full support of a comprehensive range of expert knowledge in the operation of his business in the form of the 'head office organization' of the franchisor.

There have been many attempts at a definition of a franchise in the USA, the home of modern franchising. Most of them seek to provide a concise expression of the elements of the transaction, which has the effect of omitting much which should be included. While this book does not seek to lay down a concise definition, the definitions which have been established for various purposes must be considered. It is hoped that this book will provide a basic commercial understanding which will enable the reader to put these formal definitions into perspective.

Before reviewing the definitions which have been prepared for legal purposes we shall examine the definitions which are used by the International Franchise Association (IFA), the US franchisors' association and the British Franchise Association (BFA).

First we shall consider the IFA definition.

A franchise operation is a contractual relationship between the franchisor and franchisee in which the franchisor offers or is obliged to maintain a continuing interest in the business of the franchisee in such areas as know-how and training; wherein the franchisee operates under.a common trade name, format and/or procedure owned or controlled by the franchisor, and in which the franchisee has or will make a substantial capital investment in his business from his own resources.

This definition is concise and quite comprehensive, yet at the same time it leaves many questions unanswered and omits features which should be included. For example, it refers to the franchisee making an investment in his own business, yet nowhere does it say that the franchisee must own his business. This point, which is a fundamental feature of a franchise, is implied rather than asserted. Another fundamental feature which is omitted is the payment of fees or other consideration by franchisee to franchisor. Excellent as the definition is, it will be far better understood by those who already have a working knowledge of the underlying commercial rationale of franchising; the definition is not for those who seek an underlying understanding.

We now examine the elements of the IFA definition.

1.   A franchise operation is a contractual relationship . . .

It should clearly be established at the outset that the franchise relationship is based upon a contract. It is no different from any other formal contract in that the terms upon which the contract is made are expressed in the contract. Perhaps it is just that bit more important that a franchise contract contains each and every term which has been agreed, for it is a contract with which the parties are going to have to live for a very long while. Moreover, in most cases it is going to be the sole provider of bread and butter (and hopefully a little jam) to the franchisee, as well as, in many cases, enabling the franchisee to pursue a dream, so that any material omission may have an effect on the whole course of his life.

2.   . . . the franchisor offers or is obliged to maintain a continuing interest in the business of the franchisee in such areas as know-how and training . . .

Of course the franchisor must maintain a continuing interest in the franchisee's business, but first, at least, get the business started. This is the first point which is omitted from the definition. It is the franchisor's obligation to introduce the franchisee to and initiate him in the business which he will be acquiring. It is also the franchisor's obligation to decide responsibly whether the prospective franchisee is in fact the right sort of person for that particular type of franchise. Nothing could be more disastrous for both parties than to place a square peg in a round hole. It is the franchisor's responsibility by pre-opening training to introduce the franchisee to all the relevant areas of the franchisor's know-how which he requires for the satisfactory establishment, conduct and operation of the business.

Know-how is one of those meaningless all-embracing terms, until one defines what is intended to be included in the expression. It will, of course, differ from case to case. Know-how for one fast food operation will differ from another—between hamburgers and pizza, for example. Even the know-how in one hamburger operation can differ from that employed in another.

Before the franchisee opens for business this vital part of the blueprint which he is being sold must be given to him. Know-how in franchising, broadly speaking, covers merchandising as applied to the particular operation, application of the principles of business management appropriate to the nature and type of business, operational methods, accounting procedures, business methods, the franchisor's secret and confidential systems, methods, and in some cases formulae. The franchisee must be fully trained in all these aspects before he is let loose in his own business, and when he is let loose he should have any necessary on-the-spot support to assist him in successfully opening the business.

Having reached this stage, the franchisee should have a full grasp of know-how applicable to that particular business; the franchisor should continue to maintain these services on a regular and updated basis coupled with the provision of field support to assist the franchisee through any difficulties which he encounters and promotional assistance to help maximize the beneficial exposure of the operation to the public to the mutual advantage of franchisor and franchisee.

3. ... wherein the franchisee operates under a common trade name, format and/or procedure owned or controlled by the franchisor ...

This brings us to the crux of the matter; it relates to the central feature around which the blueprint is developed. In all franchises there is a common trademark, service mark or trade name, the common format is the identical nature of the business carried on by all franchisees wherever they are. Included in this format are those features which make each operational unit run by franchisees appear to be part of the same network. In a premises-based franchise one would expect to find the identical appearance of each unit by the presentation of common shop front, shop signs, layouts, decor, colour scheme, equipment, fixtures and fittings. If the franchise is in the service sector and the operational unit is essentially an office there will not be a shop front but the other elements are likely to be found. In a van-based franchise (i.e. where the franchisee travels to customers) one would expect to find an identical vehicle colour and livery as well as the common fitting out of each vehicle with the necessary tools of the trade or, if product sales are involved, shelving and displays of the products. The common procedure refers to the operational methods of conducting the business that is the subject of the franchise which has been developed by the franchisor.

This part of the definition refers to those matters which constitute the basic operation, and by which the public clearly identifies the individual operation as being part of a larger group of similar operations while, of course, the operation and all its counterparts have the advantage of being run on a day-to-day basis by the owner and not by a manager.

The fact that the trade name, format and the procedure are owned by the franchisor and used by all franchisees in common with each other is what makes an element of control over the franchisees' business essential. Whatever the degree of control which is exercised by a franchisor over any franchisee it should not be looked at by that individual merely as a restriction on his ability to run his business as he thinks fit. The franchisee in reality cannot enjoy the freedom which a non-franchisee has. The franchisee in taking up a franchised business is acquiring a right to establish a business using someone else's name and system and he must accept that of necessity in order to preserve the uniformity, uniqueness and effectiveness of the business he must run his business within the framework established by the franchisor. Anyone who does not wish to do so or is not prepared to accept such a discipline should not contemplate becoming a franchisee.

A franchisee must appreciate that the franchisor and all franchisees (including himself) are dependent upon each other for success. A customer lost at one outlet can also be a customer lost to all the others. In effect, the franchisor and all the franchisees are presenting a combined operation to the consumer. As a satisfied customer whose loyalty has been gained by good quality products and/or good service moves about the country he will patronize an operation apparently part of the group which has looked after him well before, rather than that of a competitor. The disciplines and the controls which go with them are an essential part of the mechanism by which success is achieved.

4. ... and in which the franchisee has or will have a substantial capital investment in his business from his own resources.

The franchisee owns his franchised business and all the assets which are employed in or about the conduct of that business. He must also have the right to sell the equity which he has developed in the business. At this point it is well to clarify an issue which raises much confusion, namely the question of 'goodwill'. There are two types of goodwill involved in franchising.

First, there is the goodwill which attaches to the branding, i.e. the trademark, the service mark and/or the trade name and the system. Since the branding and the system belong to the franchisor the goodwill generated by the use of the branding and system accrues to the benefit of the franchisor. In the franchise agreement (as will be seen in Chapter 12) the franchisor will grant the right to the franchisee to trade using the franchisor's branding and system and to benefit from the goodwill associated with them. Franchisees will enter the franchise system and eventually leave, and when they leave, for whatever reason, they lose the right to continue to use the branding, the system and to benefit from the goodwill.

How a franchisee leaves the system is very relevant for the consideration of the other type of goodwill. This goodwill is that which arises for accounting purposes when a sale of a business takes place at a price which exceeds the value of its net assets. The excess is called goodwill. If a franchisee sells the franchised business (subject to the controls normally imposed in a franchise agreement; Chapter 12) for a sum in excess of the value of its net assets, that excess belongs to the franchisee. If that were described as the value of the franchisee's equity in his own business, which is what it is, rather than goodwill there would be no confusion. This equity represents the value of the business as a going concern and the ability to build it is one of the motivating factors for franchisees.

The reference to the capital investment is not superfluous. It is important that a franchisee makes a significant capital investment from his own resources. This goes a long way in providing him with the necessary motivation. A person who has the money which he has invested at stake, and who can see that he has the opportunity to control the destiny and growth of his equity by his diligent attention to the correct operation of the business, will put everything he can into the business and not the lesser interest of a manager.

So far there has been no mention of payment. No franchisor is going to give anything away for nothing. If it appears that he is doing so this is something which should be investigated. No one is in business to make gifts of his products or services. Franchisors are no exception to this general rule. Payment is made to the franchisor in any number of ways. He may ask for a franchise fee by name. He may sell a package which has the franchise fee included in the price. He may receive a fee calculated as a percentage of the franchisee's gross receipts. Whichever way the fees are to be taken by the franchisor he will be paid both for his initial services and for the continuing service which he provides.

One other factor which must be touched upon at this stage is the problem of territorial rights, which is dealt with in more detail in Chapter 12. This is a subject on which there can be no general rule, save that franchisees will seek some assurance that where there are fixed premises the surrounding area will not be over-saturated to their detriment. Where there is a mobile franchise the question of territorial scope becomes more significant. This issue can create many problems, for some franchised operations will thrive upon a massive saturation of an urban area while others will, by their nature, require a carefully defined and protected area of operation. Apart from the business considerations there are legal implications which arise from the application of competition laws. These considerations and implications are dealt with in detail later in this book.

We now examine the BFA definition and contrast it with the IFA definition which has just been considered.

A contractual licence granted by one person (the franchisor) to another (franchisee) which:

(a)   permits or requires the franchisee to carry on during the period of the franchise a particular business under or using a specified name belonging to or associated with the franchisor;

(b)   entitles the franchisor to exercise continuing control during the period of the franchise over the manner in which the franchisee carries on the business which is the subject of the franchise;

(c)   obliges the franchisor to provide the franchisee with assistance in carrying on the business which is the subject of the franchise (in relation to the organisation of the franchisee's business, the training of staff, merchandising, management or otherwise);

(d)   requires the franchisee periodically during the period of the franchise to pay to the franchisor sums of money in consideration for the franchise or for goods or services provided by the franchisor to the franchisee; and

(e)   which is not a transaction between a holding company and its subsidiary (as defined in Section 154 of the Companies Act 1948) or between subsidiaries of the same holding company or between an individual and a company controlled by him.

Apart from paragraph (e), which clearly has a technical basis, and is calculated to exclude 'in-house' arrangements, the definition embodies much of the IFA definition which has been analysed above. The following points of comparison will be of interest.

The definition:
(i)   confirms the contractual nature of the relationship;
(ii)   confirms that there is a right or licence granted to the franchisee to carry on the business. The definition however does not:
   (a) provide that the franchisee must own his own business;
   (b) state that the franchisee must provide for his investment out of his own resources; and
   (c) confirm that the franchisor will be obliged to provide initial training;
(iii)   deals with the question of control by the franchisor over the manner in which the franchisee carries on the business;
(iv)   confirms the obligation of the franchisor to provide the continuing assistance which is so essential; and
(v)   deals with the question of the payment of franchise fees.

Like all definitions, it has been coined for a particular purpose, and no doubt it was the intention of the BFA to frame its definition on such a basis that membership will be available to companies whose franchise, while not strictly a 'business format' franchise, is still a franchise of a more limited nature (see Chapter 5 for a discussion on other types of franchise). Membership of the BFA carries with it responsibilities, and it is clearly in its interests and in the interest of members of the public that, so long as the business to be conducted is what may be reasonably described as a franchise within the generic sense in which the term is understood in business circles, such a franchisor should have the ability to join the BFA. The BFA is dealt with in detail in Chapter 17.

It is significant that the definition omits reference to the initial training in setting up the business, and it is also significant that the definition omits the requirement that the franchisee should have made a substantial capital investment out of his own resources in the business he would operate. The parallels between the two definitions are quite clear, and from these definitions and this discussion emerge the following basic features which must be present in every 'business format' franchise.

1. A franchise relationship is founded upon a contract which should contain all the terms agreed upon.
2. The franchisor must first develop a successful business format (the system) which is identified with a brand name which may be a trademark, service mark and/or trade name.
3. The franchisor must initiate and train the franchisee in all aspects of the system prior to the opening of the business so that the franchisee is equipped to run the business effectively and successfully and assist in the opening.
4. After the business is opened the franchisor must maintain a continuing business relationship with the franchise in the course of which it provides the franchisee with support in all aspects of the operation of the business.
5. The franchisee is permitted under the control of the franchisor to operate under the branding (trademark, service mark, trade name) format the business systems developed and owned by the franchisor and to benefit from the goodwill associated therewith.
6. The franchisee must make a substantial capital investment from his own resources.
7. The franchisee must own his business.
8. The franchisee will pay the franchisor in one way or another for the rights which he acquires and for the continuing services with which he will be provided.

Having looked in outline at the commercial arrangement which lies behind the franchise method of marketing and the definitions used by two major franchise associations we now examine the approach adopted by those who have established legal definitions of franchising. Before doing so it is important to understand that legal definitions do not seek to explain, they seek to establish a method of identifying a particular business practice with which it is proposed to deal in the legislation in which the definition appears. There are four legal definitions which will be considered.

First there is a definition of franchising in Section 75 of the Financial Services Act 1986:

> franchise arrangements, that is to say, arrangements under which a person earns profits or income by exploiting a right conferred by the arrangements to use a trade name or design or other intellectual property or the goodwill attached to it ...

This definition is scarcely helpful for understanding and is flawed: what is intended to be meant by income which is earned as distinct from profits, and why the use of 'or' when detailing the intellectual property element and goodwill when 'and' would be more appropriate? Since the definition of franchise arrangements is intended to exclude them from the definition of 'a collective investment scheme' which clearly does not include franchising, the worthlessness of the definition, to put it at its most charitable, for the purpose of the discussion is clear.

The next definition is that which appears in the Block Exemption Regulation for Franchise Agreements, which was adopted by the European Commission on 30 November 1988. This Regulation provides exemption from the competition laws of the European Community for those agreements which comply with its terms. The scope and effect of the Regulation is explained in Chapter 12. The Regulation defines a franchise in the following terms:

> 'franchise' means a package of industrial or intellectual property rights relating to trademarks, tradenames, shop signs, utility models, designs, copyrights, know-how or patents, to be exploited for the resale of goods or the provision of services to end users.

This definition is limited and technical but clearly recognizes the role of branding and know-how (the system). However, it is confined to franchises where the franchisee is selling goods or providing services to an end user (i.e. the ultimate consumer). The definition is deliberately limited since the European Commission made it plain in the preamble to the Regulation that industrial franchises (i.e. those which concern the manufacturing of goods) are not intended to be governed by the Regulation since they consist of manufacturing licences based upon patents and/or technical know-how, combined with trademark licences. The definition also excludes franchises involving the sale of goods at wholesale level since the Commission lacked experience of such franchises without which it did not feel able to legislate.

The Commission definition does not stop at the treatment of the word 'franchise'; it goes on to define a 'franchise agreement' and it is in this definition that many of the business features, which we have discussed, emerge.

The expression 'franchise agreement' means an agreement whereby one undertaking, the franchisor, grants the other, the franchisee, in exchange for direct or indirect financial consideration, the right to exploit a franchise for the purposes of marketing specified types of goods and/or services; it includes at least obligations relating to:

- the use of a common name or shop sign and a uniform presentation of contact premises and/or means of transport
- the communication by the franchisor to the franchisee of know how
- the continuing provision by the franchisor to the franchisee of commercial or technical assistance during the life of the agreement.

Some of the words which are contained in this definition are themselves defined:

'contact premises' means the premises used for the exploitation of the franchise or, when the franchise is exploited outside those premises, the base from which the franchisee operates the means of transport used for the exploitation of the franchise (contract means of transport).
'know-how' means a package of non-patented practical information resulting from experience and testing by the franchisor which is secret, substantial and identified.

The expressions 'secret', 'substantial' and 'identified' are also defined but for the purpose of this discussion they are not relevant. They are discussed in Chapter 12. Chapter 12 also contains a definition of the expression 'master franchise agreement'.

These two definitions of 'franchise' and 'franchise agreement' should for our purpose be read together. They blend the definitions of what franchising is with some of the techniques which are used in structuring franchise arrangements. However, if we review these definitions against the basic features listed on p. 11 we find the following elements present.

1. There must be a contract (see definition of franchise agreement).
2. There must be a system developed (see definition of know-how).
3. There must be training (i.e. communication of know-how).
4. There must be continuing support (i.e. the continuing provision of services).
5. There must be the grant of the right to operate the business using the system and branding (i.e. one party grants to the other the right to exploit a franchise and 'the use of a common name or shop sign').

6, 7.   These are barely implied in the definition but since the Regulation is conditional upon the franchisee indicating its status as an independent undertaking it seems the Commission takes these features for granted. Certainly the status of a franchisee as an independent business is recognized in the preamble to the Regulation.

8.   There must be payment for the rights (i.e. 'in exchange for direct or indirect financial consideration').

As well as providing a legal definition for the purposes of the Regulation it will be seen that the Commission has also incorporated a number of the commercial features which form part of the overall description of a franchise as well as the techniques for implementing a franchise programme which are discussed in this book.

The final definitions to which reference should be made are those which are to be found in the USA, where there is much legislation in which franchising is defined. There are two definitions to which reference will be made; the first is that which appears in the state of California legislation, which was the first franchise legislation when introduced in 1970.

'Franchise' means a contract or agreement, either express or implied, whether oral or written, between two or more persons by which:

(1)   a franchisee is granted the right to engage in the business of offering, selling or distributing goods or services under a marketing plan or system prescribed in substantial part by a franchisor;

(2)   the operation of the franchisee's business pursuant to such plan or system is substantially associated with the franchisor's trademark, service mark, trade name, logo type, advertising or other commercial symbol designating the franchisor or its affiliate; and

(3)   the franchisee is required to pay, directly or indirectly, a franchise fee.

The definition is extended to include contents involving petroleum dealers and there are also definitions of franchisor, franchisee and franchise fee.

This definition of 'franchise' is less extensive than the European Commission's definition and is typical of those which have been adopted in statutes in the USA which affect franchising.

The second US definition at which we shall look is that which appears in the Federal Trade Commission Franchise Rule. This rule was introduced in 1979 and defines franchise as:

(a)   The term 'franchise' means any continuing commercial relationship created by any arrangement or arrangements whereby:

(1) (i)(A) A person (hereinafter 'franchisee') offers, sells, or distributes to any person other than a 'franchisor' (as hereinafter defined) goods, commodities, or services which are:

(1) identified by a trademark, service mark, trade name, advertising or other commercial symbol designating another person (hereinafter 'franchisor'); or

(2) indirectly or directly required or advised to meet the quality standards prescribed by another person (hereinafter 'franchisor') where the franchisee operates under a name using the trademark, service mark, trade name, advertising or other commercial symbol designating the franchisor; and

(B) (1) The franchisor exerts or has authority to exert a significant degree of control over the franchisee's method of operation, including but not limited to the franchisee's business organisation, promotional activities management, marketing plan or business affairs; or

(2) The franchisor gives significant assistance to the franchisee in the latter's method of operation, including, but not limited to, the franchisee's business organisation, management, marketing plan, promotional activities or business affairs; provided however that assistance in the franchisee's promotional activities shall not, in the absence of assistance in other areas of the franchisee's method of operation constitute significant assistance; or

(ii)(A) A person (hereinafter 'franchisee') offers sells or distributes to any person other than a 'franchisor' (as hereinafter defined) goods, commodities or services which are:

(1) Supplied by another person (hereinafter 'franchisor') or

(2) Supplied by a third person (e.g. supplier) with whom the franchisee is directly or indirectly advised to do business by another person (hereinafter 'franchisor') where such person is affiliated with the franchisor; and

(B) The franchisor:

(1) Secures for the franchisee retail outlets or accounts for said goods, commodities or services; or

(2) Secures for the franchisee locations or sites for vending machines, rack displays, or any other product sales display used by the franchisee in the offering, sale, or distribution of such goods, commodities or services; or

(3) Provides to the franchisee the services of a person able to secure the retail outlets, accounts, sites or locations referred to in paragraph (a)(1)(ii)(B)(1) and (2) above; and

(2) The franchisee is required as a condition of obtaining or commencing

the franchise operation to make a payment or a commitment to pay to the franchisor or to a person affiliated with the franchisor.

The terms 'franchisor' and 'franchisee' are broadly defined:

The term franchisor means any person who participates in a franchise relationship as a franchisor as denoted in paragraph (a) or this section [i.e. the paragraph defining 'franchisor'].

The term franchisee means any person (1) who participates in a franchise relationship as a franchisee as denoted in paragraph (a) of this section or (2) to whom an interest in a franchise is sold.

There are exceptions which briefly include:

- 'fractional franchises' where the franchisee has another related business and the franchised business does not represent more than 20% of the dollar sales volume of the franchisee;
- the total of payments to the franchisor or person affiliated to the franchisor are less than US$500 during the first 6 months of operations;
- employment relationship;
- partnership relationship;
- membership of a bona fide co-operative association; or
- a bare trademark licence.

It will be appreciated that while the first part of the definition relates to business format and product distribution franchises the second part relates to the wider business opportunities field. Good examples of the sort of opportunities which the definition includes are rack jobbing and vending machine rounds. Some of these opportunities can be structured as business format franchises.

The US definitions are limited to the 'nuts and bolts' and do not add to these basic elements, what might be described as the methods of implementing a franchise in practice which the commercial and European definitions all contain.

The basic elements in these US definitions include many of the eight features listed above.

1. There must be a contract (but it need not be in writing to be caught by the US statutes).
2. There must be a system.
3. There must be a branding, i.e. trademark, service mark, trade name, etc.

4. There must be a grant of rights.
5. There must be payment of money.

How all the elements are combined together and the techniques which are employed to enable a franchise to be established and operated will be discussed in the chapters which follow.

Chapter 2

The history and development of franchising

EARLY HISTORY

It is possible to search through history and find examples of trading practices which have a resemblance to franchising. The guild system which was introduced in the City of London in the twelfth century is one such example. Many quote the pub-tied house system as an example of franchising although it is merely an exclusive purchasing arrangement lacking many of the features of a franchise. In strict legal terms the word 'franchise' means a grant of rights from the crown and in other countries, e.g. the USA and Australia, it has been held by the courts that the word 'franchise' means a grant by a governmental authority. To this day there exist in the UK ancient franchises to hold fairs, markets and to provide ferries, bridges and fords across rivers and streams.

The technique of franchising with which this book is concerned is generally thought to have started in the USA when, following the Civil War, the Singer Sewing Machine Company established a dealer network. The Singer Company in the UK is today a full member of the British Franchise Association, thus perpetuating the link with the early days of franchising history.

Whatever claims may be made by franchising communities in various parts of the world one must credit the United States' business community with the ingenuity which has led to such a widespread use of the technique which is described in this book.

The technique of franchising did not derive from one moment of inventiveness by an imaginative individual. It evolved from the solutions developed by businessmen in response to the problems with which they were confronted in their business operations. It may be said that at the beginning of the twentieth century driving and drink (but not alcoholic) were the catalysts for franchising activity followed by a trickle of developments until the 1930s, when Howard Johnson started his famous restaurant chain in the USA, and the 1940s and 1950s, which saw the birth of so many of the modern giants of the franchising community.

CATEGORIES OF FRANCHISE

During these distinct phases different categories of franchising emerged and involved all levels in the chain from manufacturer to consumer. Thus we find franchise arrangements between:

- manufacturer and retailer;
- manufacturer and wholesaler;
- wholesaler and retailer; and (lastly but certainly not the least)
- retailer and retailer.

Each of these categories is explained in some detail in Chapter 5.

THE GROWTH OF FRANCHISING

In examining the growth of franchising one must start in the USA as not only is it the cradle of modern franchise development, but also it is the largest market-place for franchising systems and also provides the best statistics. It is undoubtedly the largest exporter of franchising systems despite the great advances which have been made in other countries, notably Canada, Japan, Australia, France, Germany and the UK. Franchising in some form exists in over 80 countries and that number will continue to grow although in many cases the number of franchise systems will be very small.

When one bears in mind that it was only in the 1950s that franchise systems began to develop in large numbers, the growth rate in the USA has been apparently impressive. According to the US Department of Commerce publication *Franchising in the Economy* which is published each year (now published by the International Franchise Association):

Franchising sales of goods and services in more than 509,000 outlets were expected to reach $640 billion in 1988 about 7 per cent higher than a year earlier and about 91 per cent over the level of sales at the start of the 1980s. Employment in franchising, including part time workers will probably reach 7.3 million by the end of 1988.

Product and trade name franchising, which typically include automobile and truck dealer petrol filling stations and soft drink bottlers, have achieved a growth in sales despite the reduction in the number of outlets. Almost the whole of the reduction is attributed to the closure of petrol filling stations. The publication shows sales of £72 billion in 1972 from 262,100 establishments compared with sales of £281 billion in 1988 from 140,820 establishments.

Business format franchising has been responsible for much of the growth of franchising in the USA since 1950. The publication shows sales of £17.9 billion in 1972 from 189,640 establishments compared with £118.8 billion in 1988 from 368,458 establishments—a rise of 6.62 times in sales and 1.94 in establishments. Although the figures which represent the position in 1988 are themselves impressive one must question whether the increases over a 16-year period fully justify the tremendous 'hype' which in the USA is attached to the growth rate of franchising. The number of business format franchisors offering their products and/or services to prospective franchisees has also been rising steadily from 909 franchisors in 1972 to 2177 franchisors in 1986.

That the numbers involved are growing is undoubted but many of the increasing number are small and there are many whose lifespan in the statistics for whatever reason is quite short. It is also probable that there are more franchisors than the figures suggest bearing in mind the difficulties in identifying and locating those who are franchising.

The impact of franchising in the USA is due in no small measure to large franchisors, those with 1000 or more units each, who dominate business format franchising, with 56 companies accounting for 48% of all sales and 49% of all establishments in 1986, the last date for which figures are available. From the author's observations it is reasonable to suggest that this same pattern exists in many countries. It is no bad thing because these giants give franchising the favourable exposure which it needs to encourage the ambitious and to maintain its progress.

Notwithstanding the great increase in volumes of sales and numbers of outlets the percentage of retail sales by franchise outlets of the total retail sales in the USA has remained remarkably constant over the last 11 years, fluctuating between 31 and 34% (Table 2.1).

According to a survey prepared for the International Franchise Association it is projected that this figure will rise to 50% by the end of the century. Franchising activity will have to penetrate retail marketing in a spectacular fashion over the next 9 years if the forecast is to become a reality.

The USA and Australia are the main countries in which government-sponsored statistics have been available but there are statistics available from other countries which vary from the professionally prepared in, for example, Canada and the UK, to best estimates made by franchise associations derived principally from information supplied by their members and obtained from other market sources. There are other surveys but many of them seem to

Table 2.1 Franchise sales as a percentage of total retail sales

Year	Franchise sales (%)
1978	32
1979	31
1980	32
1981	32
1982	33
1983	33
1984	32
1985	33
1986	34
1987	33
1988	34

draw their information in the main from other published sources (including franchise associations) rather than from independent research. The information shown in Table 2.2 appears to be the best which is available and indicates the level of franchising activities in some of the major economic markets.

Table 2.2 Franchising activities

	No. of franchises	No. of outlets	Sales (£)
Australia (1989)	230	10,303+	N/A
Austria (1988)	30	1,363	N/A
Belgium (1987)	77	4,045	2.00 bn
Canada (1987)	1000	45,000	32.31 bn
Denmark (1989)	60	500	N/A
France (1988)	675	29,698	10.00 bn
FRG (1987)	180	9,000	3.38 bn
Italy (1988)	197	11,500	2.10 bn
Japan (1988)	619	102,397	27.69 bn
Netherlands (1987)	244	8,252	3.60 bn
Norway (1988)	120	850	0.30 bn
Spain (1990)	195	20,000	N/A
Sweden (1988)	60	1,000	1.50 bn
UK (1990)	375	18,200	4.73 bn

These figures exclude sales of gasoline for automobiles and trucks, and soft drink bottles.

Comments on the UK market

It is perhaps a sobering thought for us in the UK to appreciate that Mc-Donald's and Kentucky Fried Chicken, the two largest franchise operations worldwide, have between them more outlets than the entire franchise community in the UK. Indeed it is probable that the 20–25 largest franchisors have between them more outlets than are to be found in the entire European Community—sobering perhaps but not surprising in the light of the earlier reference to the stranglehold which large franchisors have over franchising in the USA.

This potential presents opportunities for British franchisors since there is no European Community member state which can be said to be over-franchised given this perspective. So far as we in Britain are concerned we must accept that the franchisor and outlet numbers are well below our potential and that this provides opportunities to others to take up the challenge. If one applies the same proportionate exercise to Britain only in population terms then Britain will need to increase franchisor numbers by 221 and outlets by 62,729 in order to catch up with the US size of market penetration.

Despite the difficult trading conditions, the 1990 NatWest–BFA Franchise Survey revealed that in the year to 31 May 1990 the number of franchised systems in the UK increased by 28% from 295 to 379. The number of franchised units rose by 10% from 16,600 to 18,260 while sales rose by 11% from £4.73 bn to £5.24 bn. Those directly employed in franchising numbered 184,000; it will be appreciated that there will be many, working in companies who supply products and services to franchised businesses, who owe their employment to franchising. Appendix A gives a summary of the NatWest–BFA Franchise Survey results over the period from 1986 to 1990.

Elsewhere

A summary of the Australian government survey issued in May 1989 by the Bureau of Industry Economics provides a wide range of statistical information making some interesting comparisons with the US market. For example, the number of franchisors per million of population is 13.9 in Australia compared with 8.4 in the USA; and the number of outlets per million population is 671 in Australia and 1456 in the USA. Although the figures given in Table 2.2 indicate that there are 230 franchisors in Australia the survey indicates that some sources suggest that there could be as many as 600.

In Spain there was rather slow development of franchising activity but the effect on franchising of Spain's joining the European Community has been dramatic. The Spanish franchise community is now among the most significant in Europe. According to a survey by Euromarket, although franchising was rare in Switzerland up to the mid-1980s by 1988 some 200 companies were offering franchises.

The growth of franchising internationally has spread throughout all continents and regional zones with varying degrees of activity. The different levels of growth reflect business climates, availability of spending power, legal and political problems. The East–West political divide has been penetrated by franchising with Holiday Inns and Kentucky Fried Chicken in Beijing and Pizza Hut and McDonald's in Moscow; McDonald's also has a restaurant open in Budapest.

Franchising is being considered as a method of marketing goods and services by an ever increasing number of companies and is likely to grow at a considerable pace not only in the UK and the European Community but elsewhere in both the developed and undeveloped world.

Chapter 3

Why franchise your business?

There are two fundamental advantages to a businessman who decides to franchise his business. Both flow from the fact that it is a feature of franchising that the growth of the network is achieved by using the resources of the franchisees. (Note: for convenience, 'businessman' will be used throughout to refer to a business person of either sex.)

The first franchisee resource of which use is made is financial. Each franchised outlet which is opened does so with capital provided by the franchisee. It could not really be otherwise since it is the franchisee who will own the assets to be employed in that outlet. The opening of each outlet does not therefore require the provision by the franchisor of capital. This does not mean that a franchisor does not need to find capital for his business—he does (Chapter 6), but the capital requirements for his business will not extend to the cost of establishing each outlet in his network. The provision by the franchisee of the capital required to open each outlet enables the franchisor to achieve a rapid growth rate without the normal constraints imposed upon a business which has to raise capital or borrow to fund its development.

There are broader advantages available since financial institutions find it more attractive to lend where the risk is spread. Franchising helps them achieve this objective. Since each outlet opened by each franchisee to whom financial assistance is given represents a separate loan there is a spread of risk compared with lending to one business to assist it in opening a number of outlets. (The approach of banks to franchising franchisees is discussed in Chapter 7.)

The second franchisee resource of which use is made is the manpower resource which the franchisee represents. The franchisee will have responsibility for the day-to-day conduct of the business. The franchisee will provide the local controls and will operate the franchisor's system with the interest of an owner of the business. He will recruit, train, motivate and supervise his staff. He will bring his skill and whatever entrepreneurial abilities he has to bear upon his business and hopefully maximize the opportunities with which the franchisor's name and system provide him. His will be the concern of an owner and not an employed manager, and the result should be a well-run and more profitable outlet.

From these two fundamental resources flow a number of other benefits. In addition, there are benefits which flow from adopting the franchise method of marketing. These may be summarized as follows.

1. The franchisor will only require a compact organization, consisting of a few highly specialized managers in the various aspects of the business with which the organization is concerned, and their support staff.

2. The franchisor can earn a reasonable profit without becoming involved in high capital risk or in the day-to-day detail and problems which arise in the management of scattered outlets.

3. Since the franchisor is using others' resources and can by his training programmes equip them to carry on his business system, his organization has an ability to expand more rapidly on a national, and eventually on an international, basis, using a minimum of risk capital and management resources.

4. The franchisor will find it easier to exploit territorial areas which are not already within the scope of the organization as franchisees with local interests and knowledge can be obtained.

5. The introduction of a franchisee to an existing branch in a multiple chain can convert a loss-making, or marginally profitable, outlet into a profitable outlet, thus enabling a business presence to be maintained when otherwise it might have to be closed down. This outcome is also achieved by removing from the profit and loss account for the outlet such expense items as the cost of employment of the manager and staff, including the cost of holiday and sickness staff cover, as well as the proportion of head office overheads which will normally be allocated to the outlet. Although a franchise fee will be payable it will be considerably less than these items. The use by a business of the technique of converting part of its network to franchising is dealt with in Chapter 5.

6. A franchisor has fewer staff problems with which to cope as he is not involved in the staff problems of each individual outlet.

7. The local management of each franchised outlet will be keen, well motivated, and extremely alert to minimize costs and to maximize sales—much more so than would be the case with a manager.

8. A manufacturer can secure outlets for its products by establishing a franchise at wholesale or retail level which deals in such products.
9. A wholesaler which has under-utilized storage and distribution facilities can establish a retail franchise dealing in the products which it distributes, thus providing additional outlets for those products and enabling it to make more economic use of its facilities. There can be some legal problems for wholesalers who embark upon this course in the light of competition law. These problems are discussed in Chapter 12.
10. An existing business with multiple outlets can raise capital to enable it to reduce borrowing or to diversify its business interests by selling off some or all those outlets and simultaneously entering into a franchise agreement for the future operation of those outlets. This will require the proper establishment of a franchise system as well as the overcoming of a number of problems which are discussed in Chapter 5.
11. Franchising offers the scope to an existing single owner of a multiple chain to develop its future outlets by a franchise system rather than expanding its own outlets, thus reducing the calls upon its capital and manpower resources.
12. Certain types of franchise schemes are able to benefit from the development of national accounts. There are many large industrial concerns having a number of factories, offices and depots throughout the country which require the services offered by some franchise networks. Franchisors are able to negotiate with them for each franchisee to service the requirements of the local branches within his franchised area. None of the franchisees would have the ability or the capacity to negotiate or service arrangements of this nature on his own, yet the group as a whole has the capacity to do it. Each franchisee by the quality service which he provides to the franchisor's customer ensures that the group as a whole retains the business of the large national multiple outlet company.

There is of course a down side as with so many things in life. We have seen that there are two fundamental advantages to a business in adopting a franchise, but there is one area which causes more difficulties to franchisors than any other: the franchisees themselves. This may seem a drastic statement but most of the problems with which a franchisor will be confronted will arise from his dealings with the franchisees as 'people'. The subject of franchisor and franchisee relations is so important that two chapters in this book (Chapters 10 and 11) are devoted to it. The personal relationship between franchisor and franchisee, and the way in which it is managed, are crucial to the success or failure of the franchise.

This relationship is constantly and repeatedly put under strain. Many of the symptoms are clearly and regularly experienced by many franchisors, and include the following.

1. A franchisee may well develop a feeling of independence: he is successful; his business is running well and he is earning what he was told he could expect to earn or perhaps even more. He tends to wonder why he needs the franchisor at all. He becomes convinced that the reason for his success is that he is running his business well on his own initiative. This presents a challenge for the franchisor. After all, the franchisor may be doing his job well and helping his franchisee achieve success only to find that the franchisee now thinks that he is the person who was responsible for his success and the franchisor is superfluous to his requirements. This is a matter which calls for a correct response and a skilful exercise in franchisor–franchisee relations.

2. A franchisor has to ensure that standards of quality, of services and of goods are maintained throughout the franchised chain. His field support staff will act as supervisors of these standards as well as providing support to the franchisees. The franchisor's staff who deal with franchisees must be aware of the problems involved in dealing with franchisees who will often see nothing wrong in trying to cut corners and in adapting the disciplines of the system to suit their own convenience. Firm, close direction may well be needed in some cases and one must always be conscious that a small untreated deviation from the system today can become a larger problem tomorrow and much more difficult to cope with.

3. Despite the belief that franchising produces well-motivated franchisees there are some franchisees who are not alive to the opportunities with which their business presents them. This problem could be symptomatic of more than one underlying cause:
   - the franchisee may not really be suitable for self-employment and may not be able to cope;
   - the franchisee may have made a mistake in his selection of franchise and the franchisor may have compounded that mistake by not employing the right selection procedures. For example, the franchisor's business may require the franchisee to be a good salesman and the franchisee may not possess the necessary personality or determination;
   - the franchisee may have reached a level of satisfaction with his lot in life: he is earning more than ever before in his life and can afford all he needs; he does not see the point in working harder to achieve more. What he fails to appreciate is that no business can stand exactly still where one would like it to be; it should get better but if growth is neglected it will get worse;

- the franchisee may not be operating the system properly.

Each of these causes will require a different approach to be adopted and each will require a different solution. Above all the franchisor must never forget that the franchisee does own his business. The franchisee has to be educated and coaxed into accepting that the franchisor's suggestions in response to the problem do amount to sound advice. It is not the same thing as saying to the manager of a business 'it is now company policy that "so and so" should be done and therefore you must do it'. A franchisee can never be treated in this way. If the franchisor's reasoning and explanations are good it should be possible for him to make the franchisee see how much more sensible he would be to do what he is advised by the franchisor to do.

4. A breakdown of trust can develop between the franchisor and franchisee arising out of the incompatibility between the franchisee and the individual within the franchisor's organization with whom the franchisee has to deal.
5. A franchisor may well believe, with some justification, that in training a franchisee he is in fact preparing a possible future competitor.
6. The franchisor must be sure that the person selected for the franchise is suitable for the particular type of franchise and has the capacity to accept the responsibility of owning his own business. The franchisor owes it to prospective franchisees and to the growth of his own business to ensure that no one who is unsuitable is allowed to take a franchise.
7. There is often difficulty in obtaining the co-operation of franchisees in investing in the decoration and renovation of their premises and upgrading of equipment so that the consumer is always given service in the manner stipulated in the franchise agreement and in a manner consistent with the brand image and reputation of the franchised network.
8. There are some franchises where the franchised business forms part of a larger business which is carried on by the franchisee. An example of this sort of business would be a car hire franchise owned by a motor dealer and run from the same premises as his main business. (Such a franchise is often referred to as a fractional franchise, i.e. the franchised business is a small fraction of the franchisee's total business.) The franchisee can find an interaction and conflict between the staff of the two types of business which may operate to the detriment of either or both.

9. Effective communications plays a great part in effective franchisee management. Chapters 10 and 11 deal with this issue in detail.
10. The amount of profit in cash terms which will flow to the franchisor from a franchised outlet will be less than the profit potential of the franchisor-owned outlet, although as a return on capital the franchised outlet is likely to produce a better result.
11. The franchisor will be running the risk that where (as is usually the case) the franchisee is paying franchise fees calculated as percentage of gross income, he may not be fully disclosing his gross income (this issue is dealt with in Chapter 12).
12. There may be difficulties in the recruitment of a sufficient flow of suitable persons as franchisees.

In summing up the disadvantages with which a franchisor is faced, it will be appreciated that most of the disadvantages for a franchisor arise from his dealings with the franchisee as an individual and the personalities involved. 'People problems' would also confront a non-franchisor businessman. However, there is a vital and subtle distinction for the franchisor between running his own business and running a franchised business, in that the franchisee owns his business and he will resent the franchisor trying to impose the same regime on him as if his business were merely a branch of the franchisor's company. Each party must appreciate how essential are co-operation and mutual dependence and a tolerance and understanding of the way in which the other thinks.

Chapter 4

Why take up a franchise?

In Chapter 9 there is a detailed review of the considerations which a prospective franchisee should bear in mind when deciding upon whether or not to become involved in self-employment and how to 'check out' a particular franchise and franchisor. A prospective franchisee will have to become a businessman capable of making decisions, and before embarking upon his venture he has to make two vital decisions: whether or not to embark upon a business venture which involves franchising, and which particular business and franchisor he should select.

In making a decision about the former, an assessment has to be made of the advantages and disadvantages of franchising from the franchisee's point of view so that the prospective franchisee can compare becoming involved in franchising as a franchisee with establishing his own non-franchised business. It is helpful to review the pros and cons of franchising and in particular the restrictions which a franchisee has to accept and which will exist throughout the franchise relationship.

When a new business is established the owner may or may not have had previous experience of running his own business or of running a particular type of business which may represent his attempt to prove that his own ideas work. Such a person will have to discover by trial and error the most cost-effective way of running the business, including the investment of capital. The question to be resolved is whether the owner will succeed in achieving sufficient profitability before his financial resources are used up. If he does he will not join the sad statistic of 25% of new business ventures which fail in the first 2 years; if he continues to do well he will not join the 40% of new business ventures which fail in the first 5 years. Franchising provides the prospective franchisee with a business opportunity which has been through this high-risk phase of its existence; the cost of establishing the business as a viable business in the market place which is capable of being successfully franchised has been borne by the franchisor who has developed it. This type of exercise by the franchisor is called a pilot operation and its scope and purpose is detailed in Chapter 6. What the franchisee is buying into is the research development and investment of the franchisor, thus reducing the high risk inherent in establishing a new business. While the risk level is considerably reduced, this does not mean that there is no risk. Franchised businesses fail for a variety of reasons which are discussed in Chapters 6 and 9, but the failure rate for new franchised businesses for whatever reason is, so far as one can ascertain, somewhere between one-eighth and one-tenth of the failure rate for non-franchised new businesses. From this opportunity to lock into the proven success formula established by the franchisor and from the concept of franchising flow a number of advantages from which a franchisee can benefit.

1. The franchisee's lack of basic or specialized knowledge and experience is overcome by the training programme of the franchisor.
2. The franchisee has the incentive of owning his own business with the additional benefit of continuing assistance from the franchisor. The franchisee is an independent businessman operating within the framework of the franchise system. This provides the opportunity to the franchisee through hard work and effort to maximize the return from his business and the value of his investment.
3. In most cases the franchisee's business benefits from operating with the benefit of a name and reputation (a brand image) and goodwill which are already well established in the mind and eye of the consumer.
4. The franchisee will usually need less capital than he would if he was setting up a business independently because the franchisor, through the experience gained from pilot and other operations, will have eliminated unnecessary expense.
5. The franchisor provides the franchisee with a range of services which are calculated to ensure, so far as is practicably possible, that the franchisee will enjoy the same or a greater degree of success as the franchisor has achieved. These services will include:
   - the application of developed criteria for the selection and identification of trading locations, or if the franchise is based upon mobile operations, the area of such operations;
   - guidance to the franchisee to assist in obtaining occupation rights to the trading location, complying with planning (zoning) laws, preparation of plans for layouts, shop fitting and refurbishment

and general assistance on the calculation of the correct level and mix of stock and in the opening launch of the business;

- the training of the franchisee and staff in the operation of the business format and the provision of an operational manual with detailed instructions;
- the training of the franchisee and staff in any methods of manufacture or preparation which may be appropriate;
- the training of the franchisee in methods of accounting, business controls, marketing, promotion and merchandising;
- the purchase of equipment;
- obtaining finance for the establishment of the franchisee's business; and
- getting the newly franchised business ready for trading and opened.

6. The franchisee receives the benefit, on a national scale (if appropriate), of the franchisor's advertising and promotional activities. It is usual for each franchisee to make a contribution towards the funds which are expended for this purpose.

7. The franchisee receives the benefit of the bulk purchasing power and negotiating capacity which are available to the franchisor by reason of the existence and size of the franchised network.

8. The franchisee has at his disposal the specialized knowledge and experience of the franchisor's 'head office' type organization while remaining self-employed in his business.

9. The franchisee's business risk is reduced. However, no franchisee should consider that because he is coming under the umbrella of the franchisor he is not going to be exposed to any risk at all. Any business undertaking involves risk, and a franchised business is no exception. To be successful, the franchisee will have to work hard, harder than ever before perhaps. The franchisor will never be able to promise great rewards for little effort. The blueprint of a way in which to carry on business successfully and profitably can rarely be the blueprint to a way of carrying on business successfully without working.

10. The franchisee has the services of field operational staff provided by the franchisor to assist him with any problems which may arise from time to time in the course of business.

11. The franchisee has the benefit of the use of the franchisor's patents (if any), trademarks, service marks, trade names, copyright material, trade secrets, know-how and any secret process or formulae.

12. The franchisee has the benefit of the franchisor's continuous research and development programmes designed to improve the business, to keep it up to date and competitive.

13. The franchisor assembles the maximum amount of market

information and experience which is available to be shared by all the franchisees in the network. This should provide the franchisee with access to a breadth of information which would not otherwise be available to him if he were not a member of the franchised network.

14. There are sometimes some territorial allocations in appropriate cases which protect the franchisee against competition from the franchisor or another franchisee within a defined area around the franchisee's business address or in the case of a mobile franchise a defined area of operation. This will invariably involve issues under UK and European Community competition law which are dealt with in Chapter 12.

15. The recognition by the banks of the advantages of franchisee financing (Chapter 7) have made lending sources and terms available to franchisees which are more attractive than those offered to non-franchised new businesses.

In addition to the aforementioned advantages, there are also disadvantages to the franchisee.

1. Inevitably, the relationship between the franchisor and franchisee will involve the imposition of controls. These controls will regulate the quality of the service or goods to be provided or sold by the franchisee to consumers. It has been mentioned previously that the franchisee will own his business. However, the business which he owns is one which he is licensed to carry on in accordance with the terms of his contract. He must accept that for the advantages enjoyed by him, by virtue of his association with the franchisor and all the other franchisees, control of quality and standards is essential. Each bad franchisee has an adverse effect not only on his own business, but indirectly on the whole franchised chain of businesses and all other franchisees. The franchisor will therefore impose standards, and demand that they are maintained so that the maximum benefit is derived by the franchisee and indirectly by the whole franchised chain from the operation of the franchisee's business. This is not to say that the franchisee will not be able to make any contribution or to stamp his own personality on his business. Most franchisors do encourage their franchisees to make the contribution to the development of the business of the franchised chain which their individual talent and qualities permit.

2. The franchisee will have to pay the franchisor for the services provided and for the use of the 'blueprint', i.e. initial and continuing franchise fees, although there are many ways in which a franchisor may obtain income from the activities of the network (Chapter 7).

3. A prospective franchisee may find it difficult to assess the quality of the franchisor. This aspect is dealt with in detail in Chapter 9.

4. The franchise contract will contain some restrictions against the sale or transfer of the franchised business. This is a clear inhibition on the franchisee's ability to deal with his own business but, as with most of the restrictions, there is a reason for it. The reason is that the franchisor will have already been most meticulous in his choice of the franchisee as his original franchisee for the particular outlet. Why then should he be any less meticulous in his approval of a replacement? Naturally he will wish to be satisfied that any successor of the franchisee is equally suitable for that purpose. In practice there is normally very little difficulty in the achievement of successful sales or transfers of a franchised business. (This is discussed in detail in Chapter 12.)

5. The franchisee may find himself becoming too dependent upon the franchisor and fail to produce the personal drive which is necessary to build up a successful business and to take full advantage of the foundations for business development which the franchisor's business format provides. Some franchisees lose their perspective. They delude themselves into believing that the franchisor has a duty to be so concerned about their particular business that he should ensure that the franchisee has a flow of customers and to provide a degree of day-to-day involvement, both of which are inconsistent with franchising as a concept.

6. The franchisor's policies may affect the franchisee's profitability. For example, the franchisor may wish to see his franchisee build up a higher turnover (from which he gets his continuing franchise fee) while the franchisee may be more concerned with increasing his profitability, which does not necessarily flow from increased turnover.

7. The franchisor may make mistakes of policy; he may make decisions relating to innovations in the business which are unsuccessful and operate to the detriment of the franchisee. This is why franchisors are always urged to market test innovations thoroughly before their introduction and to be able to demonstrate to franchisees the cost-effectiveness of the introduction of new ideas.

8. The good name of the franchised business or its brand image may become less reputable for reasons beyond the franchisee's control.

These are the advantages and disadvantages which every franchisee must weigh up and consider before making the decision on whether or not he wishes to enter into a franchised business. In Chapter 9 there is detailed guidance on selection of a franchise. The advantages and disadvantages listed here must be taken into account when considering the factors mentioned in that chapter.

Chapter 5

What can be franchised?

This book is concerned to a large extent with the business format franchise which is described and analysed in Chapter 1. It has already been explained that there are other types of franchise. Franchise arrangements, in the widest commercial use of the word, are those transactions in which one person grants rights to another to exploit an intellectual property right involving, perhaps, trade names, patents, trademarks, equipment distribution, a fictitious character, or a famous name, but not amounting to the entire package, or business blueprint, which is the essential feature of the business format franchise.

There are thus franchises involving transactions between:

- manufacturers and wholesalers;
- manufacturers and retailers;
- wholesalers and retailers;
- retailer and retailer.

In order to illustrate the four categories of transaction there follow examples of the types of arrangement involved in each case.

MANUFACTURERS AND WHOLESALERS

This first category came into existence when soft drink manufacturers established the practice of franchising their bottling facilities. Briefly, what they did (and indeed still do) was to grant the right within a defined area to use a concentrate of syrup manufactured by and obtained from them. The bottlers' functions included making up and bottling (or canning) the drink using the manufacturer's syrups and in accordance with the manufacturer's requirements and to distribute the resulting products. Prime examples of this category are Coca-Cola, Pepsi-Cola and Schweppes.

MANUFACTURERS AND RETAILERS

This category is involved with what are frequently described as 'first generation franchises' and includes some of the oldest of this type of franchise arrangement. It developed out of the arrangements made by the automobile industry in the early years of its existence. The problems with which they were confronted resulted in the establishment of franchised dealer networks.

There are also the arrangements made between petrol companies and their filling station proprietors. So many of the elements of the business format franchise are present in these arrangements that they may appear to be quite close to achieving that status. Indeed, many motor manufacturers' 'main dealer' arrangements are business format franchises. There are within the scope of the petrol companies' arrangements with filling station proprietors, different types of transaction ranging from a licensee or tenant of premises owned by the petrol company to a sales agreement with the owner of the filling station which may or may not be exclusive. In recent years many of the petrol companies have added convenience stores to the forecourt of their filling stations and in some cases have varied their arrangements with licensees to something much closer to a business format franchise.

WHOLESALERS AND RETAILERS

This category is not so clearly identifiable, at a glance, as being distinctly different from the manufacturers and retailers category. There can really be no commercial reason to differentiate between them except that the franchisor is a wholesaler rather than a manufacturer. The types of business which come within this category include hardware stores, chemist's shops, supermarkets and automobile aftercare businesses.

RETAILER AND RETAILER

For this category, one need only look as far as the traditional well-known business format franchises. It is not necessary to look to the USA for examples; there are some well-known UK franchises which illustrate this type of growth. Prontaprint is a good example. This was started as a pilot operation which was expanded to three stores and then, as was the intention from the outset, the concept thus developed was franchised. Another UK example, a mobile franchise, is Hometune. This started by offering the service to the consumer and expanded by the use of the franchise system. The vast majority of 'high street' franchises have developed in this way: franchising has been chosen by the franchisor as the marketing method most suited to the expansion of the concept.

The above categories do not amount to some of the traditional methods or practices described in Chapter 1 as being the business methods from which the business format franchise evolved, namely agencies, distributorships, licencing, and know-how agreements. We shall therefore briefly examine the nature of these arrangements and compare them with franchising.

In the first place there are agencies. An agent is a person with either expressly given authority to act on behalf of another person or one who, by the nature of his relationship with that other person, is implicitly authorized to act on his behalf. The authority given may be a special authority which is limited to doing one or two specific acts or it may be a general authority giving the agent unrestricted power to act. Fundamentally, an agent does not act on his own behalf and he is not a buyer and seller of his principal's products. He acts on behalf of and in the name of his principal. There is no separation of principal from agent in the eyes of third parties dealing with them. Whatever the agent says or does is completely and effectively binding upon his principal. Between the agent and the principal, there are duties which each owes the other, but the third party is not usually concerned with whatever these private arrangements may be.

In all franchise arrangements the parties usually go to great lengths to ensure that no agency relationship arises. Indeed, invariably in franchise agreements there is a specific provision to establish that the franchisee is not the franchisor's agent or partner and has no power to represent himself as the franchisor's agent or as being empowered to bind the franchisor. Agreements should require the franchisee prominently to state that he is a franchisee or licensee of the franchisor so that the consumer or others who deal with the franchisee are in no doubt as to the position.

The expression 'agency', like the expression 'franchise', is used quite often in the wrong context. It is, in fact, often used in the context of distribution arrangements. A distributor is, in essence, usually a wholly independently owned and financed wholesale operation which is granted certain distribution rights in relation to a product.

The real relationship between the parties is that of seller and buyer. The distributor is a completely independent businessman. Unlike the agent, in his dealings he does not bind the person by whom he has been granted the distribution rights. He may carry a range of products in respect of which he has a distribution agreement and he may have competing or conflicting lines.

The business he conducts is his own business, and he is no doubt motivated purely by commercial considerations in deciding whether or not to accept any restrictions which may be imposed upon him in a distribution agreement. The distributor buys for his own account and takes the full risk of whether or not he will be able to resell at a sufficient profit. The buyer and seller relationship may also be present in a franchise agreement, but in most cases it should only be a feature and not the whole substance of the arrangement.

Licensing and know-how agreements are, invariably, the same thing. A licence is descriptive of the nature of a transaction by which one party authorizes another to carry out or perform certain functions. A know-how agreement is a particular type of licence agreement and is most widely to be found in relation to the manufacturing process. These types of arrangement largely arise out of patent or trademark exploitation and will usually authorize the manufacture of a product or a piece of equipment. This is not necessarily the only business carried on by the licensee: he may well be combining his activities under the licence or know-how agreement with many other activities. It may be that the product which is being manufactured under licence is complementary to, or an accessory of, something else that he does or makes. Alternatively, it may just make a useful addition to his existing range. Again, like the distributor, he is an independent businessman. He runs his own business; he does not act by or on behalf of the person who granted him the rights. This type of transaction is the closest analogy there is to a business format type of franchise and differs from it in at least the sense that there is no obligation upon such a licensee to adopt and comply with the business format and system imposed by another.

How does franchising differ in practice? Let us take as a simple example a company which manufactures meat products and introduces a hamburger as one of its new lines. Experience shows that the hamburgers sell well and are very popular. A bright young man in the marketing division suggests that the company opens up its own restaurant to sell the hamburgers—which it does.

The company could, at that point in time, have decided to obtain a wider distribution for its product by entering into a licensing agreement with other meat manufacturers for the same hamburger to be manufactured according to the same recipe in various parts of the country or territory with which we are concerned. It may do this in any event. It may have a distribution network of its own or it may distribute through meat wholesalers under distribution agreements. It may also consider using its existing sales force or appointing one.

In this case, however, the company has decided, in addition to using these traditional methods, to open up a retail outlet, and it develops a limited-menu fast food operation built around its hamburger. It has thereby provided an additional method of exploitation of its product and secured retail outlets for the sale of the hamburgers. It has gone directly into the retail market but it does not have sufficient capital, or does not wish to commit the necessary large amount of capital, to open rapidly a chain of what could prove to be very successful hamburger bars. Accordingly, it decides to exploit the distribution of the product at retail level by granting franchises or licences to others who will run identical hamburger bars modelled on exactly the same basis as the 'pilot operation' which the manufacturer has set up. The franchisees will trade under the same name which has become established by the franchisor, the same format, the same procedures and they will sell the same product. A consumer should feel on entering each store that it is part of the same organization and that the service and product are identical in each store. In other words the company establishes a business format franchise.

The manufacturer has expanded its distribution network; it has secured additional selling points; at the same time it is utilizing the staff and facilities of its head office by providing a back-up to the franchisees in various stores. It is therefore making a far more economic use of the amount of expertise available in its organization. Rapid growth of the retail outlets can be achieved without the franchisor having to make available a considerable amount of capital resources or to stretch its manpower resources, which, perhaps, it can ill afford or it is reluctant to do.

What is the franchisee's position? He is certainly not an agent. He is not acting on behalf of the franchisor and he is not binding or committing the franchisor. He is his own man. He owns his business, he is an independent businessman, he puts the necessary capital into the business and he runs it and manages it. He is not a distributor in the ordinary sense, although he is part of the franchisor's distribution network. His position is not incompatible with a distributorship for he is certainly buying a product and selling it, but he is applying a process to the product before resale. He performs his activities as a principal. He does not have other lines; he is not running any other business independent of this franchised business. So although there is a contrast with a distributorship, both franchisee and distributor are part of the chain in the supply of products to the consumer except that the franchisee operates at retail level while the distributor operates at wholesale level.

How does the franchise compare with licensing and know-how agreements? In fact the same sort of contrast can be found as exists with the distributorship, although licensing and know-how agreements are even closer relations of franchise transactions than a distributorship. One is inclined to the view that the business format type franchise is directly analogous to the know-how and licensing arrangement. Let us therefore take another look at the franchise arrangement which has been described.

There is a licence granted permitting the franchisee to trade under the trade name and in the particular format. There is certainly a know-how agreement. Know-how is imparted in all aspects of the franchised business. Before he is established in business the franchisee will require to be trained in the basic business skills relevant and limited to this particular type of business and in the operational requirements. He will also expect assistance in site selection, design and remodelling of the store, equipment, marketing and promotion. The franchisee will also expect a continuing interest to be taken in him by the franchisor providing guidance when needed, promotional activities, innovation, and so on.

What makes the franchisee's position different from the other arrangements is that uniquely the franchisee operates under the trade name of the franchisor and using the franchisor's business system. With *traditional* arrangements the agent, the distributor, or the licensee has his skills and experience which he is making available with the framework of the agency distributorship or know-how agreement. In the *franchise* arrangement the other party (i.e. the franchisee) does not have the skills, or experience, so he is to be given them and then sustained to the extent that he needs it.

One element which is missing from the equation is the agency element, 'agency' being used in the strict sense. No franchisor would want to enter into a franchise arrangement in which the formal relationship between him and the franchisee was that of principal and agent. If that were the case, with all the inherent risks, he might just as well operate his own branch and employ a manager.

Franchising, therefore, is not merely an alternative, it is in reality another weapon in the armoury of the manufacturer, wholesaler or retailer which can be utilized to expand his business in addition to the other methods available to him. It will therefore be appreciated that there is very little that cannot be franchised. Any business which is capable of being run under management is capable of being franchised. This does not mean that any such business will franchise successfully. The successful franchises are usually built round novel concepts, patented equipment, and trademark associations. They are invariably novel approaches to an existing concept and, indeed, the food industry demonstrates this factor more readily than most.

A restaurant or a café is a class of business which has existed for many years, yet, when Wimpy emerged on the market in the UK in the 1950s, the new type of approach (the limited menu concentrating on doing a little but well) brought immediate success. A further illustration of this point is that in the USA there are at least 19 different types of food operation under franchise.

The franchise scheme should aim to fill the gap in the market by providing a service or product which is not readily available or available at all. Its introduction should also be timed correctly, for there is no point in introducing a franchised scheme for a service or product which the public have outgrown and do not want or which is on the wane. Temporarily fashionable ideas should also be avoided; they may not have staying power. The clearest idea that can be obtained of what can be franchised is to examine the experience of others. Over the years many lists and classifications of business under franchise in the USA have been published. The following list appeared in the first edition of this work in 1970 and remains valid.

1. Accounting/Tax Services. This embraces tax preparation, computerized accounting systems for specialized professions, small business, and traders.
2. Agribusiness.
3. Art Galleries.
4. Auto Diagnostic Centres.
5. Auto Rentals/Leasing.
6. Auto Supply Stores.
7. Auto Transmission Repair Centres.
8. Auto Washes/Products/Equipment.
9. Automotive Products/Services.
10. Beauty and Slendering Salons.
11. Building and Construction.
12. Business Aids/Services.
13. Campgrounds.
14. Catalogue Sales.
15. Chemical Maintenance Products.
16. Children's Products/Services.
17. Cleaning/Maintenance/Sanitation Services.
18. Cosmetics.
19. Credit/Collection Services.
20. Dance Studios.
21. Dispensing Equipment (Food and Beverages).
22. Domestic Services.
23. Employment and Temporary Help Services.
24. Entertainment.
25. Food Operations. This category is broken down into 19 types of operation:
    Barbecue
    Cantonese
    Chicken
    Donuts
    Fast Foods
    Full Menu
    Hamburgers/Frankfurters
    Italian
    Mexican
    Mobile Units
    Pancakes/Waffles
    Pizza
    Roast Beef
    Sandwiches
    Seafood
    Smorgasbord

Speciality

Steaks

Miscellaneous Food Operations (e.g. Bakery routes)

26. Fund Raising.
27. Glass Tinting.
28. Health Aids/Services.
29. Health Clubs.
30. Hearing Aids.
31. Home Improvement.
32. Industrial Supplies/Services.
33. Lawn and Garden Care.
34. Marketing Sales Promotion.
35. Motels.
36. Nursing Homes.
37. Office Machines/Systems.
38. Paint/Chemical Coatings.
39. Paint Stripping.
40. Pest Control.
41. Pet Shops and Services.
42. Physical Conditioning Equipment.
43. Printing/Duplicating Services.
44. Publishing.
45. Rack Merchandising.
46. Rentals and Leasing (General Equipment).
47. Safety Systems.
48. Sales Training.
49. Schools/Instruction.
50. Scientific Social Introductions.
51. Sewer Cleaning.
52. Signs.
53. Sport/Recreation.
54. Stores (Retail). These include such stores as: dry cleaners; shoe and heel bars; ice-cream; bridal salons; jewellers'; gift shops; and coin-op laundries.
55. Swimming Pools.
56. Telecopy Systems.
57. Television Systems.
58. Travel Agencies.
59. Tree Services.
60. Vending Operations.
61. Vinyl/Plastic Repair.
62. Water Conditioning Systems.
63. Weight Control.
64. Wigs/Hairpieces.

65. Miscellaneous Products and Services.

The British Franchise Association's membership covers the following 46 business classifications with an additional 38 subclassifications:

1. Motor Vehicle Services.
    (a) Rust Proofing.
    (b) Car Tuning Service.
    (c) Motor Accessories; Cycles; Cycle Accessories; Camping; Caravaning and Leisure Goods.
    (d) 24-hour Mobile Windscreen Replacement Service.
    (e) Exhaust Systems Replacement.
    (f) Vehicle Security System.
    (g) Car Valet Services.
    (h) Automobile Parts.
2. Brewers.
3. Car Hire.
4. Drain and Pipe Cleaning.
5. Print Shops.
6. Fast Food.
    (a) Fried Chicken.
    (b) Hamburgers.
    (c) Fish and Chips.
    (d) Baking and Coffee.
    (e) Pizza.
    (f) Baked Potatoes.
7. Home Improvements.
    (a) Double Glazing.
    (b) Woodworm/Dryrot Eradication Services.
    (c) Damp Proofing.
    (d) Leaded Windows.
    (e) Kitchen Renewal.
    (f) Security Locks.
    (g) Window Blinds.
    (h) Internal Decoration.
    (i) Kitchen and Bathroom Furniture.
    (j) Bedroom Furniture.
8. Parcels Delivery Services.
9. Hairdressing.
10. Retail.
    (a) Coffee, Tea.
    (b) Ladies Fashion.
    (c) Aquatic Centres.
    (d) Household Furnishings.

(e) Soft Drinks.
(f) Health and Skin Care.
(g) Shoes.
(h) Garden Buildings and Sheds.
(i) Internal and External Door Furniture in Brass and Other Metals.
(j) Sewing Machines.
(k) Confectionary.
(l) Neckwear and Accessories.
(m) Pharmacies.
(n) Non-branded Foodstuffs.
11. Chauffeur Services.
12. Haircare and Beauty Products.
13. Employment Agency.
14. Industrial Cleaning Services.
15. Hire of Marquees.
16. Business Transfer Agency.
17. Estate Agency.
18. Ceramic Tiles.
19. Stained Glass.
20. Industrial Vehicle Cleaning.
21. Accounting Services.
22. Convenience Stores.
23. Bathroom Suite Renovations.
24. Removal and Storage Facilities.
25. Industrial Chemicals.
26. Landscape Maintenance Services.
27. Hot Bread Kitchens.
28. Instant Picture Framing Services.
29. Office and Industrial Cleaning.
30. Maids Services.
31. Hotels.
32. Tool and Equipment.
33. Repairing Service for Brick and Stone Buildings.
34. Stripping and Restoration of Furniture.
35. Roof Thatching.
36. Concrete Delivery Services.
37. Investigation Bureau.
38. Workshop Consumables and Maintenance for Industrial Users.
39. Milk and Dairy Produce Distribution.
40. Motoring School.
41. Manufacture and Sale of Name Badge Signage, etc.
42. Distribution and Automotive Hand Tools.
43. One-hour Film Developing and Printing.
44. Insurance Brokers.

45. Vinyl Coverings Repair and Restoration.
46. Secretarial and Word Processing Training Centres.

In assessing whether a business may be franchised the following criteria should be considered.

1. The concept including the products and services must be proved in practice to be successful.
2. It should be distinctive both in its public image and in its system and methods.
3. The system and methods must be capable of being passed on successfully to others.
4. The financial returns from the operation of the franchised unit must be sufficient:
   — to enable the franchisee to obtain a reasonable return on the assets employed in the business;
   — to enable the franchisee to earn a reasonable if not good reward for his labours; and
   — to enable the franchisee to make payment to the franchisor of a reasonable fee for the services which he will continue to supply to the franchisee.
5. The income generated by the franchisor from the operation of the franchise must be sufficient to cover the franchisor's overheads and to earn a reasonable profit.

A word of caution, however; a prospective franchisee must decide whether he is being offered a franchise at all. A franchise scheme must contain the elements of a franchise as described in Chapter 1 to qualify as a business format franchise.

A number of business opportunities offered in good faith are often loosely described as 'franchise opportunities'. Examination of the elements of the transaction by reference to the principles contained in Chapter 1 will assist in reaching a conclusion as to whether or not it is a franchise. The types of business that are likely to be within this category are distributorships, sales agencies or sales representatives and dealerships as described earlier in this chapter. These have certain elements of a franchise, but usually a vital element such as the continuing relationship as well as a business format and system is almost completely lacking. While these other types of business do not amount to a business format franchise they are frequently conceived and developed by the application of the principles upon which such a franchise is based.

New schemes amending and adopting these principles will arise from time to time. This is only natural. It is, however, important that any prospective franchisee should recognize the extent of the services and facilities being offered to him. The fact that a particular business on offer does not amount to a business format franchise does not of itself mean that it is not worthwhile.

The ingenuity of businessmen has fully demonstrated the versatility of franchising as a business method. Unfortunately, however, the ingenuity of the modern businessman has not been limited to the pursuit of legitimate, ethical franchising. Indeed, franchising offers scope for the fraudulent as the transaction involves a continuing relationship. If, therefore, the initial franchise fee is set too high, allegedly to cover some of the continuing services which are never intended to be provided, the scope for fraud is obvious.

There developed what has become known as the 'pyramid selling' scheme, which is also sometimes described as a multi-level marketing scheme. Such schemes involve the sale of distributorships to purchasers who may divide and subdivide them and sell them on to those whom they recruit as subdistributors. Expansion of these enterprises takes place on the chain-letter principle. The ostensible object is to build up a sales force which will sell the company's products or services from door to door. In fact, selling the goods or services is difficult; they are usually expensive, and areas are often saturated with other distributors. Selling distributorships is much more lucrative and becomes, effectively, the company's business.

There is a very good description of a pyramid selling scheme in a 1972 case in the UK in which the then Secretary of State for Trade and Industry brought proceedings to wind up two companies which were engaged in a pyramid selling scheme. The case was heard by Mr Justice Megarry (as he then was), who described the scheme in that case in the following terms:

The sale of cosmetics is conducted through a hierarchy of individuals. At the lowest level there are 'Beauty Advisors', who sell the company's products direct to members of the public. Above them there are the 'Supervisors', who not only themselves sell to members of the public, but also each recruits and supervises a team of beauty advisers. Above the supervisors are the 'Distributors', who constitute the top rung outside the company, and may have a team of supervisors under them. As I have indicated, the rights that go with the position of distributor or supervisor are embraced by the term 'franchise'. The company allows a discount of 60 per cent on its products, and when a beauty adviser makes a sale, he or she received half that discount, and the other half is shared equally between the supervisor and distributor above the beauty adviser in the chain. On direct sales by a supervisor, the supervisor receives a commission of 45 per cent, and a commission of 15 per cent goes to his distributor. On direct sales by the distributor, the full 60 per cent commission goes to the distributor.

In addition to any profit that the company makes on the sale of cosmetics, the company has the other source of income that I have mentioned. A distributor has to pay £1,500 to the company for his position. If he has been recruited by another distributor, that distributor receives a commission of £795 from the company, the company keeping the balance of £705. On the other hand, the supervisor pays the company £700 for his position, and for his recruitment the company pays a commission of £245 keeping the balance of £455. If the new supervisor has been recruited by a distributor the distributor keeps the whole of the commission. If the new supervisor has been recruited by another supervisor, the commission is in effect split between the supervisor and his distributor, the supervisor receiving £140 and the distributor the remaining £105.

After a supervisor has been appointed, he may secure his promotion to distributor on paying a further £800 to the company, this sum bringing his initial £700 up to the requisite £1,500. On such a promotion occurring, the distributor who originally recruited the new distributor, or whose superior recruited him, receives a commission of £550, the company keeping the remaining £250 out of the additional £800.

The financial incentive to recruit distributors or other participants in the scheme is self-evident. The lack of incentive to sell products was reflected in the evidence from which it emerged that average sales of products during the period July 1971 to January 1972 reached a peak of between £8 and £9 per week per participant. On the other hand, one distributor had received £5625 for the sale of rights to participate.

The main emphasis by the companies in marketing the scheme was placed upon the money which could be earned by the recruitment of distributors and supervisors. The rewards could be considerable. If a distribution could each month promote one supervisor to be a distributor and the supervisor appoint another to take his place the distributor would earn £10,800 in a year. The company of course would have been paid £13,920. There is no mention of the income to be generated by sale of products.

Evidence was given by the Government Actuary that if each distributor achieved the targets indicated in the manual after 2 years there would be over 16 million distributors. If on the other hand each distributor achieved as encouraged in the manual, double the rate, there would be 16 million distributors after 1 year, over 66 million after 13 months and over 280 billion in 2 years. The judge concluded that the projected figures in the manual were 'utterly devoid of reality'.

The fundamental difference between franchising and pyramid selling lies in the objective of the participant which, when fulfilled, will earn him profit; the franchisee intends to and can only make his profit from conducting his fast food restaurant, mobile service or other business. The pyramid participant gets his main profits from recruiting equal- or lower-status participants. Supplying goods or services to consumers is incidental and may be of so little advantage that the participant does not bother with it. A franchisee, on the other hand, gets nothing from recruiting others. A pyramid participant (except at the lowest level) gets practically nothing from anything else.

These pyramid schemes have been recognized as containing elements which are dishonest and, accordingly, the Fair Trading Act 1973 contains provisions which define pyramid-type schemes. The Act also contains provisions which permit the making of regulations (which have been made):

(a) to control or prohibit the issue, circulation, or distribution of documents, circulars, notices, advertisements and announcements which contain invitations to persons to participate in a scheme; and

(b) prohibiting the promoter of a scheme from performing functions which are vital to the operation of such a scheme:
  (i) a limit of £75 on the value of goods to be supplied to a participant until 7 days has expired from the date of the contract;
  (ii) the prohibition of payments as security for future liabilities for the supply of goods;
  (iii) the prohibition of charging for the provision of training facilities to a participant unless the participant has the free choice whether or not to make use of such facilities;
  (iv) the participant has to be given the right at any time without penalty to terminate the agreement by 14 days notice which provides a discharge from all contractual liability to the promoter.

One of the basic weaknesses of the regulations is that they do nothing to restrict statements made orally at sales meetings held by those who promote pyramid or other multilevel distributorships. These meetings were the technique employed for selling pyramid schemes and were used to generate a high level of infectious enthusiasm which lowered the guard of those attending and played upon their greed for making money. The regulations do nothing to control or prohibit the use of this technique.

It is vitally important to be able to recognize involvement with a pyramid-type scheme. And obviously before signing a contract or parting with money one should take proper professional advice. But it is a matter for suspicion if one is offered or told that there will be a reward (i.e. payment, supply of cheaper products, or any other disguised benefit) for doing something totally unrelated to the sale of the basic product or service with which the scheme is involved. For example, one may be offered a percentage payment of any sum paid to the promoter of the scheme for recruiting another participant, or for persuading such participant to purchase a higher position in the scheme. Other rewards could include a profit or commission on sales, or the provision of services or training to other participants in the scheme, or a commission on sales effected by other participants in the scheme. Attendance at meetings of the nature described above should be avoided but if one is tempted to join such a meeting the temptation to sign up on the spot must be resisted so that appropriate professional advice can be taken. If one is not permitted to remove the documents one should never sign and should not pursue the proposition further.

Pyramid selling schemes have cost some unsuspecting people a great deal of money; there are many legitimate franchises in which to invest without becoming involved in pyramid schemes. No legitimate franchise will do what the pyramid schemes do and that is to promise rich rewards quickly and without hard work. Whatever is being franchised legitimately will offer reasonable prospects of good rewards in return for the hard work and application which is the lot of all successful self-employed businessmen.

There are six situations in which existing established businesses have become involved in the franchise method of marketing.

1. The expansion of an established retail chain by:
    — adding new franchised stores, thus reducing the need for additional capital and manpower;
    — a combination of franchising of existing stores as well as franchising additions to the chain.
2. The turning over to franchising of marginally profitable or unprofitable stores in a retail chain. By removing from the profit and loss expense items such as the cost of employment of staff, including holiday and sickness cover and head office overheads, and replacing them with a franchisee working for himself and paying a franchise fee, the performance of the store can be dramatically and favourably transformed.
3. By the sale of selected operations coupled with the grant of a franchise to the purchaser a business can raise capital either to enable it to reduce borrowings or to enable it to diversify its business interests.
4. A company with underused wholesale storage and distribution facilities can establish a franchise providing additional outlets for the products in which it deals, thus enabling it to make more economic use of its facilities.
5. A manufacturer can establish a franchise in order to secure outlets for its products.
6. From a prospective franchisee's point of view there are those franchised businesses which can conveniently be added on to an existing business with which it is compatible. A good example of this sort of 'marriage' would be the establishment of a car hire business on the forecourt of a motor dealer. This sort of add-on business is often described as a 'fractional franchise'.

Undoubtedly further applications will be developed. One must avoid approaching franchising as a rigid, closely defined business method. It is quite the reverse: it is a flexible marketing method from which many lessons may be learned and applications developed.

Chapter 6

How to become a franchisor

There are seven basic elements involved in creating and developing a franchised business.

1. The basic business concept.
2. Pilot operation.
3. Developing the franchise package.
4. Developing the operational manual.
5. Marketing the franchise package.
6. Selecting franchisees.
7. Developing the franchisor's organization.

Although these elements are listed in a sequence there are many areas of overlap and some of the elements will be developing in parallel with others. A good example of this overlap is element 7 since the franchisor's organization clearly will be developing throughout the whole process. We shall consider each element in turn when the way in which they interact will be evident.

THE BASIC BUSINESS CONCEPT

The establishment of a franchise system invariably arises in one of two ways. The first is when it is decided to expand an existing business by use of the franchise method of marketing. The second, and one which is becoming more common, is when a positive attempt is made to set up and establish a business with a view to franchising from day one.

The latter case is not to be recommended for the beginner, and although an experienced franchisor may be able to proceed in this way significantly few have succeeded. The usual course is for the proprietor of an existing business, which has the potential for a more rapid expansion rate than its capital and staff resources would permit, to turn to franchising as the means to exploit that potential to the fullest extent possible.

It should be understood that franchising is not a path to salvation for an ailing business. It will not produce, if ethically and soundly run, an immediate positive cashflow and profits. On the contrary, it will require to be developed in the same way as any other business method. Capital and manpower resources will have to be devoted to the development of the concept, its marketing and sustenance. As will be seen in Chapter 7, it may be some years before profits and positive cashflow can be expected. Franchising must, therefore, be developed from a sound financial and business base, which will not make calls upon the resources which will have to be devoted to the franchising activities.

It is essential, if one is intending to franchise, to keep the business simple. Others will have to be taught to operate it as successfully as the innovator, and the more complex it is, the more difficult it will be to recruit, train and sustain franchisees. So basically, the scope must deliberately be limited to a framework which is manageable by others. It is also important that the business be easy to set up in terms of installation and its equipment requirements.

Let us look at a fast food operation as an example. The simpler the design and layout of the kitchen and preparation areas, the more standardized the decor, design and layout of the take-out and/or restaurant area, the easier it will be to adapt premises to the design and the more quickly one can cope with the establishment of each operation.

There is also the paramount need to keep the menu simple, so as to reduce the inventory requirements and make it possible to keep the preparation and serving of the food simple, quick and efficient and at the same time to keep portion control at an effective level. One is more likely, with a simple and restricted menu, to limit the amount of equipment to be employed and thus reduce the requirements of the business in terms of space, levels of investment and maintenance.

Retail outlets provide another example of the activities which the franchisor must try to keep simple. Apart from the design, decor and layout, which are all vital, there is the question of the stock inventory. The more extensive it is, the broader the range, the more complex is the task of all who have to deal with it, and the greater the likelihood of financial loss through poor stock choice, control and mismanagement. The overall aim should be to simplify control, reduce paperwork and make the system as foolproof as possible. On the whole, these basic principles will apply whatever the business being franchised.

Another objective must be to provide franchisees with a support service and information which no single trader in business with aggressive competitors could ever hope or expect to match. Thus, we see that the development of the concept requires meticulous planning and anticipation of needs.

It is also important to define clearly the market at which the business is aimed. There is little point in having a good idea and a great business in prospect if, for example, as can be the case, one is dependent for referrals upon others in the particular trade, who do not see the need to deal with one's business, or who are already coping with the aspect of the business in which one is interested and will see no benefit to themselves by dealing with another business providing a similar service or product.

The dangers inherent in aiming oneself at the ultimate consumer, if that consumer is likely to go to the established trade first, must be considered. This could arise if one is intending to provide a specialist service which is catered for by existing, more comprehensive business services. In such a case, there will probably be a heavy promotional cost to deliver the right message to the market-place before the business becomes accepted in its own right. That is a burden which falls on the franchisor, and its cost and likely effectiveness will be a factor in his decision taking.

There are five other factors to consider.

1. Franchisees with finance: will one be able to attract franchisees with, or able to acquire, sufficient financial resources to enable them to become established and to provide an adequate level of working capital?
2. Franchisee skills: will one be able to attract franchisees with the necessary basic ability to enable them to acquire the skills required in the operation of the franchised business and to teach those skills to their staff?
3. Premises: can a sufficient flow of suitable premises be found at rental levels which will enable franchisees to trade profitably?
4. Consumer demand: has the franchisor demonstrated or can he afford to devote, adequate resources to establish a sufficient market demand?
5. Market sector: is the business sector healthy or in decline; is the product a temporary fad or a flash in the pan? Does it have staying power?

One should aim to make the business distinctive in its total image. Each franchised business which is successful has its own innovative concept, which sets it apart from other businesses of the same type. This is what makes consumers choose to patronize that business as well as, or instead of, others in the same category. The existence of competitors can often be very healthy.

It can help to develop the overall market and act as a stimulant to both franchisor and franchisee alike.

Do not simply copy or imitate others. In the long run this is not a profitable course to adopt. They may have legal sanctions which they can apply, but even if they have not, they are probably already working out how to update and improve upon what they are presently doing. They will no doubt, through the development of their business and their experience, always keep one step ahead. It should also be understood that the copier does not have the benefit of laying the foundations of his knowledge through experience and that a shallow base makes his business vulnerable.

In order properly to protect the exclusive recognition of the business image it is best if at all possible to base it upon trademark or service mark registration. In selecting a trademark or service mark there are some basic principles which experience and market research have shown to be wise.

1. It should be easily pronounceable, compact and roll off the tongue.
2. It should not be capable of being translated. What sounds good in English may be offensive when translated into a foreign language.
3. It should be an invented, or coined, word, so as to be more readily registrable as a trademark or service mark.
4. It should be short.

Not only will the franchisee's business have to provide sufficient profits to enable the franchisee to obtain an acceptable return on capital and a reasonable income from his work, it must also provide sufficient revenue to enable the franchisee to pay a fee to the franchisor for the provision of all the continuing services which will be available. Unless the business can generate sufficient revenue for these purposes it probably is not capable of being established as a franchise.

Most successful franchises are businesses where a high degree of personal service to the customer is important (e.g. retailing, fast food, quick printing) and they require the personal presence and commitment of the franchisee at the point of sale. Regular features of such businesses are long hours, coupled with fast, reliable and friendly service. The length of hours to be worked by the franchisee will not necessarily be confined to the hours during which the business is open to the consumer. There will always be work to do, administrative, accounting, marketing and promotion, as well as 'thinking time'.

It is worth reiterating here the criteria to be borne in mind in assessing whether or not a business can be franchised.

1. The concept must be proved by practical experience to be demonstrably successful.
2. The business should be distinctive in its brand image and in its system and method.

3. The system and method must be capable of being passed on successfully to others within an economically sensible time frame.
4. The financial returns from the operation of the franchised business must be sufficient to enable:
   (a) the franchisee to obtain a reasonable return on the capital employed in his business;
   (b) the franchisee to earn a reasonable, if not good, reward for his labours; and
   (c) the franchisee to make payment to the franchisor of a reasonable fee for the services which he will continue to supply to the franchisee.
5. Can the franchisor make a sufficient on-going profit from fees received from franchisees?

THE PILOT OPERATION

Having developed a business concept, it is essential that at least one pilot operation, and in many cases a number of pilot operations, should be established. How many pilot units are required will depend upon how representative of the planned outlets in the network are the locations of the pilot operations. It may be that before the franchisor can be sure he is ready to provide a range of experience to franchisees, experiments have to be made in different areas. It may also be necessary to keep the pilot operation running for extended periods generally over 12 months, particularly where seasonal factors have to be taken into account. A franchisor with an established business may be able to benefit from experience gained from the operation of existing outlets, but even if they exist he should still operate at least one pilot operation under the same conditions as will apply to the proposed franchise system to ensure that the system works in practice. It will be prudent to run more than one pilot unit so as to eliminate any distortions arising from the results of one unit through the close attention it receives or the uniqueness of its location.

It has been suggested to the author that a pilot operation is not always possible or relevant, and that the franchisor can guarantee the operation on a money-back basis. In the author's view, this is a dangerous attitude and one which negates the fundamentals upon which business format franchising is established.

Fundamentally and essentially, the franchisor is selling a sophisticated package of proven know-how. If the franchisor has not proved his ability to operate his package with success and put his own money at risk he has no right to market the franchise. Nor, indeed, will he have established the goodwill, reputation and identity of the name which is associated with his package. It is irresponsible to seek to establish a franchise by trial and error, and at the expense and risk of the initial franchisees. Initial franchisees do not have as their function the operation of pilot units.

A guarantee of money back is no substitute for a lost business, a lost opportunity or in some cases a lost dream. In any event, how, with an untried and untested concept, does one ensure that the franchisor will be there with adequate money to pay back those who claim? Even if the franchisor and the money are there, inevitably there will be disputes about whether the failure was that of the franchisor's concept, or of the franchisee in not complying with the franchisor's guidelines.

The great responsibility which a franchisor has to his franchisees cannot be emphasized too strongly. Franchisees will be invited to part with what are for them substantial sums of money (which may often represent their life savings), change their whole way of life, and to become to a great extent dependent upon the franchisor and the concept for the welfare of themselves and their families.

Apart from these justifications for the pilot operation, it will fulfil the following functions.

1. The viability of the concept in practice will be developed and established as acceptable and exclusive in the mind and eye of the consumer. In the light of European competition law (Chapter 12) this process of experimentation and trial and error by a franchisor assumes a greater importance than it previously had.
2. It will identify problem areas and enable the franchisor to provide solutions in relation to:
    (a) marketing;
    (b) acceptability and availability of product or service;
    (c) methods of marketing, promotion and merchandising;
    (d) local by-laws;
    (e) building regulations;
    (f) fire regulations;
    (g) health and safety at work requirements;
    (h) planning requirements;
    (i) streamlining of shopfitting methods;
    (j) staff availability and training requirements;
    (k) taxation, including VAT, and customs and excise duties (if any); and
    (l) other factors of a legal and business nature relevant to the particular type of business.
3. It will enable the franchisor to experiment with layouts (see later comments) and to discover the best combination of equipment as well as the cost-effectiveness of resources in its acquisition. Alternative presentations of the decor and design of the interior and exterior of the premises can be tried out so that the most effective can be used.

4. The potential and actual trading experience of different types of location can be obtained. This will include experimenting with opening hours to discover what the optimum hours are during which the business should be operating. It should be borne in mind that in deciding which hours to open, consideration must be given to staff hours and shifts if need be. It could be that the ongoing costs of remaining open for extended periods, involving the need to introduce additional staff, will be uneconomic. On the other hand, trade may sometimes only develop slowly at certain 'non-traditional' times (e.g. late at night or on Sundays). It may not develop at all unless a commitment is made to be open at those times for at least a period of several months.

5. It will be appreciated that as training in the operational side of the business is necessary, so too is training in business management and accounting techniques. In developing the pilot operation, particular attention should be paid to the introduction of simple and effective systems of accounting, stocktaking and controls (e.g. in a food operation, portion and quality).

6. The franchisor will need an operations manual. The pilot operation will provide the basic information from which the operations manual will be prepared and the franchisor must be careful to record the lessons learned so that they are effectively employed for the benefit of the franchisees.

The requirements of layout of the premises will obviously differ from case to case. Some businesses are very dependent upon the way in which goods are merchandised, while others will not be.

Taking a fast food business as an example, the layout will have to be carefully planned so that the preparation progresses by logical steps without the need, so far as possible, to retrace one's steps. The whole operation of preparation will in all probability be timed and if the layout is such that a few unnecessary seconds per operation are inevitably required this could add up to the need for an additional employee. The availability within easy reach of what is required is essential if staff are not to be continually getting in each other's way. This is essentially the practical application of basic work study techniques. Portion control and size will have to be established to ensure customer satisfaction and to enable guidance on pricing policies to be established. If these factors are not properly resolved they could reduce the profitability of the operation, and the cumulative effect of failure to pay attention to such details could make the difference between a scheme which could be franchised and one which could not.

Even when the viability of the concept has been proved with the pilot operation this does not mean that the need for continuous 'pilot' operations ceases. The need, in fact, is greater, except that from being called 'pilot operations' they become what are called company-owned units.

The franchisor has to remain ahead of the game. He must continually be experimenting and developing, and by being in the field in the market-place he will be able to put his experiments and developments into practice on his own outlets. He will be able to show the franchisee that what he suggests is proved and tested in the field. It is just as important that the continuing developments are proved and tested as it was to prove and test the initial concept by the establishment of the pilot operation.

A franchisee may at some time need to be persuaded that his store needs refurbishment; that equipment should be replaced; and that he must update the appearance of his store. What better way is there to persuade him than to be able to demonstrate by the performance of the company-owned stores what can be achieved? 'Do what I have done' is infinitely better than 'do what I say'.

DEVELOPING THE FRANCHISE PACKAGE

The successful running of the pilot operation is essential to the preparation of the franchise package. The experience obtained in setting up and running the pilot operation will provide the basis upon which the elements in the package are structured. The package involves bringing together the elements of the business, reflecting the accumulation of the franchisor's total operational experience in a transmittable form.

It might be considered appropriate at this stage to consider employing the services of a consultant. In doing so regard should be had to the factors set out in Chapter 18.

The franchisor will have to know where one can establish an outlet and the criteria by which the site or the scope of a territory can be judged. Clearly, the factors which are dealt with in this chapter will not necessarily apply in all cases. Some franchise operations are dependent upon the specific location from which trading is to be carried out, others may depend upon advertising and marketing, followed by telephone contact. Retail and fast food franchises are typically in the former category, while such franchises as Hometune and ServiceMaster are in the latter. Furthermore, experience with the pilot operation should have indicated when custom is likely to produce the peaks of business activity.

It is suggested that the following considerations should be taken into account in assessing the degree of business activity a particular site may be capable of generating. The requirements will differ in some cases and so may the conclusions to be drawn from the information revealed by enquiries.

It may be thought that these criteria would apply to every business whether or not it is franchised. That is so, but in franchising, since one is offering to provide know-how to others, the franchisor's research must be done thoroughly to ensure that the franchise sold and the advice given are soundly based.

1. **Type of street**
   (a) Dual carriageway—is there a centre barrier?
   (b) Local road or trunk road.
   (c) The availability of motorway services sites is restricted.
   (d) Is car parking available?
   (e) Would the proposed use of the premises create a traffic hazard?
   (f) Roadside locations have been established but are still difficult to obtain.

2. **The environment**
   The environment is an increasingly important factor in assessing the suitability of sites and the appropriateness of the type of business. There is and will in the future be much legal regulation involving environmental considerations; they will be ignored in the future at considerable peril.

3. **Foot and/or road traffic volumes**
   The volume of traffic must not be permitted to mislead. For example, road traffic may not be able to stop if it is travelling too quickly, or if there is too much congestion, or risk of congestion. Similarly, foot traffic can be quite large, but uninterested for various reasons, such as commuter foot traffic at a railway station. Those who commute are invariably in a great hurry and may only stop for a quick purchase or may not stop in the numbers sufficient to justify the establishment of the proposed business. One should not ignore developments which are increasingly taking place at many railway stations or travel facilities which include shopping areas as a feature and which attract non-travelling shoppers. Do not be misled by the proximity of a pedestrian crossing. Crossings take people away from as well as bring them towards a site. If the crossing is leading to a town centre, or shopping area, it could place the site just outside the main flow of the pedestrian traffic.

4. **The degree of identification to which the premises are exposed**
   This will depend for its importance on the specific franchise involved, but clearly the better the exposure to the consumer of the franchisor's established identity, the greater the prospects of business.

5. **Landmarks and business which they may generate**
   (a) Museums
   (b) Schools
   (c) Cinemas, pubs, discos
   (d) Youth clubs

(e) The proximity to the leading multiple stores in a high street or shopping centre, e.g. Marks & Spencer or Sainsbury's

(f) Office blocks

(g) Sports facilities (which may provide evening and weekend business)

(h) Travel facilities, e.g. railway stations (subject to the above comments), tube stations (in London), coach depots, car parks

(i) Tourist attractions

In the case of a mobile franchise, where the franchisee visits the customer, careful evaluation has to be made of catchment areas and an assessment of what are realistic territorial allocations. Experience will have to be obtained of the different considerations which apply to urban and non-urban areas. Examples of mobile franchises include Hometune, Colour Counsellors and ServiceMaster (see the case studies in Chapter 15).

Having decided that the particular location is acceptable by the relevant criteria, one also has to assess the premises for their suitability for the purposes of the specific business. This would be the case, of course, regardless of the fact that there will be a franchise involved. The factors to be considered, and the effect they may have on the business, would include the following.

1. The size of the premises and whether one can fit into them all the necessary fixtures, fittings and equipment (if any) while still providing sufficient selling space or space for providing any on-site services.

2. The suitability or otherwise of the premises for conversion into the end product. This must take into account such factors as the need to provide adequate ventilation and to comply with health and safety requirements so far as may be appropriate to the type of business.

3. The availability of the necessary public utility services at the premises.

4. The amount of any premium which may have to be paid to acquire the premises, and the amount of rent and business rate.

5. The terms upon which the lease will be granted.

6. An assessment of the cost and the likelihood of obtaining the following, drawing upon the experience gained in running the pilot operation:

   (a) planning consents;

   (b) building by-law consents and fire certificates;

   (c) complying with any of the statutory or local authority by-law requirements which apply in the particular case; and

   (d) landlord's permission to carry out any works and to the assignment of the lease.

In the case of a mobile franchise it is the assessment and selection of the area of operations which is important; the location of trading premises is a secondary factor and in many cases, certainly in the early stages, the franchisee can run the business from his home. The need to be visible and uniform in appearance is achieved by the use of the same type of vehicle which is decorated in a distinctive livery so that each operational unit is a moving advertisement for the franchise and the franchisee's business.

Marketing of these sorts of operation is calculated to ensure that potential customers are aware of the service being offered and that when they require that type of service they will think of the trade name of the franchisor: use by consumers of these services is invariably on an occasional 'as-the-need-arises' basis and the most frequent point of contact is the telephone. These schemes tend therefore to be marketed by the use of their telephone numbers in association with their name and to be heavy users of Yellow Pages and other telephone directories and guides. In some cases the franchisor will provide a toll-free centralized number through which consumers can make contact with the network. In cases where the franchisees market their own phone numbers the control by the franchisor of the telephone numbers associated with the trade name is essential and the franchisor will tend either to become the subscriber or to require that on termination of the franchise agreement the franchisee will surrender the use of the number, preferably by transfer to the franchisor.

The experience gained in running the pilot operation will enable the franchisor to prepare standardized plans, specifications, packages of equipment and/or shopfitting which can be varied and amended so as to fit in with the requirements of particular premises. The basic needs in terms of fixtures, fittings and equipment will have been established, as will the correct layout. The franchisor will also have to be able to give advice on the decor of the store so that it reflects the established brand image. It should also be possible with the information available to the franchisor to streamline the preparation of any applications that are necessary for planning and by-law requirements. These applications can often be supported with brochures which explain and illustrate what is proposed.

The franchisor, drawing on his experience with pilot operations, will also prepare operational manuals which will provide the franchisee with all the information he will require in order correctly to operate the franchise business. The manual will invariably be used in training, and thereafter, while the franchisee is running his business, he will have it available to him at all times so that he can obtain guidance, or refresh his memory on any aspect of the business. Most manuals contain detailed guidance on the tasks to be performed by each individual member of the staff of the franchisee. The manual is an essential part of the process whereby the franchisor transfers his know-how concerning the running of the franchised business to the franchisee.

The franchisor will make arrangements with suppliers of the basic materials or products in which the franchised business deals for their sale to franchisees at competitive prices. These arrangements may extend to suppliers of any bags, boxes or other materials which are utilized at the point of sale. It will also usually be arranged that these materials will bear the franchisor's trademark, service mark or trade name. Arrangements will have to be made with equipment suppliers so that proper supplies are available to meet the franchisee's demand for equipment and spare parts and for their repair and servicing.

Systems of work will have to be put into written form. Job descriptions will have to be prepared explaining the scope and all the facets of each employee's activities so as to fit in with the overall scheme. Promotional literature, including point-of-sale material, will have to be created, as will any common format literature and notepaper.

The franchisor will have to set up training schedules and training facilities for franchisees and their staff. The importance of a properly structured training programme cannot be over-emphasized. This is not something which can be relegated to the category of 'I will work something out when we see the first franchisee'. The training requirements for the franchisee and his staff should be identified, the length of the course and how it will be presented must be carefully structured. The contact between franchisor and franchisee in the initial training phase will have a considerable bearing on the quality of the relationship. The training course will have to cover all facets of the conduct of the franchisor's business system so that the franchisee is, on its completion, capable of running the business and complying with his contractual obligations. However, while standards must be high the course must not be so long that the franchisee cannot afford to attend it and remain financially viable. The franchisor will prepare simple accounting procedures and business systems which are to be operated by the franchisee. The training course would include tuition in the use of these systems. The accounting procedures and business systems will fulfil two purposes. The first is to ensure that the franchisee has the correct flow of information available to enable him to see where his operation is going wrong or, if it is going right, that it is, in fact, proceeding according to plan or better. The second is to provide the franchisor with the information to enable him to provide continuing advisory and follow-up services as well as forming part of his control mechanisms. The franchisor will also have crucial financial information available which can be used in his dealings with prospective franchisees.

The franchisor will develop the necessary information to enable him to give advice to the franchisee about the leasing of premises or equipment, and other contracts into which the franchisee may have to enter with suppliers and with those who provide maintenance services for the equipment which is used in the franchised business.

The franchisor will need to explore the availability of financial facilities for his franchisees. In doing so he will learn whether he has prepared his franchise proposition sufficiently well to convince the sources of such facilities that it is acceptable. The banks have established an influential role in franchise development as a result of expertise which they have acquired (Chapter 7).

DEVELOPING THE OPERATIONAL MANUAL

The need for an operational manual (or manuals) has already been pointed out. In practice, the franchisee will first have contact with the manual when he attends for his training and then it will be loaned to him to be available as a continuing guide to the conduct of his business.

The manual will contain in written form the complete method for conducting the franchised business. It will invariably have the benefit of copyright protection which an oral explanation could not have. It thus forms an essential part of the legal methods by which the franchisor protects his ideas, know-how and trade secrets. It will, therefore, be appreciated that the manual should be extremely comprehensive and cover in detail all aspects of the day-to-day running of the franchised business.

Since the adoption by the European Commission of a block exemption regulation for franchise agreements (Chapter 12), the role of the manual has become more significant. This is because the regulation stipulates that the franchisor's 'know-how' must be described in a sufficiently comprehensive manner to make it possible to verify that it fulfils the criteria of secrecy and substantiality which are prescribed in the definition of a franchise agreement.

It is difficult in any publication to cover all types of franchised operations. This chapter will deal with what might be regarded as the sort of provisions one would expect to find in every manual, and then provide some specific suggestions which may be appropriate for particular types of franchised businesses.

Introduction

Each manual should contain some introductory remarks explaining the basic nature of the operation and the business philosophy of personal service which underlies it. The introduction should spell out in broad terms what the franchisee can expect from the franchisor, and what the franchisor will expect from the franchisee.

Operational system

There should then follow a detailed description of the operational system which explains how the operation is set up, and how and why the various constituent elements fit in with each other.

Equipment

A section in the manual should deal with the equipment which is required for the operation of the business. It will give a detailed explanation of what the equipment is, its function, and how to operate it. Guidance should also be given on how to troubleshoot basic and common faults which are likely to develop. There will be a directory of telephone numbers in the manual and this will include the telephone numbers of supply and service centres for the equipment (see below).

Operating instructions

This section will probably be broken down into a number of subsections. The following are suggested.

1. Opening hours/days.
2. Trading patterns.
3. Staff schedules and rotas.
4. Standard forms and procedures.
5. Requirements as to staff appearance (e.g. uniforms).
6. Staff training procedures.
7. Procedures for employing staff and compliance with statutory obligations.
8. Procedure for disciplining staff and the statutory obligations imposed on the franchisee as an employer.
9. Pricing policies. (It is likely that it will be illegal for the franchisor to seek to impose prices on the franchisee. This will not prevent the franchisor from issuing a recommended price list, but the recommendations must not be enforced.)
10. Purchasing policies (these can be affected by legal considerations (Chapter 12)) and delivery arrangements.
11. Product standards (quality and quantity) including customer complaints procedures.
12. Service standards.
13. Staff duties: a detailed job description for each member of the staff should be included which sets out not merely the nature and extent of the duties, but also the methods and procedures to be adopted in performing them.
14. Payment of franchise fees: the detailed procedure for calculating and accounting for fees with specimens of the appropriate forms.
15. Accounting: the specified accounting methods to be employed by the franchisee and the flow of information required to be provided to the franchisor. Advice on VAT requirements and PAYE and how to complete the necessary paperwork should also be given.

16. Cash control and banking procedures, including procedures for dealing with cheques, cheque cards and credit cards.
17. Advertising and marketing: basic guidance on standard point-of-sale advertising, marketing and selling techniques, with a list of dos and don'ts.
18. Requirements in regard to the presentation of the franchisor's house style and the way in which the franchisor's trademark and/or service mark should be used.
19. Insurance: details of cover recommended and any schemes offered by or through the franchisor. Alternatively, guidance on how to go about getting the cover required.
20. Stock control procedures.

Standard forms

There should be a section devoted to standard forms which will include all those already referred to above. Additionally, there could be the following.

1. Contracts of employment which comply with current legal requirements.
2. Agreements with managers or staff requiring them to keep the franchisor's trade secrets, methods, etc., secret and confidential and not to use or disclose them for any purpose except for the discharge of their responsibilities as employees.
3. Contract forms to be used in dealings with customers in the course of the conduct of the franchised business.

Technical supplement

This would contain more detailed technical information about equipment than is contained in the section dealing with detailed operational methods. It is not uncommon to see manufacturers' explanatory literature supplemented by detail contributed by the technical staff of the franchisor's organization.

Franchisor's directory

A directory of who's who in the franchisor's organization, and whom to contact for any particular aspect of the franchised business.

Telephone directory

A directory of all useful telephone numbers, such as service centres, suppliers, etc.

The above provisions are what one would expect to find in most manuals, with certain variations from business to business. In appropriate cases (two are now offered as examples) one would expect to find further sections, as well as some consequential variation of the sections previously mentioned.

Fast food

- Recipes
- Methods of preparations of food
- Kitchen procedures, including kitchen layout
- Times for preparation, cooking, holding and serving of each menu item
- Portion quantities, including how many portions should be produced from a given quantity of ingredients
- Stock requirements (range as well as quantities)
- Display and merchandising techniques
- Local advertising, promotion and public relations
- Menu content and variations according to time of day
- Customer complaints procedures
- Special industry applicable legal requirements, e.g. health and hygiene
- Planning, by-laws, disposal of litter, night operations, noise, parking, work permits for foreign staff
- Cleaning routines

Retail outlet

- Stock requirements in terms of approved or nominated suppliers, quality, quantities, range and shelf-life of products
- Store layouts
- Display and merchandising techniques
- Customer relations
- Issuing guarantees and dealing with claims
- Customer complaints procedures

The list could be almost endless as one looks at the variety of franchise offers: Hometune, Budget Rent-a-Car, ServiceMaster, Fastframe and Prontaprint are but a few diverse examples. The specific manual requirements of each will differ both in nature and scope.

All franchisors should be conscious of the need constantly to keep their methods under review and to introduce changes and variety so that their operation is at the forefront of the market. Such changes and variations should be reflected in supplements and amendments to the manual or manuals so that the franchisee is always kept informed and up to date.

MARKETING THE FRANCHISE PACKAGE

The best way for a franchisor to market a franchise package is based upon his ability to demonstrate his success. Pilot operations should have been established to prove the concept works in practice. If, through the operation of these pilots, the franchisor is able to demonstrate success (without which, of course, there is little, if anything, to franchise) this in itself will be the best marketing tool in the launch of the franchise.

Many franchisors maintain a low profile in the marketing of the initial few franchises. It can be very tempting to respond to many requests (as often happens) for franchises from prospective franchisees in the early days when the franchisor has spent a considerable amount of money in developing the franchise and is anxious to generate a positive flow of income. Many franchisors have suffered a great deal of difficulty with early franchisees whose recruitment was premature and whose credentials were not as thoroughly assessed as they should have been because the franchisor was more interested in responding, or under financial pressure to respond, to the short-term need for cash flow rather than the careful development of his network.

In marketing franchises, many have found that editorial comment in local and national newspapers is a very effective method of attracting enquiries. This can only be achieved if the franchise, or someone connected with it, provides newsworthy material. There is also luck to be taken into account since even newsworthy items may be dropped if something better turns up. One could employ public relations consultants, but doing so might involve a greater expense than most franchisors could afford at such an early stage. However, since this approach can be very effective it should be investigated thoroughly before being dismissed.

Most franchisors make contact with their franchisees in one of the following five ways.

1. A customer of one of the pilot operations may ask to become a franchisee.
2. The prospective franchisee is attracted to the opportunity by a friend who has taken up a franchise, or by talking to an existing franchisee.
3. The prospective franchisee responds to a news item or feature in a newspaper or magazine mentioning the franchise.
4. The prospective franchisee has seen an advertisement in such media as *Franchise World* or the business opportunities sections of the various daily or Sunday papers.
5. The prospective franchisee meets the franchisor at a franchise exhibition.

Before a franchise opportunity can be advertised in the national press the prior approval of the Newspaper Publishers' Association must be obtained.

This will involve the completion of a questionnaire providing detailed information about the franchisor and the franchise operation and the consideration of the franchisor's contractual documents. This must be taken seriously since the scrutiny to which applications are subjected is thorough and approval is by no means guaranteed.

A grand opening of one or more of the pilot operations can create a public event at a relatively modest cost, which could attract media attention. Attention to detail is essential, for little credit will be given to a spectacular launch where the arrangements go wrong. Suppliers may be persuaded to provide products at special discounted prices and/or to take advertising space in a special feature in a local newspaper.

Having achieved some measure of public awareness through the visible success of the pilot operations, the franchisor will then wish to make some similar public display to mark the decision to expand using the franchise method of marketing. It is crucial that the early franchisees, and their locations or territories, are carefully chosen. At all costs, the franchising operation must avoid a false start. Successful early franchisees are a very effective demonstration of what their successors may hope to achieve. By contrast, if the early franchisees experience difficulties, whatever the reason, it will be more difficult for the franchisor to attract new franchisees.

The financial terms (i.e. initial franchise fee, plus on-going turnover-based fees, or mark-up on supplies or other sources of the franchisor's income) must be structured to ensure that the franchisee will obtain an attractive return on his capital and income for his labours.

The opening of the first franchised unit may be approached in the same 'grand opening' manner as the pilot operation. It is useful to provide the press, particularly the local press, with a thumbnail sketch of the franchisee involved so that human interest and personal finance/investment stories can be written, together with appropriate information about the franchisor and his results to date.

All the facts and data provided must be truthful and accurate, and presented in a direct, positive manner which can be easily assimilated. It is likely that a well-organized grand opening event will be so hectic and well attended that there will be little time for lengthy explanations with complex details. This means that the written material made available is important. It will invariably form the basis of any editorial comments which may subsequently appear in the press.

The aggressive approach does not appeal to all, nor indeed is it necessarily the right approach in each case. Some may take the view that they do not want significant publicity at such an early stage of development. Such people consider a quiet buildup of the network to be more important; more extensive publicity can follow when the franchise is soundly established and ready to move forward at a quicker pace.

However, one factor which is undoubtedly essential is that the franchisor must be patient at this crucial stage. He must not try to expand more quickly than his capacity to attract well-qualified franchisees and to service them allows.

The franchised business will be advertising for customers for its products/ services and the side-effect of such advertisements may well be to generate enquiries from prospective franchisees. Having gained publicity or obtained a lead for a prospective franchisee, the franchisor must not produce, in response to enquiries, a brochure or other literature which does not do the franchisor justice. There are many franchisors who let themselves down by the poor quality of their printed material. It must never be forgotten that the material supplied in response to enquiries will be part of the franchisor's 'shop window'.

It will thus pay to prepare an attractive set of literature. This should explain who are the people involved in the franchise and their experience, and it should give the history of the business and a description of the franchisor's services. It is always a good idea to include some pictures of the business premises and/or vehicles and of the people involved in the business. By this stage, the franchisor should have a business of which he is proud and will be pleased to promote its virtues to prospective franchisees.

Many franchisors follow a set procedure when marketing the franchise. It should be appreciated that out of every 100 enquiries, 80 will probably never get beyond the initial communication, 10 will on submission of personal details be unsuitable, 10 may be worth meeting and discussing the proposition with, and two or three may be suitable and finally buy a franchise.

Marketing the franchise requires considerable patience (no apology for repetition—it is important). No franchisee worth having is waiting with pen poised to sign the contract.

The franchisor must consider the suitability of the prospective franchisee. This involves the consideration of a wide range of factors which are considered below, but consideration should also be given to factors which are calculated to ensure that the prospective franchisee has considered his position very carefully and that certain basic elements are present. These include the following.

1. Is the prospective franchisee suited to the rigours of self-employment with the stress involved?
2. Is the person fully committed to and capable of undertaking all that is involved in running the franchise?
3. Will he fit in and get on with the franchisor's head office and field team?
4. What is the prospective franchisee's past history?
5. Does he have adequate financial resources?
6. Is his commitment supported by a spouse (if there is one)?

The franchisor should bear in mind that not only is it in his own interests to ensure that his franchise and self-employment are right for the prospective franchisee, but also it is in the prospective franchisee's and all other franchisees' interests.

The franchisor will also have the task of explaining the contract and the reasoning behind its provisions, which will call for thoroughness and a great deal of patience. It must be remembered that, for the franchisee, this can be the biggest decision in his life. There will be disappointments for the franchisor because some prospective franchisees whom the franchisor would consider ideal will decide against buying the franchise.

What then is the procedure? It is very important to get this right. First impressions always count a lot and the written presentation will tell a lot about the franchisor and just how business-like is his operation.

1. Normally, the franchisor will receive a letter or phone call from the prospective franchisee. The initial contact may be made at a franchise exhibition when such preliminary discussions can take place. No franchisor should ever 'sign up' a franchisee at the exhibition at which the first meeting has taken place. All normal investigations and procedures must still be followed, particularly in a case where the prospective franchisee may have been influenced by the euphoria of the event. The franchisor will respond by sending out or handing over an illustrated presentation describing the franchise company and its success story. Sometimes this is presented in a question-and-answer form. Some companies explain briefly what franchising is. The franchisor may find it convenient at some stage to send prospective franchisees a copy of *How to Evaluate a Franchise* (published by *Franchise World*). Franchisors find that this guide puts franchising into perspective for potential franchisees and their professional advisers, who may never previously have had contact with a franchise transaction.

2. The presentation is often accompanied by an explanation of what the franchisor does for his franchisees in terms of setting them up and in continuing to service their needs and requirements thereafter.

3. Some financial information is also usually despatched with the initial material. This is very rarely presented as a guarantee of what one will achieve. Rather, it will illustrate a profit performance which may be achieved if certain levels of sales are reached. These figures must be prepared with care and contain a proper explanation of what they do represent so that the prospective franchisee is not misled and so that the franchisor is not creating possible problems for himself later on if things go wrong.

4. The franchisee will also be invited to complete an application form to provide the franchisor with details about the franchisee to enable the

franchisor to find out whether the franchisee has the financial resources and is a suitable person with whom to proceed further.

5. These items may be accompanied by a letter inviting the prospective franchisee to contact the franchisor to discuss the matter further. The better course would be to wait until the application form is submitted. A franchisor should understand that many of the requests he receives will not be serious enquiries and may be from other franchisors or prospective franchisors who wish to see what he is offering.

It is to be emphasized that considerable time and effort will be involved in finalizing the first few franchise contracts and getting the new franchisees open for business and trading. The process will be even longer where suitable property has to be acquired and converted. The franchisor should not rush his fences, or expect rapid results in the initial stage of his franchise programme.

SELECTING FRANCHISEES

The selection of franchisees is not an easy subject on which to give advice, particularly as it is of crucial importance. It is one of the ironies of life that one has to learn by one's mistakes in order to gain experience. Franchising is no different, and the skill of choosing the right franchisees is, of necessity, developed with experience.

It is not uncommon to find that a franchisor will have more problems from among the first 10 franchisees than from those who subsequently join the network. It is also not unknown for some of those early unsatisfactory franchisees to poison the atmosphere later on by stirring up the network.

One of the most common mistakes which is made by new franchisors is to be too ready and willing to establish initial franchisees and to give them special deals. This is quite understandable, since at that point the franchisor has spent a great deal of time and money on establishing his franchise and in running his pilot operation. He wants to expand quickly and see a return on his investment as soon as possible. He is at the point of maximum vulnerability just when he requires the strongest nerve. It is a great mistake to accept as a franchisee someone who is willing to buy the franchise unless he matches up to the franchisor's requirements in every respect. That is just as important with the first as it is with the hundred-and-first franchisee. Standards of selection must never be relaxed or compromised. There are many franchisors who, having become established, express the wish that they could be rid of some of their earlier franchisees who were accepted because they were available, and not because they matched up to the franchisor's requirements. These franchisees would not qualify for acceptance at the present stage because the franchisor is now established and can afford to be more selective and patient. Would one set up a pilot operation in a totally wrong location merely because it was available, or would one wait patiently for the right site? One would, of course, wait for the right site. So with the initial franchisees it is essential to be patient. Wait for the right person. It will pay in the long run.

There are those franchisors who give special deals to initial franchisees to lure them in, again as a means of starting up quickly. This is also a mistake and, as experience shows, on the whole builds up problems later on when one has to exercise control over such franchisees, who still rate themselves as 'special cases' and feel that they are thus entitled to 'special treatment'. Additionally, franchisees do talk to each other, and special deals cause ill feelings with attendant difficulties for the franchisor as the later entrants to the network discover that they have different terms, which they will resent.

Many franchisors develop what they call a franchisee profile as the number of their franchisees increases. This reflects the pattern of qualities and qualifications of the franchisees which they have set up in business. As an example, a franchisor may be able to say that his franchisee is most likely to be a married man, aged 39–45 years with two children and the following attributes and attitudes: he has had a successful career in middle management, is fed up with lack of prospects and stifled by company policies, is keen and anxious to be his own boss, is supported by his wife in his ambitions, has no previous experience in the type of franchised business on offer, and has adequate finance backed by a fairly good equity in his house on which he can borrow.

It is important that the prospective franchisee has enough money to get started, but possibly not much more. While the franchisee may have to borrow some of the funds, say up to 50%, or even as much as 70% (which some banks are prepared to offer), the rest should be his own cash. Any borrowing should be arranged with an ethical source of funds (e.g. a reputable bank, finance house or insurance company) and over a satisfactory length of time to enable the business to generate sufficient to enable payment of the borrowed funds, and the interest thereon, while leaving sufficient for the franchisee's reasonable living expenses. Five- to 10-year loans should be satisfactory for most purposes.

It is as well to remember that if the franchisee has not put in any funds of his own, he may be tempted to walk away from the franchised operation if difficulties are encountered, rather than work his way through them. A financial commitment the loss of which would be felt by the franchisee is a considerable incentive and is usually regarded as an essential feature of a franchise transaction.

An ambitious, committed individual is an ideal prospect likely to prove to be a successful franchisee but one must be certain that his ambition will not lead him to become creative so far as the franchisor's system is concerned. No matter how ambitious, the franchisee must accept that he is operating someone else's system and not his own.

In some cases large companies have become good franchisees, and there are some very successful multiple franchisees, notably in hotel, fast food and retail businesses. The large corporate franchisee, by contrast with the small proprietorial corporate franchisee, can present problems for a franchisor. It is more difficult in such a case to control the spread of the franchisor's know-how, and secret and confidential information. An economically strong franchisee, who may be more financially powerful than the franchisor, would be a powerful opponent in the event of any disputes. Also, the large company may find the constraints imposed upon it by franchising too restrictive and may gradually introduce what it thinks are improvements to the system. Such a situation is challenging since the large company may consider that its experience in its own operations equips it better than the franchisor. For these reasons it may be sensible for most franchisors not to deal with large companies as franchisees, certainly not until the network is strong enough for the franchisor to be able to withstand the pressures to which he could be subjected.

However, the more common type of relationship is basically one between the franchisor and the individual franchisee (who may form a company) and is a very personal one. The success of the personal relationship is indeed the key to the successful growth of the whole operation. An individual franchisee must be healthy and vigorous enough to withstand considerable physical and nervous strain. The hours will undoubtedly be long. There may be fetching and carrying, and he may be on his feet for extended periods. The nervous strain can come from the entirely novel experience of having his complete wealth and livelihood at stake in the franchised venture. He cannot hold his hand out for wages at the end of the week to anyone but himself.

It is important from the customers' point of view that the franchisee looks healthy, clean and tidy, particularly in any operation where he is handling or serving food. The franchisee who is clean, tidy and healthy himself is likely to keep his operation clean, tidy and 'healthy'.

The franchisor should have at least one meeting with the prospective franchisee and spouse in their own home. Seeing them together, and the way in which they live, and keep and maintain their home, can tell a lot about them. Those who live in a sloppy manner are likely to run their business in the same sloppy way. Do not find out too late when a simple additional procedure can provide the information required. Meeting both together will also enable the franchisor to judge just how committed the spouse is to the proposed venture and how likely to interfere.

Most franchisors do not require their franchisees to have prior experience of their particular trade as full training will normally be provided. Indeed, some franchisors believe that the person with experience of their type of business will be more difficult to train in the franchisor's particular methods.

It can be difficult effectively to 'untrain' someone and retrain him so that in the future he will not ignore the system. On the other hand, there can be some businesses where a background knowledge of the trade or technical know-how is essential and since it cannot be taught within an economically viable time frame the prospective franchisee must have the requisite knowledge. In such a case, the franchisor's training will have to be very thorough and so will the continuing supervision of operations.

Age is relatively unimportant in many cases so long as the prospective franchisee's health is good, although advanced age may render people unsuitable for some particular kinds of business. In some franchises, a husband and wife team is an ideal combination with both partners active in the business. Even where this is not required, it is important that the prospective franchisee has the total support of his spouse. There may be telephone messages to be taken and relayed at unsocial hours of the day and night, normal mealtimes will often be missed, and there may be widespread disruption of the normal pattern of social and domestic life.

The prospective franchisee must be independent enough to be able to manage a business on his own. However, he must be dependent enough to want to work within the rules of the franchise and not continually to be challenging the franchisor and the system and seeking an excuse to break away.

It is essential in view of the relationship which exists in a franchise for the franchisor and franchisee to have mutual trust and respect. The franchisee must be someone whom the franchisor can trust with his name and goodwill. Will he be honest in his financial returns on which the management services fee income will depend? Will he give his staff and customers honest and fair treatment? On the other hand, can the franchisee trust the franchisor, and does the franchisor deserve that trust? The franchisor must demonstrate a successful record of ethical business practice.

Can the prospective franchisee, with the franchisor's help, cope with running his own business, probably for the first time? The first couple of meetings should provide clues on this score, as will a visit to his home. The franchisor should be able to tell if the prospective franchisee is serious in his approach by the way he asks questions about the operation and also the effort which he puts into visiting outlets and generally vetting the franchise proposition. The prospective franchisee should be encouraged to ask questions and to talk about himself and his aspirations.

Will the franchisee be receptive to the training and guidance which he will be given? Does the franchisor feel that the franchisee will have the capacity to cope with the assimilation of information and be able to apply it in practice?

Finally, the franchisor will have to decide whether he likes the applicant. Since both parties will doubtless see (and hear) a lot of one another and are mutually dependent, it is most important that they get on well with one another and have mutual respect. The 'chemistry' must be right. After all, both parties will be working considerable hours for the same end—the success of the franchise. The franchisor does need the franchisee to be successful. The success of both the franchisor's and the franchisee's business will be inextricably interwoven.

The ultimate decision must be made by the proprietor of the franchisor, as the decision has long-term consequences for both parties. The principals on both sides must be happy with the arrangement.

If the franchisor chooses to make use of the services of a consultant, the two must work very closely with each other. The reputable consultant will know that it is the franchisor who should appoint franchisees and he will want the franchisor to be interested and involved. An ethical consultant may help the franchisor in acquiring the skills involved in selecting the right franchisees, but the consultant should never sell franchises. The consultant should be paid a professional fee for services actually rendered and never a commission on sales (Chapter 18).

In summary, the franchisor should select his franchisees deliberately and cautiously, and allot sufficient time to do the job properly. Remember, it is a crucial decision for both parties. The franchisee will often have at stake his whole life savings and life-style. The franchisor for his part will have at stake the reputation of his business, his future income and his credibility in selling further franchises.

DEVELOPING THE FRANCHISOR'S ORGANIZATION

As in any business, it is sensible for the franchisor to set up and expand his organization gradually in line with the development of his business. It would not be financially sensible to take on too many additional staff initially when there are as yet no franchisees. On the other hand, it is essential that all the franchisees (especially the early ones) are fully serviced, so the franchisor must have properly trained staff available to deal with the requirements of the network and may not leave the hiring of the requisite staff until after franchising commences. It is a matter of timing and judgement on the part of the franchisor to ensure that he has sufficient staff resources and skills to provide for the franchisee's needs. It can make a lot of sense for the franchisor to recruit his managers of pilot operations with a view to their broader involvement in the network's development.

There will undoubtedly be expenses incurred in establishing the franchisor's organization to accommodate the development of franchisee recruitment before there is any income. It is very likely—indeed, it is invariably the case—that the franchisor will suffer net losses in the first years. How many years it will be before profits are made will vary from case to case and will be affected by the growth rate of the business, but the time span can be as much as 3 to 5 years. There will be unavoidable expenses of trademark and/or service mark registration, brochure production, staff salaries, office over-heads, expenditure, travel, advertising, promotion, legal and accountancy advice, etc. before and while the franchisees become established and the fees on turnover, or mark-up on the supply of goods, begin to flow to the franchisor.

The franchisor is faced with expenses in the early stages which his income from the franchisees will not cover. However, he should not despair as his income should grow faster than his expenses. The staff required to cope with five franchisees may well be able to cope with 25. Each new franchisee who commences operations represents additional income for the franchisor and, as the turnover of each franchisee increases, the franchisor's income will also increase. The financial aspects of franchising and fee structures are dealt with in Chapter 7.

Source of income

Each franchisee should represent a secure and growing source of income to the franchisor, provided that the franchise is a good viable system, and is kept that way by the sensible management of the franchisor. Furthermore, suc-cessful existing franchisees will provide a source of additional expansion for the franchise network as they seek to reinvest their profits by opening further units. It is not uncommon to find that existing franchisees are a significant source of recruits for new outlets.

The long-term nature of the franchise contract with its continuing obli-gations is a major advantage over the normal sales operation, where, say, packets of tea have to be sold to the same grocer every few weeks. The latter type of operation needs a large sales force, heavy continuous advertising, and there is always the fear that the customer will choose to buy a competitive product or even the same brand from another supplier.

These factors have an important impact on the type of organization which the franchisor should develop in the early stages. Basically, he will need few, but competent people who have a broad knowledge and are hard-working. 'Hard-working' is not lightly said, since the franchisees will in many cases be working long hours, sometimes 7 days a week, and, having invested their life savings in the franchisor's idea, will generally expect to be able to contact the franchisor whenever they feel the need. Running a franchise involves a great deal of unsocial hours, time and effort.

Breadth of knowledge is also important as the franchisee will want answers on all sorts of subjects and will prefer to cover them all in the one conver-sation with the particular person to whom he is talking, or with whom he is accustomed to deal. The functions most franchisors need to emphasize are finance (accounting), franchise sales, marketing and operations (including innovations). Each of these are examined in turn.

Finance (accounting)

For the new franchisor, the financial aspects should be capable of being dealt with by the staff who deal with his own company operations. They should be able to devise and develop a simple accounting system for the franchise network and be capable of giving financial advice to franchisees and in relation to the operation of the accounting system. Regular returns and accounts will be required from franchisees and it is vital that each franchisee understands from the outset exactly what is required in this respect. This understanding should be instilled in franchisees during training.

The information which is required should fulfil two objectives.

1. It should enable the franchisor to monitor each franchisee's performance as well as provide the basis for calculating the fees to be paid.
2. It should enable the franchisee to see for himself how his performance compares with his business projections and with the objectives, which he and the franchisor have set, and with the other franchisees in the network.

The task of providing the information should be made as simple as possible, but that does not mean that essential steps should be avoided. The information required will be in three categories:

1. Gross revenues.
2. Profit and loss statements.
3. Capital expenditure.

There will be provisions in the franchise contract requiring the franchisee to submit the various categories of information at stated intervals.

GROSS REVENUES

Information relating to gross revenues will be required by the franchisor at the same intervals as the franchisee fees are required to be paid. The period fixed for such payment should be as short as possible, weekly if feasible, so that the franchisee will be required to discipline himself to attend to his financial records each week and to write out a cheque for fees each week. If his finances are shaky and fees are delayed, the problem is then discovered sooner rather than later so that remedial action can be taken. The disciplines of attending to financial records each week will ensure that up-to-date financial management information will be available to him and the franchisor. The franchisor should require the franchisee to provide him with a copy of the relevant information.

A simple form for weekly reporting might look as follows. It is assumed that the week finishes at the close of business on a Saturday.

Weekly gross revenues—fee remittance form/tax invoice

Address of store/operation ....

Store no. ....

Accounting reference no. ....

Week ending ....

Franchisor's VAT no. ....

Franchisee's name and address ....

	1 Total gross revenues	2 Less VAT	3 Total for fee calculation	4 Number of customers	5 Average value per customer
Sun					
Mon					
Tues					
Wed					
Thurs					
Fri					
Sat					

Fee calculation

Total revenue (per column 3)		£ ....
Management services fee	... % thereof	£ ....
Advertising contribution	... % thereof	£ ....
Total		£ ....
VAT at 17.5% thereon		£ ....
Total remitted by cheque herewith		£ ....

I certify that the figures set out above are true, correct and complete.

Signed ....

Name in full .... Franchisee

Date ....

PROFIT AND LOSS STATEMENTS

A profit and loss statement will identify whether margins have gone astray and can help identify existing or developing problems. Again, the more frequently the information is available, the better. If possible a profit and loss account should be prepared weekly. In most businesses, the five most important factors to check are sales, gross margins, stock, cash and wages. They are the chief variables. It is important that all should be checked on a weekly basis. If the level and range of stock are such that weekly checks are impracticable a monthly check should be carried out. Any longer period results in inadequate financial information being available to franchisees and to the franchisor, which is not a sensible way to manage a business.

The sales should be checked frequently with takings being reconciled between cash register and amounts banked at least every day. If the business operates a shift system, the takings should be physically counted and agreed at the end of each shift before those responsible for the shift which is ending leave the premises. Some fast food operations take hourly till readings to develop information to assist in the anticipation of the business flow.

Where credit is given, great care must be exercised to ensure regular payment of receivables as cash flow is as important as sales. There is no point in achieving high sales if the money is not available to be used by the franchisee. A lack of positive cash flow could destroy what could otherwise be a successful business. The higher the level of receivables the more capital the franchisee must have available to finance his business.

If the business involves product sales, a system must be devised for checking the stock of products at regular intervals. The longer the interval the less valuable the information available. Without this information, there is no check on shortages, theft or gross profitability. Proper ordering is difficult if the franchisee does not know what he has. The advent of computerized cash registers (electronic point of sale) which can record stock movements can assist, but cannot replace actually checking physically to ensure that what the machine says is what is really there.

A typical profit and loss statement is as follows:

Profit and loss statement

Gross revenues	£ . . . .
Less VAT	£ . . . .
Total revenues	£ . . . .
Less cost of sales	£ . . . .
Gross profit	£ . . . .

It should be noted that there may be differences in the breakdown of these items. In a fast food operation, there could be a breakdown between the cost of food and cost of packaging. Where there are separate elements involved it may be wise to break them down to assist in the monitoring of performance and controls. Additionally, if the operation involves the carrying of stock, the opening and closing stock figures have to be taken and netted off to provide an accurate gross profit figure.

Other deductions need to be made before the net profit figure can be calculated:

Less: Operating expenses
Salaries/wages
Rent, rates, service charges
Management services (franchise) fee
Advertising fee
Additional local advertising
Insurance
Telephone
Electricity
Gas
Repairs and renewals
Travel expenses
Sundry expenses
Bank charges and interest

Allowance will have to be made for depreciation before the net profit is accurately stated.

Upon receipt of the profit and loss statement, the franchisor should check the figures to see whether they reveal any departure from the performance criteria which he has established.

In order to facilitate the rapid production of the required information, the franchisor should provide simplified profit and loss statement forms. The variable items of revenue, cost of sales, gross profit, wages and franchise fees are entered every week with standard amounts entered for the other items, e.g. rents, rates, etc. This method enables useful information to be produced within a day or two of the end of the week so that the franchisee himself and the franchisor are both rapidly aware of any problems and how the business is developing in general. The standard amounts can be updated and changed as they vary.

A useful check is for the franchisor to make available the key performance criteria of the network, e.g. revenues, cost of sales, wage percentage, spend per customer, etc., to all units (franchised and company-owned), on a weekly basis, accompanied by a brief commentary on any significant features. The figures will be of interest to franchisees and can often create competition between franchisees to become the best performers in the network.

CAPITAL EXPENDITURE

Capital expenditures are more difficult to control. The danger is that a franchisee does not appreciate that his expenses have to be deducted from his gross revenues before he has any profit for himself. There is a tendency to spend prematurely on the good things in life. It is wise to call for a balance sheet at periodic intervals so that some indication of the financial health of the business is available.

It is useful to have full accounts reviewed every quarter (or at least every six months) by external accountants and audited accounts on an annual basis. The franchisor's existing financial and administrative staff can provide advice and a brief guide to matters such as the payment of wages, employment regulations and VAT returns.

In time, it may be necessary to have additional accounting staff for the franchised side of the business, but certainly not initially. Indeed, there is much to gain from using the existing staff. They will be able to advise from a basis of knowledge and experience of the business and also they will doubtless deepen their own understanding of the company's business in the process.

Some franchise companies develop in-house computer capacity and provide an accounting service to franchisees, which in turn provides a greater ability, both to the franchisor and franchisee, to monitor and control the franchisee's business.

Franchise sales

On the sales side, the proprietor of the business will initially have to do the selling himself; indeed, there is a considerable case for him to continue to do that. Selling, used in its normal sense, is not necessarily an appropriate word. It is more a case of explaining the proposition, the services offered, the contractual basis and terms. The proprietor of the business is the appropriate person anyway, as he will fully understand the motivation and concerns of the prospective franchisee about to go into business on his own, probably for the first time.

Recruiting a specialist salesman from outside is potentially dangerous at any time but is particularly so in these delicate early stages; such a person would not know the business and the franchisor would not know him well enough to rely utterly on his judgement and his ethics when it comes effectively to parting people from their life savings. The use of outside consultants for the sale of franchisees is not recommended.

When extra help is required on the sales side, those to be involved should be taken on one at a time, with impeccable references from previous employers, very carefully screened and thoroughly trained. They must also understand the ethics of franchising and that they must become experts at the 'soft sell'. Hard selling has no place in franchising. Alternatively, the franchisor could consider transferring someone from his own operational organization to assist on the sales side. The advantage of recruiting from existing staff is that they will have the systems knowledge and their integrity is known.

These comments concerning the proprietor carrying out the sales function are made on the assumption that the franchisor is a proprietorial company. Where this is not the case (e.g. where the operation to be franchised is part of a large organization), then the head of that division—the director in charge, or the managing director of the subsidiary company—should similarly devote himself personally to the selling effort.

One last word on the question of sales. Any individual specializing in this activity should be paid a good salary, with regular reviews, good conditions of service, plus a modest performance bonus. The aim should be to attract and retain a career-minded individual with a view to a long service career, who will produce a steady flow of high-quality results. He will provide an essential future link with franchisees, who will often consult him as an 'uncle figure' when problems arise. Ethical franchising is not a foot in the door, immediate performance, high bonus, or 'you're out' type of selling operation. Therefore, the financial incentives used to attract that type of salesman are totally inappropriate in franchising.

Marketing the product or service

In the early days of franchising activity it is unlikely that the franchisor will need any specialist additional marketing staff. If the franchisor already has a marketing capability for company operations, it should be used. If the franchisor employs an advertising agency, they should also be briefed on the franchising plans. If the franchisor does not have an advertising agency it is recommended that one be appointed. If the franchisor is too small at this stage for an agency to be interested the franchisor should obtain experienced assistance.

Expenses must be carefully watched, especially in the early stages when little can be afforded. However, good design work to establish the image will be needed. Some of this may already exist, but in switching to a franchise it may be wise to take another look at existing material and perhaps ensure greater distinctiveness. There are specialist design firms who offer such a service.

There will be advertisements to place, and public relations events and releases to be handled. All these items should be carefully considered and it is best to start with a modest programme and ensure that the money spent is wisely invested. At this stage, more than any other, it is vital to obtain full value for money.

Although specialist agencies exist, as the franchisor's organization grows so too will the capacity to do a great deal of promotional, marketing and design work in-house. The franchisor should have staff who specialize in promotion, marketing and design work. He will need to liaise with specialist agencies and with the franchisees in the field. Considerable advantage will be gained from discussions with franchisees about various marketing and promotional ideas. Point-of-sale material is often worth trying with company-owned outlets and then with selected franchisees before its introduction throughout the network.

A continuous and positive approach to marketing and promotion from within the franchisor's organization is also good for the morale of franchisees; it preserves continuity and will assist in demonstrating in practice the franchisor's concern with success of the franchisee's businesses.

Operations (including innovations)

The franchisor will undoubtedly need sufficient staff to provide franchisees with the detailed help they require to prepare and launch their new venture. The franchisor has the obligation to continue to monitor and advise the franchisee and if necessary control him after the launch.

The obvious source for a candidate will be one of the existing operational staff from a company operation. At first only one person will be required, someone who is an experienced all-rounder, particularly good in practice. He must be able personally to perform all the tasks necessary and be prepared to roll up his sleeves and actually work alongside the franchisees in the early days. The preparation of the operations manual should also be the responsibility of the person chosen to be in charge of operations.

In the early days, training is likely to be carried out at company-owned opeeerrations by one of the franchisor's experienced managers, using the manual which has been written. If the company already has a training officer, well and good, but most new franchisors will not be so well blessed and will need to maximize the use which can be made of the franchisor's existing operational staff and facilities. It should be recognized that franchising is different from employment and the person engaged in training will have to adjust his thinking to the different discipline which is required in dealing with franchisees.

As the franchise network develops the franchisor will be able to provide a classroom with a mock-up of an operational unit. This may be sited conveniently on the floor above, or in space behind, an existing company operation. The staff involved in operations will expand with the growth of the business and the operational support side of the franchise business will develop along a number of paths.

1. There will be the initial training of new franchisees and staff.
2. There will be the continuing retraining of franchisees and staff. Much of this can be done at the franchisees' premises. Its main purpose will be to work out operational flaws, to eliminate bad habits developed by the franchisee, and to introduce new methods. Field staff will also be able to train the franchisee in new techniques and systems.
3. There will be a team in the field offering on the spot operational advice.
4. There will be those dealing with product or service innovations and experimental ideas. These should always initially be tried out in the franchisor's company operations.

The quality of the franchisors' field support and monitoring services is important. The franchisor, even in the early stages of his development, has to contemplate that there will be difficulties. He must be ready to cope.

The franchisor will also have to consult with his bankers, accountants and solicitors. The franchising project should be fully explained to them at an early stage, as it is possible that they may not know too much about the subject. The bankers may be helpful in providing finance for franchisees and may be able to introduce the franchisor to their franchise managers for investigation and guidance. It is not generally sensible for the company to be involved in financing franchisees themselves, either by lending funds or by providing guarantees. The function of the franchisor should be limited to introducing the franchisee to the sources of finance which are available and to provide any necessary information which the source reasonably requires.

The accountants can be asked to advise on methods of monitoring the franchisees' financial performance. Solicitors will advise the franchisor about the protection of his rights; they will prepare the contractual documentation and review any franchise sales literature.

In summary, the initial organizational requirements for the new franchisor with limited resources are the following.

Franchise sales
> Proprietor or managing director himself, plus a good secretary.

Marketing of the product or service
> Proprietor himself, plus a good secretary, plus advice from outside designers and an advertising agency.

Operations
> One person transferred from one of the franchisor's existing operations, who may be a manager selected with this role in mind.

Shopfitting and equipment
> The operations person, plus outside suppliers/shopfitters.

Training
> A manager of one of the franchisor's own operations.

Finance and administration
> Existing company personnel, plus help from the franchisor's bankers, accountants and solicitors.

There remain three important considerations to remember.

1. The owner or managing director of the franchise must be fully involved personally since he must be prepared to demonstrate his faith in his business and in franchising.
2. The maximum use should be made of existing company staff for reasons not only of economy, but also knowledge, experience and

dependability. The choice of initial supporting and managerial staff is, therefore, vital and should be made with an eye to the future.

3. There can be no franchise activity unless and until a successful and sufficiently profitable pilot operation is first established.

Chapter 7

The financial aspects of franchising

In franchising the franchisee earns his revenue from the operation of the individual unit. The franchisor earns his revenue from the income which he can generate principally from selling franchise packages, continuing franchise fees and mark-up on product sales. As will be seen below there are other potential sources of revenue for the franchisor. The franchisor cannot expect to generate a flow of revenue which is not justified by the quality and range of the services which he provides to franchisees. Furthermore it must be remembered that the basic business which the franchisee is running must generate sufficient profits to enable the franchisee to:

- obtain a return on his investment;
- earn a reward for his labours;
- enable him to make the contracted payments to the franchisor.

If the franchisee's business cannot achieve that there must be a question mark about the viability of the proposition as a franchise. Furthermore the franchisor must be able to generate a sufficient flow of revenue to enable him to cover his overheads and make a profit on his operations as franchisor.

The franchisor should by his pilot operation be able to establish how profitable the franchisee's business is likely to be. This knowledge is essential to enable the franchisor to assess the level of revenue which a franchised business is capable of generating and affording.

Establishing franchise fees is not to be done by guesswork; it is a matter of proper calculation. If fees are established at a wrong, low level the franchisor may not be able to trade profitably. If fees are established at an excessively high level the franchisee may not be able to trade at a sufficient level of profitability.

Establishing fees for the supply or provision of services is not so easy as it is to establish the price for goods. In the case of goods the direct and indirect cost of production and distribution can be calculated with some degree of accuracy. The cost of provision of services is more difficult to ascertain. The franchisor in many cases will be providing services and will find it difficult to know how to calculate the proper level of fees. Where there is a supply of products by the franchisor on which the franchisor is obtaining a mark-up as well as the requirement for the franchisee to make a payment of continuing franchise fees there is a risk that the franchisee will be vulnerable to over-charging by an adjustment of the product mark-up. While in practice there is little that a franchisee can do to negotiate a franchise fee he must be aware of the sources of revenue for the franchisor arising out of the activities of the franchisees in the network:

- the franchisee must know how franchise fees are calculated so that he can judge whether they are fair;
- the franchisee must be able to relate the level of fees to the range and quality of services which he receives. If he does not receive, in return for those fees, services of an added value in excess of the amount of the fees, the involvement of the franchisor may be difficult to justify;
- the franchisee should examine the franchisor's approach to franchise fees; this will provide an insight into the franchisor's attitude;
- if the franchisor is the supplier of the product the method of adjusting prices will be important.

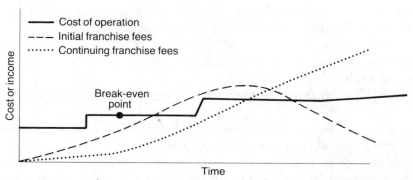

Figure 7.1 *Costs and incomes over time in the development of a franchise network.*

Figure 7.1 shows the sort of trend one might expect to find in the development of a franchise network. The initial fee income is shown as providing the main sources of income in the early stages and then being caught up and overtaken by continuing franchise fees. The figure illustrates the way in which the expense of running the franchisor's organization grows in steps (there may well be more steps than shown in the figure). Each step prepares it to cope with the expansion which follows to the point where the organization is developed and the rising continuing fees result in an increasing profitability because the organization has reached its optimum level. The staff required to cope with five franchisees may well be able to cope with 25 franchisees and those who cope with 35 may well be able to cope with up to 50 and so on. The figure makes clear the need in the early stages for the franchisor to provide adequate working capital to finance the initial deficits; indeed, the time span before the break-even point is achieved can be as much as 3–5 years. The figure ignores any profitability from pilot or company-owned store outlets.

We shall now review the various potential sources and revenue for a franchisor and comment upon each.

INITIAL FRANCHISE FEE

In most cases the franchisee will be charged an initial franchise fee. How this will be identified will depend upon how the franchisor structures his franchise package. In its simplest form the franchisor will provide a range of services to help the franchisee establish his operational unit and will charge a fee. The fee will cover the provision of these services as well as training and may include an element which is attributable to the value of joining the franchised network represented by the strength of the name and the goodwill associated with it.

In a more complex arrangement the franchisor may well acquire and fully equip the trading premises for the franchisee and upon completion of the franchisee's training hand over the 'key' to the franchisee. This approach is called a 'turnkey operation' and the franchisor will charge an initial franchise fee by way of a mark-up on the cost of the elements contained in the package including training.

In another approach the franchisor may in addition to the provision of a range of services sell to the franchisee an equipment package comprising all the initial equipment requirements of the franchisee's business. The sale price will include an initial franchise fee by way of mark-up on the cost of the equipment.

There are some who express the view that the franchisor should set the initial franchise fee as low as possible so as to reduce the franchisee's cost of setting up to a minimum level. Others do not share that view and will charge a full initial franchise fee which takes into account all the cost factors as well as a mark-up. These cost factors will reflect the total cost of recruiting, evaluating, training and establishing the franchisee in business including legal accounting and site finding fees. In the case of some franchises an element will be included for the cost of joining the network which will vary depending upon the level of maturing of the network and the value of the name and of membership of the network.

In the early stages of the franchisor's development the income from initial franchise fees will be an important source of revenue for the franchisor and the buildup of other sources will be slower depending upon the buildup of the franchisees' businesses (Fig. 7.1). Of course if there is a product mark-up the ongoing revenue flow will build up more rapidly.

The franchisor will have to accept that while his flow of franchisees is being developed his income will be far less than his cost of operations; indeed it could well be 3–5 years before the franchisor achieves the break-even point on his franchise activities. This factor means that the franchisor must face up to a requirement to produce adequate capital resources to enable him to sustain his operations until break even is reached. In this sense the franchisor's needs and requirements are no different from any other new business which will take time to develop a level of profitability. There are those who believe that setting up a franchise will produce immediate positive cash flow and profitability and thus solve the problems with which a business which is experiencing difficulties is confronted. That is a fallacy, as is the belief that a business in difficulty is a good base upon which to build a franchise system.

It is also unrealistic for the franchisor to seek to shorten the period which it will take to reach the break-even point by charging high initial franchise fees, for, quite apart from the issues referred to above, the higher the cost of entering the fewer prospective franchisees who can afford it and the greater the return from operations will have to be to justify the outlay.

If one examines the level of front-end franchise fees the average seems to fall within the range of 5–10% of the total cost of the franchise package, i.e. the total investment cost to the franchisee of getting into business and opening. Therefore, with an investment level of £50,000 to £60,000 an initial fee in the range of £2500 to £6000 seems to cover the current average. In the case of the smaller and less expensive packages, e.g. ServiceMaster and Hometune, the percentage can of course exceed the 5–10% range.

As the initial investment grows the percentage fee in cash terms may be too high in relation to the initial supply of services. Thus a fee of £5000 rather than £10,000 might be charged for a franchise package involving investment in the region of say £100,000, although it will be noted that this is still within the 5–10% range. The franchisor should, as mentioned above, relate the amount of the initial franchise fee to the expense incurred by him in selecting, assisting and preparing the franchisee in the establishment of his business.

It may be possible to raise the initial franchise fee in the course of time to reflect the growing strength and success of the franchise. In some cases membership of the network in itself is of great value. It would also be prudent to review the fee to reflect inflationary pressures on overhead expenses. The franchisor would do well to remember that his success will, in the long run, be dependent upon his ability to help the franchisee make the most of his money. This objective can be assisted by keeping the initial investment level as modest as possible; there are more potential franchisees with £25,000 to invest than there are with £50,000 or more.

It would be very unusual for the initial franchise fee to be the only fee the franchisor will ever receive, otherwise he would have no capacity to finance the continuing relationship. While such a fee is often taken it is invariably tied to one or other of the fees which are described below.

SALE OF THE FRANCHISE PACKAGE

The franchisor can structure the sale of the franchise package in a number of ways.

Turnkey

This method of approach involves the franchisor in acquiring the necessary premises, shopfitting and equipping them so that they are ready for occupation by the franchisee and for the commencement of business. In such a case the franchisor would contract with the franchisee to provide these services and the franchisee would undertake to pay for them. Such payment would in all probability be made in stages during the period while the work was proceeding. The price which the franchisor will charge will invariably include a mark-up on the cost to him of the services. That mark-up may also include the initial franchise fee or the franchisor may still separately charge the initial franchise fee. In any event the franchisor will have the opportunity to earn a profit by the mark-up which he charges.

This does not provide the franchisor with a blank cheque to charge as he pleases. The charges made should fairly represent the added value represented by the franchisor's contribution in organizing the acquisition of the premises and carrying out the appropriate works. If the franchisor loads the cost of the initial package unrealistically he runs the risk that:

- the price will be deterrent to a prospective franchisee particularly when compared with the price of entry to competing networks;
- the financial structure will not permit the franchisee to obtain a reasonable return on his investment;
- a bank or other lending institution from which the franchisee seeks financial assistance will conclude that the figures do not justify their involvement;
- the long-term prospects for the franchise system will be harmed.

These factors apply not only to the 'front-end' charges which a franchisor may make but also to all sources of income of which the franchisor takes advantage. Quite apart from the franchisor seeking too many sources of income it should be a fundamental principle that the franchisor should never make a secret profit at the expense of franchisees. Not only will this invariably involve unfairly reducing the franchisee's margins, it may also prevent franchisees from obtaining the benefits of the negotiating power of the network. In addition, the discovery by franchisees of the existence of a secret profit will at worst destroy the trust and confidence which franchisees should have in their franchisor or at least seriously undermine the relationship.

Equipment package

The franchisor may, by contrast, provide the franchisee with specifications and plans so that the franchisee can, after acquiring the premises, organize the requisite shopfitting. The franchisor may offer to sell to the franchisee an equipment package which will comprise all the equipment which is required to be installed in the premises for the purposes of the franchised business. The franchisor will, no doubt, have bought in the equipment from suppliers (including manufacturers) at a discount below the market price. The franchisor will usually charge a mark-up to cover the cost to him of putting the package together and to make a contribution to his general overheads.

Equipment purchasing

In another type of approach the franchisor may, as in the case of the equipment package, provide the franchisee with specifications and plans so that the franchisee can, after acquiring the premises, organize the required shopfitting. So far as equipment is concerned the franchisor will provide the franchisee with a list of branded or otherwise specifically described equipment which is approved by the franchisor and which the franchisee is free to obtain from any supplier of such equipment.

Leasing the equipment

Some franchisors arrange for the leasing of equipment to the franchisee rather than a sale so as to reduce the cost of the initial package. The franchisor may receive a commission from the leasing company. Alternatively, but less frequently, the franchisor will lease the equipment direct to the franchisee and take a profit on that transaction. Indeed, in some cases where the franchisor's system involves the use of specialized patented equipment, it is only possible for a franchisee to arrange to lease that equipment, the franchisor being reluctant to sell it. With the increasing cost of financing the establishment of a new business, finance packages which are prepared will often include leases of equipment. Rental of equipment can also often be arranged with suppliers.

What the franchisee must know is the extent to which the franchisor can add to his capital cost and the cost of running his business by receiving commissions from suppliers or lessors of equipment who are approved or nominated by the franchisor.

Specialized equipment

In some cases there may be an obligation imposed upon the franchisee to purchase future supplies of novel or essential equipment from the franchisor. Such sale will undoubtedly include a profit element for the franchisor. In a franchise which is dependent upon a specialized piece of equipment the obligation may extend to the purchase and use of later and improved versions of the equipment. In such a case the franchisee should be satisfied about two aspects; first that new equipment cannot be imposed upon him when the existing item of equipment is doing the job perfectly well, whatever refinements the newer equipment may have, and second that the franchisor cannot over-charge the franchisee by unreasonably increasing the mark-up. Any change of equipment for a later model which the franchisor wishes the franchisee to purchase should be justified in terms of increased efficiency and output resulting in a cost-effective alternative.

LEASING OF PREMISES

Leasing is a complex aspect of franchising, with problems which arise not only from the legal implications but also the attitudes, practices and balances of negotiation power which are prevalent in the property market at the relevant time.

1. Sometimes the franchisor will be able to negotiate terms for leasing a suitable site on extremely good terms in view of the value of the covenant which the franchisor is able to offer the landlord. The franchisor may decide to sublet these premises to the franchisee at a higher rent, thus earning a profit rental for himself. Whether or not the franchisor becomes involved in the leasing of premises will be a structural decision to be made when the franchise package is brought together (Chapter 6). If the franchisor has decided not to involve himself in the ownership of the premises he may nevertheless find that, owing to pressure from landlords or their estate agents, he must become involved, in order to secure the best locations. There is no inherent reason why a franchisor should not be involved in property; there are many significant franchisors (e.g. McDonald's) who have property involvement as a fundamental policy.
2. The franchisor may, in some cases, own or acquire the freehold of the

  premises from which the franchisee is to trade and will grant a lease
  to the franchisee.
3. In both cases the franchisee should take care to ensure that the terms
  contained in the sale are those which prevail in the market, allowance
  being made for the risks taken and the support given by the
  franchisor. Care must also be taken to ensure that the franchisor does
  not use the lease to impose unreasonable conditions which he would
  not be able to impose in the franchise contract.

FINANCING ARRANGEMENTS

The franchisor may make arrangements with a finance company for a commission to be paid to him on the introduction of franchisees to the finance
company. As a much rarer alternative, the franchisor could set up his own
finance company and make a profit on financing franchisees' financial
requirements.

CONTINUING FEES

Management services fees (royalties)

In order to finance the provision of continuing services to franchisees the
franchisor has to secure a regular flow of income. This is normally achieved
by charging what are usually called management services fees or royalties
together (in the case of a production distribution franchise) with a mark-up
on the supply of products (see Chapter 12 for an explanation of the legal
problems which are involved in the supply of products).

  It is difficult to know how one should fix the level of continuing franchise
fees. Given the general difficulty which there is in fixing fees for the provision
of services the answer is not readily apparent. In seeking to establish the level
of fees to be charged the franchisor has to take a medium- to long-term view.
It will take time for the network to reach the size which will produce
economic viability. As explained above this can take 3–5 years. The franchisor must prepare a 5-year business plan with realistic projections of growth
and calculate what level of continuing franchise fees will enable him to
achieve a healthy financial structure for his business. In doing this the same
exercise will have to be undertaken in respect of the franchisee's business so
that the right foundations have been laid down for the franchisor's business
plan. Furthermore the franchisee's business will have to be judged on the
basis of a level of continuing franchise fees which can be afforded, bearing in
mind the principles discussed in this book, and be competitive with other
franchise systems. The overall average amount of continuing franchise fees is

in the region of 6.5% of gross revenues of the franchisees. This does not include advertising contributions (see below), which overall average 1.3% of such gross revenues. (The figures quoted are taken from the 1990 NatWest–BFA Franchise Survey; see Appendix A.)

Most franchisors charge a straight percentage fee on the gross revenues of the franchisee. It is possible, although not so common, for the franchisor to establish a fixed fee or to require payment of a minimum level of fees. It should not be necessary to establish fixed minimum fees since a well-motivated franchisee should not need such targets to be set. Such a franchisee should be only too anxious to maximize the opportunities which the franchised business provides him. Fixed fees can benefit a franchisee in financial terms if their level is not too high but adjustments need to be made at regular intervals and it is not easy to produce a fair way of making such adjustments without the franchisee being vulnerable. From the franchisor's point of view the fixed fee basis may be superficially attractive but it does not take care of inflation or reflect growth and could inhibit or prevent him from developing the business properly through lack of resources.

There are those who consider that the percentage fee is the best way as the franchisee knows precisely how much he has to pay up; he knows precisely how to calculate it; and he knows that the franchisor will not be taking fees in any other way. The franchisor also knows where he stands and benefits from the inflationary increase in gross revenues and from the growth in the business to which his efforts as a franchisor will have contributed.

The other view held by many is that this is not a good way to charge a franchise fee. The view is that psychologically the franchisee will not like parting with his money to somebody else. In the early days while the franchisee's business is becoming established and is not yet achieving profits the franchisee will not be too happy paying fees to the franchisor despite the fact that they are to pay for services which are being provided. Even when the franchise is profitable it can be painful for the franchisee visibly and frequently to part with a slice of hard-earned cash. Furthermore, as the franchisee feels a degree of independence from the franchisor, which is a feeling which many successful franchisees do develop, he will become more aware of the drain from his pocket and more reluctant to pay the franchise fee.

There are many good franchises which operate on the percentage fee basis and there are some good franchises which operate on a different basis although they are very much in the minority. Certainly, from the franchisor's point of view the percentage fee basis is a safer and more reliable method. It is easier to administer and more satisfactory from the competition law point of view. In the case of a franchise where the franchisor is the product supplier, very often there is a combination of the percentage fee and product mark-up.

One common error is to apply the misnomer of 'royalty' to continuing franchise fees. The error usually arises because franchise fees are invariably calculated as a percentage of the gross income of the franchisee rather in the same way as one calculates royalties. Royalties are what is called passive income, i.e. income arising from the use of an asset rather than an income earned in exchange for services or goods. The common examples are royalties for the exploitation of a patent or for the use and publication of copyright material. Franchise fees are a payment by the franchisee in return for the continuing services with which the franchisor will provide the franchisees. It cannot be denied that some part of the fee represents a charge for the use of the trademarks and business system of the franchisor. What proportion of the fee that part will be is difficult to judge but, for it to be significant, the continuing franchise fee would have to be much larger than the services supplied would justify. In practice this is rarely the case.

Sale of products

In some franchises, particularly those where the franchisor is a manufacturer, wholesaler or where trademarked goods are involved, the agreement will compel the franchisee to buy goods from the franchisor or a nominated supplier of the franchisor. The franchisor obtains a return by marking up the goods. This mark-up may be all he receives, so that it is, in fact, a franchise fee as well as a gross profit on the goods. Where a nominated supplier is used the franchisor can obtain income by receiving a rebate from the supplier. Rebates on supplies which reflect the bulk purchasing power of the networks arguably should be made available for the benefit of franchisees. Some suppliers will provide retrospective rebates which reflect sales during the relevant period and some will provide advertising allowances to be spent by the network. There are some franchisors who distribute rebates to franchisees. There are some who have structured their franchise fees at a level which reflects their expectation of income from this source. Advertising allowances can be applied for the benefit of the network's advertising and promotional activities.

One of the difficulties which can arise with charging franchise fees by product mark-up is that the franchisee can be at the mercy of an unscrupulous franchisor. There are undoubtedly many companies which operate this system fairly and properly, often delaying price increases to the last possible moment. It is, nevertheless, a method of payment of a franchise fee which should be carefully scrutinized by the franchisee. The franchisee should satisfy himself that the franchisor is not taking and cannot take advantage of him and that there are forms of protection upon which he can rely. If there are no proper safeguards in the contract the franchisee should question whether he should sign it.

It is essential for the franchisor to consider the alternatives available. Invariably it is fairer for both parties to have the percentage fee payable rather than the mark-up on goods. If the franchisor contrasts his income calculated as a mark-up on the goods with his income calculated as a reasonable percentage of the franchisee's gross revenue, he will often find that he is no worse off. The franchisee can look at a relatively modest percentage fee in the confident knowledge that the franchisor will not be able unreasonably to increase the margin for himself at the franchisee's expense.

Two factors clearly emerge from the above: firstly, so far as the franchisor is concerned he must make a policy decision at the very earliest moment on the manner in which he will charge franchise fees. He must budget to ensure that the flow of fees which he receives from the various sources are sufficient to show him the return which he needs to cover his overheads and to make a reasonable profit within a sensible time frame bearing in mind his growth prospects. Secondly, so far as the franchisee is concerned he must ascertain the sources of the franchisor's income. He must satisfy himself that the franchisor will not be in a position unfairly to take advantage of him.

ADVERTISING FUNDS

Most franchise schemes provide for expenditure on advertising and promotion by either or both franchisor and franchisee. Where the franchisor undertakes the obligation to advertise and promote there are three alternative methods of dealing with the expense.

1. The franchisor charges the franchisee a sum calculated as a percentage of the franchisee's gross income rather in the same way as the continuing franchise fee (management services fee) is calculated. The sums received by the franchisor from the franchisees are spent by the franchisor on advertising and promotion. Most franchisors will want to have complete control over the advertising and promotional activities upon which the sums in the fund are spent.

2. The franchisor includes the advertising expense within the continuing franchise fee and undertakes to spend not less than a minimum percentage of such fees on advertising and promotion. Again, most franchisors will wish to have the same degree of control over advertising and promotional activities.

3. The franchisor undertakes to do such advertising and promotion to such extent as he thinks fit without collecting a contribution or allocating a fixed sum for the purpose. This approach could be adopted when the franchisor is a manufacturer who is already a substantial advertiser on his own account and the franchisee will inevitably benefit.

Apart from these cases there are franchise operations in which it is considered better to concentrate on local advertising and promotion than on a national basis when the franchisor will probably require the franchisee to spend a fixed percentage of gross income each year for this purpose.

In all cases, both national and local, the franchisor will insist on control of the form and content of all advertisements and promotional material since it is his name and system which are being advertised.

FINANCIAL INSTITUTIONS

As franchising is an inherently safer way of establishing a new business it is not surprising that the banking community has appreciated the advantages of lending money to franchisees. This is not only the case in the UK; banks in many countries have also become heavily involved in franchisee financing, including the Republic of Ireland, France, Spain, the Netherlands, Australia, South Africa and Canada. In the USA, because of restrictive banking laws, franchisee bank financing has not developed to the extent that it has elsewhere.

In June 1981 the National Westminster Bank became the first to establish a franchise finance department. It was quickly followed in August 1981 by Barclays Bank. Since then the other banks have followed these initiatives, and the Royal Bank of Scotland, the Midland Bank, Lloyds Bank, the Bank of Scotland and in Northern Ireland the Ulster Bank and the Bank of Ireland have also established franchise departments. Many of the banks have sponsored franchising activities. The National Westminster Bank sponsors the annual franchising survey commissioned by the BFA (see Appendix A) and the NatWest Centre for Franchise Research at the City University Business School. The Royal Bank of Scotland has sponsored training activities by the BFA. Barclays Bank sponsors a summer school in international franchising at the City University Business School. Midland Bank sponsors the Franchisee of the Year award. Lloyds Bank has sponsored publication by the BFA of *How to Evaluate a Franchise*, which is sold to franchisees. The banks have also demonstrated their wish to have a continuing involvement in franchising by joining the BFA as affiliate members.

As mentioned above, the reason why banks entered the field of franchising is that they recognized that franchising is a safer way of establishing a new business. Furthermore, with the proven concept and the 'umbrella' of the franchisor's organization, the ability of the business to generate sufficient profit to enable the franchisee to repay his obligation and to live comfortably is more readily recognizable. This enables the banks to consider lending a greater proportion of the franchisee's set-up costs than would normally be considered appropriate.

Each of the banks which has entered the market has adopted the same approach: the appointment of a franchise manager at the centre and around whom the department can be developed. The alternative would be to educate the whole branch network in franchising and in how to evaluate a proposition. This would result in an inconsistency of approach which would be damaging and confusing and ensure that the corporate know-how of franchising was spread so thinly as to be incapable of being put to good use.

The specialist manager at the centre, with a developing team around him, enables the bank to acquire and develop its know-how in relation to franchising and pass it on to those who join the department. There is a skilled application of the knowledge acquired which enables rapid evaluation of propositions and the establishment of a consistent attitude towards each franchise system. The local manager faced with the prospective franchisee borrower can be provided, not only with a brief about franchising in general, but also about the specific proposition which he is being asked to consider.

A bank's decision about whether or not to be formally involved in any franchise is thus taken by specialists with the requisite knowledge and experience. The bank's decision on whether to lend to a particular individual is taken by the local manager, who will interview and evaluate him, supported by all the relevant information about the franchise system and the franchisor which is supplied by the bank's franchise department.

Although a bank may well be identified with a particular franchise by a franchisee promoting the availability of loans for the system by a particular bank, the banks do not warrant the viability of the franchise or its suitability for any person. The banks do point out that a prospective franchisee should make a detailed evaluation of the franchise before making his decision.

We shall examine the approach of two of the banks to franchise finance. Each has some distinction; the NatWest Bank was the first on the scene and the Royal Bank of Scotland is probably the most recent entrant.

National Westminster Bank

The franchise section of the National Westminster Bank has grown and is led by a senior franchise manager supported by a team of 12 including four other franchise managers. It also deals with financial opportunities in licensing.

The NatWest franchise section has three main objectives.

1. To support the bank's network of some 3200 branches, its Business Centres and Regional Offices with a general understanding of franchising and a specific knowledge of any franchise opportunity at the time when the local manager is discussing the financial needs of a potential franchisee.
2. To inform customers and the general public on the intricacies of business format franchising and to give general guidance to prospective franchisors on the needs of the industry and to discuss with them their proposals for franchise development.
3. To assist with the provision of finance to franchisees. Close contact is

maintained with established franchisors who are able to benefit from the ready source of finance available to their franchisees.

The bank is aware that with a properly structured business format franchise, the risk of failure is reduced and the level of finance provided to franchisees may be up to two-thirds of the total investment cost, which is greater than would generally be available in a normal 'start up' situation.

The franchise managers supplement the local knowledge of the branch manager with detailed information briefs on all franchises as back-up support to the manager when he is considering the financial needs of any prospective franchisee.

Although the bank does not warrant or recommend any particular franchise operation, it is able to provide prospective franchisees with a general information pack. This includes the bank's checklist for choosing a franchise, which assists in the evaluation of a franchise opportunity, and articles which discuss the requirements of both franchisor and franchisee.

The bank franchise section and its team of managers have also been involved in a number of activities including:

— video guide for prospective franchisors and franchisees;
— audiocassette in conjunction with the BFA and Kall-Kwick (Franchisor of the Year 1989) to assist prospective franchisees;
— in excess of 150 seminar presentations;
— the sponsorships referred to above, i.e.
  (a) the NatWest–BFA Franchise Survey and
  (b) the NatWest Centre for Franchise Research at the City University Business School.

The bank's UK franchise section has also been active in the international arena by assisting in the appointment of franchise managers in the USA, France, Spain and Ireland. The franchise section has been supportive of the franchise community in some 23 countries by providing speakers at seminars on the subject of franchising.

In short, the bank's involvement goes far beyond the provision of finance and is supportive of franchise development on a very broad basis.

Royal Bank of Scotland

The Royal Bank calls its franchise section the Franchise and Licensing Department. The bank appointed a franchise manager in 1985 whose job it was to make and maintain contact with the increasing number of franchise companies launching franchises at that time, with a view to liaising between the bank's branch managers and both franchisors and their potential franchisees. As franchising increased in popularity, the bank allocated further staff resources.

In 1988, licensing was identified as a specialist area of expertise which complemented franchising, and it was decided to add involvement in licensing to the scope of the Department's activities.

The Royal Bank's Franchise and Licensing Department now encompasses three units based in Edinburgh, Manchester and London. Each unit is under the control of a manager with responsibility for his own region. The Department has its headquarters in Edinburgh, and also includes an international section dealing specifically with franchising opportunities into or out of the UK.

The Royal Bank formed an alliance with Banco Santander (one of Spain's largest banks) in 1988, and the joint activities of the two banks have included the establishment of a Franchise and Licensing Department within Banco Santander in Madrid, modelled on the Royal Bank's UK franchise operation. The close alliance between the Franchise and Licensing Departments of the two banks provides additional assistance to franchise companies wishing to enter either market.

The bank's Franchise and Licensing Department sees its present role as twofold. Its first role is to act as a source of expertise on franchising within the bank itself, thereby assisting branch managers in providing banking services to franchisors and their franchisees. This involves the managers in the Department maintaining close contact with all the major franchise companies, so that the Department is in a position to advise branches accordingly.

The second main role of the Franchise and Licensing Department is to assist in disseminating knowledge of ethical business format franchising amongst the business sector generally, and to those individual customers and non-customers of the bank who may be interested in becoming franchisees. To this end, managers from the Department frequently talk at seminars, exhibitions and other such events on the main financial aspects of franchising. In 1989, the Royal Bank sponsored a BFA Training Foundation established to raise standards of training for franchisors.

Chapter 8

Franchisor services to franchisees

The franchise relationship involves the provision of a wide range of services by the franchisor to his franchisees. The first service provided is the establishment of the business and the proof that it is successful in operation. This service involves the franchisor in risking his own resources in opening and running a new business (or in adapting an existing business) so that the process of discovering and remedying difficulties can be thoroughly carried out in order that successive franchisees will be insulated from the risks inherent in opening a new business. The successful and skilful performance of this task by the franchisor will lay the foundations for the progress of the franchised businesses. If this part of the franchisor's job is not performed well the achievement of success by the network will be more difficult.

This task having been carried out effectively (see Chapter 6 for a more detailed discussion of development of concept and pilot operations), the services provided by a franchisor will be of two distinct types:

- those provided which are calculated to select, train and assist the franchisee in opening for business; and
- the ongoing services which are provided to the franchisee during the continuation of the franchise relationship.

Each of these types of service is important; the initial services result in the conversion of a prospective franchisee with perhaps no previous business experience into a businessman equipped to run the franchised business; the ongoing services should be calculated and provided to enable the franchisee to be sustained in his business successfully and with the benefit of the updating of relevant technical and business know-how, marketing, promotion, advertising research and development so that the market-place is properly exploited for the benefit of the network.

We shall consider each of the two types of service.

INITIAL SERVICES

These services will follow the steps which are taken by the franchisor from recruitment to the actual day of opening of the franchisee's business and sometimes for a few days beyond that day.

Recruitment

This may not usually be regarded as a service provided by a franchisor to his franchisees. However, it should be, since although the franchisor, in recruiting franchisees, is serving his own ends because he needs franchisees to expand the network he also needs to be selective. The degree of selectivity should result in the franchisor assisting the franchisee in making an objective balanced judgement about whether self-employment is right for the franchisee; that the franchised business matches the franchisee's skills and aptitudes; that the franchisor is right for the franchisee and vice versa. In providing this service to franchisees the franchisor has self-interest on his side since it is vital for the franchisor to have well-motivated, committed and well-suited franchisees if the network is to have a healthy growth rate.

A franchisor who can say 'no' when all is not completely to his satisfaction will enhance his prospects of success as well as building a network of higher quality franchisees.

Training

Training should cover two aspects. Firstly, the franchisee must be trained in basic business skills. These will include book-keeping, accounting, reporting methods and systems, staff selection, staff management and control, business procedures, documentary systems necessary for the purposes of controlling the operation, and elementary business training which will enable the franchisee to do a basic analysis of whether or not his business has developed or is developing problems and what to do about them. This training will not be so detailed that the franchisor will, in effect, be running a business management college. The training provided by a franchisor will be limited in its application and scope to providing the franchisee with the basic skills which are necessary for the purpose of conducting the particular business which he is franchised to operate.

The book-keeping system which will have been set up will have been so arranged as to provide the minimum of work and effort for the franchisee consistent with the provision of the maximum vital information for effective management. The system should be geared to produce the vital flow of financial management information which is necessary for the franchisee to see where he stands at all times. The value of up-to-date meaningful financial information cannot be over-emphasized. It should show trends, stresses and strains which, if correctly interpreted, should enable appropriate remedial action to be taken in relation to the business at the earliest possible moment. This information will be provided to the franchisor, who will be able to interpret what it reveals about the franchisee's business and his conduct of that business.

The staff selection and staff management and control training the franchisee will receive will give him the basic skills which he requires for interviewing staff, assessing their capabilities, and training them in the work which they will have to do. Handling people is largely a matter of experience, but there are nevertheless guidelines which can be given to help the inexperienced. The franchisee will, when he combines the practical experience he will obtain with the principles which have been laid down for him, find that he is achieving far more than he would otherwise have been capable of. This training should also provide the franchisee with an understanding of the legal requirements imposed upon an employer and how they should be complied with.

The franchisor will invariably design and prepare certain forms which the franchisee will have to complete. These forms will be designed to show the performance of the operation and demonstrate to the franchisor and franchisee the areas in which the franchisee needs to improve his performance. There should be a sound reason for any forms which the franchisee is compelled by the franchisor to complete. It is not the franchisee's function to operate as a source of useless information and nor should a franchisor want to clog up his own administration with unnecessary paperwork.

The franchisee should be trained so that he can develop the ability to detect problems as they arise in his business and thus be in a position to take remedial action without waiting for the franchisor's field support staff to call upon him or respond to a call for help and diagnose that avoidable trouble is brewing or has already taken its toll on the business.

The franchisee must also be trained in the operational aspects of the business. In a food franchise, for example, the franchisee will be taught portion control, quality control, preparation methods, any particular recipes, and any particular processes which will have to be applied to the food before it is passed on to the consumer. The franchisee may be required to attend a special training school to be trained in these aspects.

Above all, whether or not there is a training school, the franchisee must, after he completes his training, be capable of stepping into his own business and opening and running it without pausing to scratch his head and wonder where his next piece of inspiration will come from.

Premises

The franchisor will try to assist the franchise in acquiring suitable premises and then preparing them for use as a franchised outlet. This will involve a number of stages:

- site selection criteria
- planning and by-law compliance
- lease negotiation
- design and remodelling of outlet
- equipment requirements
- opening stock
- business launch

We shall consider each in turn.

SITE SELECTION CRITERIA

The franchisor will, with the criteria for site selection which he has established, investigate and evaluate sites for the franchisee. In some cases the franchisee will himself search for premises for consideration and approval by the franchisor. He will advise whether or not the sites come within his accepted standards, which will include not only the quality of the trading position but whether the franchise operation can be physically accommodated in the space available. At least one franchise company has instructed its site finders that unless the site which they are considering is one into which they would invest every last penny which they themselves possess they should not recommend it for the purpose of a franchisee's business. This may seem to be an extreme position but is certainly a sound principle upon which to operate. No franchisor should expect a franchisee to invest his money in something in which the franchisor would not himself invest. The franchisee should appreciate that in approving a site a franchisor is not infallible. The franchisor is exercising a judgement based on experience but he cannot guarantee that his judgement is correct. For the franchisee blindly to accept the franchisor's opinion without question can be dangerous. The franchisee should closely question the franchisor, particularly if he has doubts about the site himself, and if his doubts cannot be resolved he should not proceed.

PLANNING AND BY-LAW COMPLIANCE

There will be cases where the premises which have been found do not have planning permission established which enables them to be used for the business of the franchise system. In such a case planning permission will be necessary and the franchisor should give assistance to the franchisee in obtaining any necessary consents under the planning legislation. There are a number of ways in which the franchisor can assist, particularly as it is likely to be a problem which can be anticipated. The franchisor will in all probability have had to obtain planning permission before and will have an adviser available to assist. In cases where the concept is new many of the planning authorities need to have the concept and proposed use explained. An illustrated brochure can often assist in explaining the proposed business. Such a brochure can also be used to explain the business to estate agents representing landlords of proposed premises. Local building by-law regulations have to be complied with; the franchisor should be able to provide assistance.

LEASE NEGOTIATIONS

A further service which many franchisors offer to franchisees is assistance in negotiating a lease of the premises with the landlords or their agents. As explained above, with a new concept there may be the need for an explanatory document to assist. The franchisor's involvement in the negotiations could benefit the franchisee and assist him in obtaining premises for which he as an individual may not have been acceptable. The franchisor may find that in order to obtain the best sites he has to become involved as a tenant of the premises and sublet to franchisees or find some other way to enable a letting to be achieved.

DESIGN AND REMODELLING OF OUTLET

The franchisor should assist the franchisee in the designing and remodelling of the outlet. The outlet will have to be prepared in conformity with the franchisor's requirements. The franchisor will usually have standard plans and specifications prepared which can be adapted for the particular premises which have been obtained. In some cases the franchisor will prepare amended plans. In others he will require the franchisee to employee an architect or surveyor to prepare the plans and to pay for them. In other cases the shopfitter may prepare amended plans; this is a service which many shopfitters offer.

The franchisor may offer a complete plan preparation and shopfitting service. Alternatively the franchisor may give the franchisee assistance in deciding which particular shopfitter's estimate to accept. The franchisor may also give the franchisee support in the supervision of the shopfitters while they carry out their work. Most franchisors, although they offer such assistance, will not be prepared to accept the responsibility which the franchisee's own surveyor, for example, would accept. Specialized professional advice is the responsibility of the franchisee and should be obtained.

EQUIPMENT REQUIREMENTS

The franchisor will, if standardized equipment is not already part of the package which he has sold to the franchisee, give advice and assistance in the selection of the correct equipment at the most economic prices. He should have all the relevant information readily available and some franchisors provide a list of equipment with brand names and model numbers and specifications so that the franchisee can try to obtain a better deal elsewhere.

OPENING STOCK

The franchisor will provide the franchisee with an opening stock inventory list, and will make arrangements for the franchisee to purchase these stocks from his own purchasing department or from suppliers who are nominated or approved for the purpose.

The acquisition of stock and its delivery to the outlet on time is crucial to the success of the opening. The franchisee's training will no doubt have included guidelines on marketing and promotion as well as the techniques of merchandising products. The franchisor will in appropriate cases provide assistance with merchandising so that the products are correctly displayed; in some cases the assistance with merchandising may be provided on an ongoing basis.

BUSINESS LAUNCH

The franchisor should provide the franchisee with on-the-spot assistance in the final preparatory arrangements for the store opening. The franchisor will frequently provide opening assistance by having a team of as many as two or three people present to assist the franchisee in getting the business off the ground. Initially they may have to cope with a heavy volume of work as the public try out the business. The franchisor's opening crew will seek to ensure that the franchisee is properly putting into practice the principles which have been instilled in him during training. The opening crew should stay on the premises until they are satisfied that the franchisee has got into the swing of things and is coping well enough to be left on his own.

It is only when he is left alone after the initial shock that the franchisee will really come into his own and begin to develop his true potential. At this stage, it is important to emphasize again that the franchisee must realize that no franchisor can guarantee to him success, least of all success without work. A franchise is not a passage to wealth without effort. Most franchises will require long hours of solid work on the part of the franchisee in order to achieve success. What the franchisor is offering is a ready-made formula for carrying on business which in similar circumstances has proved to be successful. He will give to the franchisee whatever assistance he can in an endeavour to ensure that the franchisee will achieve a similar degree of success. This cannot be guaranteed, and any franchisor who offers firm guarantees of success to franchisees should be viewed with caution.

ONGOING SERVICES

The range of ongoing services which a franchisor provides to his franchisees will be such as will provide the franchisee with the proper level of support in the operation of his business. In addition the franchisor should be creating good franchisor–franchisee relations and looking to the future with research development and market testing capabilities in place. The range of ongoing services will include:

- monitoring and support
- training
- 'head office' organization
- research and development
- market research
- advertising and promotion
- communications

We shall examine each in turn.

Monitoring and support

The franchise system and contract should have built into them the structure of a reporting and monitoring system which will not only ensure that the franchisor has a method of checking that the correct fees are paid but will also provide the franchisor with the information he needs to monitor the franchisee's performance so that he is in a position to detect trends and perhaps notice warning signs.

The operation of this monitoring system is a valuable tool for both franchisor and franchisee. For the franchisee there will be the discipline of preparing meaningful information which will provide him with vital data concerning his own business and its financial performance. For the franchisor there is a record of network performances from which individual and all franchisees' performances can be reviewed and put into a global perspective.

This information by itself is not enough; there needs to be personal contact with someone who knows the franchisee and his operation and to whom the information provided will mean something. The franchisee should always know who will be available for guidance if he has problems or difficulties. The franchisor should therefore ensure that the franchisee is familiar with the franchisor's 'head office' team and that he knows who deals with what. There will often be a special point of contact with a member of the franchisor's field support team who should be in touch with the franchisee regularly both by phone and by personal visits to the franchised outlet. The franchisor's field support staff should be available at short notice if the franchisee has a problem.

The field support staff may find on a regular routine visit to the franchisee's business that all is not well and that the franchisee is not following the system correctly. Certain retraining may be necessary where, for example, bad habits have developed or the franchisee has not capitalized on notified improvements to the system. In such a case the support staff member would remain on or arrange to return shortly to the premises while he retrains the franchisee (and staff if necessary) and puts him on the right lines. The franchisee must not rely too heavily on field support; he must learn to solve his own problems; he should look to the franchisor as a shoulder upon which to lean and as a source of assistance to him when things get a bit too much.

The franchisor's field support team should be available at all times to the franchisee when required. The words 'when required' are used advisedly. The franchisor cannot be expected to know by some telepathic process that the franchisee expects help from him at any particular time. Communication is an essential feature of the relationship and the franchisee has a responsibility in this respect as well as the franchisor. The franchisee must keep in touch with the franchisor and must let the franchisor know when he has difficulties. The franchisee must not delude himself, he must face up to difficulties as they arise and not try to pretend they do not exist.

The franchisee should telephone his field support contact from time to time if he has not been visited, and have a chat with him, for out of these discussions much good can come. He must also read very carefully all literature and circulars which reach him from or through the franchisor, for by this means, if the franchisor is performing his functions correctly, the franchisee will be supplied with valuable operational information. Nothing could be more annoying than for the franchisee to call in assistance when the answer to his problems is contained in the literature which has been circulated to him and which he has just not bothered to read.

The franchisee must appreciate that the franchisor's field support staff want to work with him to help him but that he must also help himself. He cannot expect the franchisor to run his business for him. The franchisee must adjust mentally to the fact that he is a businessman in his own right and behave as one.

Whatever the benefits of franchising, the elimination of risk is not one of them. While risk is reduced and failures are lower than is the case with non-franchised new businesses, there are and always will be failures. It is important for the franchisor to understand why there has been a failure and to investigate to see whether it could have been avoided so that the lesson learned can be used to good advantage in the future. Much media treatment of franchisee failure is one-sided; it is good for the media to describe the failures but not so good to learn that the failure was more attributable to the deed and misdeeds of the franchisee than those of the franchisor. Perspective is important and there is no doubt that franchisees have failed:

- because the franchisor had not properly tested the concept before franchising;
- because the franchisor was under-capitalized;
- because the franchisor took bad decisions;

- because the franchisor was dishonest;
- because what was involved was not a franchise but some other fraudulent scheme described wrongly as a franchise; and
- because the franchisor failed to provide the continuing services properly or at all.

So clearly, the reasons which may lead to the failure of the franchisor may equally well bring down the franchisee. Unless the franchisee has the financial and business resources to seek his own salvation by continuing to trade he will fail. On the other hand, there have been franchisees who have failed despite their franchisor's support and assistance while other franchisees in the same network have succeeded.

Whatever the reason for the failure of the franchisee the symptoms will probably first show themselves as a shortage of cash. This shortage (insolvency) does not happen overnight unless of course the franchisee spends the night at the races and loses all his money in one evening.

Basically, insolvency is a developing situation and the benefit of the field support system and the franchisor's monitoring of franchisee performance should reveal the warning signs so that efforts can be made to avoid the problems which will ensue. There will always be many warning signs before the franchisee reaches insolvency: for example, he will be slow in paying—he will be slow in doing a lot of things which he should be doing to keep his business and his staff on their toes. The franchisor should be aware of the developing insolvency a long time before the point of no return is actually reached.

The reason why the franchisee is sliding into insolvency is important:

- it could be that he does not follow the system;
- it could be that he will not take advice from the franchisor (which quite often happens);
- he may not be suited to the business;
- he may be under-capitalized;
- he may be spending too much on non-essentials; or
- he may not work hard enough.

However hard one may try in selecting a franchisee it is a value judgement and one may or may not be right. Hopefully with experience one is more often right than wrong, but even so, some franchisees will be selected who are not capable of running the business.

Some franchisees who are not familiar with business assume that every pound which passes into their till is theirs to spend as they wish. They forget that they have bills and overheads to pay, and consequently their drawings out of the business are much heavier than they should be: they are not justified by the net profitability of the business. It is very difficult to tell a franchisee how much money he should draw out for himself.

There could well be other reasons which are contributory, but it is important to know why the franchisee is sliding into this situation, because without properly identifying the reason it is not possible to prescribe a cure. Therefore the franchisor should ensure that those in his organization with the right skills are brought into the picture as soon as possible.

It may well be that the circumstances are such that the franchisor will decide long before a bankruptcy situation arises that he will terminate the contract, because however much he tries, he is not able to get the franchisee to comply with the contract or the directions given to him. If the franchisor decides not to terminate, he may well think, 'I made a mistake, this is not the right man for the franchise, he's not capable of running the franchise as well as I thought he was.' The franchisor has a duty to try to help a franchisee who is running into difficulties to recover as much of his loss as possible. He also has a duty to put someone in to help the franchisee sort out the business and to see if he can sort out the franchisee and put him back on the rails. Ultimately, if the franchisee is unsuitable, the franchisor should assist him in finding a purchaser of the business on a basis which will recover for him as much as possible of his capital investment. Sometimes a franchisee will not respond, but experience shows that franchisees (with rare exceptions), if properly handled, usually do respond, and are quite relieved that someone is prepared to assist them and help them out of their difficulties.

Training

The franchisor will find that there will always be a need for training. Franchisees who do not operate the system properly may need retraining. The franchisee may need help in training his staff and in how to do it for himself. There will also be a need to train franchisees in the adoption of innovations which the franchisor will introduce from time to time. These may involve system changes or the use of new equipment, or perhaps new applications and uses of existing systems and equipment that promise to be more cost-effective for the franchisee in practical use.

'Head office' organization

Heading this activity there is, of course, the 'head office' organization of the franchisor. The organization should contain specialists in each of the fields in which the franchisee is likely to require assistance. There should be specialists in the management and accountancy aspects of the business; specialists in advertising, marketing, public relations; specialists in product quality control, equipment quality and control; specialists in all the other various aspects of the business with which the franchised chain is concerned.

Under these circumstances the franchisee is better off than the manager of a local branch within a national chain. In a national chain the accent will be on ensuring that the manager runs his branch in accordance with the policy of the company. While to some extent this would apply to a franchised organization, there is not the same rigidity. Each franchisee must be treated as an individual. His problems must be treated as those of an individual, and the approach of the team at the highest management level cannot be to dictate to the franchisee what he should do and what company policy is, but rather to try to train him and to instil in him the interest which an individual should have in running and managing his own business, albeit within the established framework. The franchisee must be persuaded to see the sense of what is expected of him.

The franchisor's interest is in seeking to achieve for the franchisee the success of which his business is capable and to bring the best out of him as an individual. The franchisor should certainly not resort to dictating to the franchisee unless the franchisee insists on breaking his contract or fails properly to operate the system.

The franchisor may also be a source for the franchisee in obtaining a prospective purchaser for his business. Whether things are going well or not for the franchisee it is quite likely that the franchisor will have contact with many people interested in taking over a business of this sort. The franchisee can often obtain valuable assistance from a franchisor when he does decide, for whatever reason, that the time has come to dispose of his business.

Research and development (including market research)

The franchisor should have research and development facilities in relation to the products, the services or the system and the market image projected. He should constantly be seeking to innovate and introduce ideas and methods for improving the business of the franchised network and the operational systems.

The research and development facilities should be experimenting with new product lines and or the introduction of new or improved services. These products and services must be compatible with the existing business and should be thoroughly market tested before they are adopted as part of the franchisor's system. A franchisor with company-owned operations can do his market research by offering the products and/or services in those operations to test the efficacy of their introduction. The franchisor may involve some selected franchisees in market testing through their operations. All changes, whether to system, products or services, should be as carefully evaluated as the original pilot operation so that the franchisor can demonstrate to franchisees the likely benefit that should result from their introduction.

The research and development activities can extend to exploiting new sources of supply of good quality materials, supplies or products for the franchisees so that their costs are kept to the most economic level possible. As the network grows its bulk purchasing power will also grow, resulting in considerable accounts with manufacturers and suppliers. This should produce valuable savings for each individual franchisee. Benefits and savings can thus be obtained for franchisees which would not be available to them outside the franchise network with only their own individual resources to bargain with.

Advertising and promotion

In most cases the franchisor will undertake responsibility for advertising, promotion and public relations for the network. The cost is invariably borne by the franchisees (Chapter 7) through the contributions they make to the franchisor for this purpose. The franchisor's advertising and promotional schemes should exploit to the full the national corporate image of the franchised network as the provider of goods and/or services.

In structuring the advertising arrangements the franchisor will have to bear in mind a number of factors.

1. First and foremost will be the need to establish and maintain a strong corporate identity for the network which is favourably received by the consumer. The franchisor will need to be in control of the way in which this identity is projected. It is the branding by which the network is known and the franchisor will thus either generate all the advertising output or subject any which a franchisee wishes to contract to an approval system.
2. Consideration must be given to what will be the most effective method of reaching the consumer market for the network's products or services. Will national advertising suffice? Will regional advertising be appropriate? Will local advertising and promotion by each franchisee be the most effective? The answers to these questions will have an influence on the franchisor's decision.
3. The franchisor will also need to consider whether to generate the materials required 'in-house' or to use outside services.
4. Will the franchisor assist franchisees with the provision of point-of-sales material out of the advertising contributions or will a separate charge be made?
5. Will the franchisor provide franchisees advertising locally with blocks, bromides or camera-ready copy which they can utilize for that purpose? This could result not only in the cost-effective use of resources but also provide the franchisor with the ability to control the way in which the advertisements display the branding.

6. What degree of consultation does the franchisor intend to have with franchisees?

The franchisor will undoubtedly need to have someone in his organization to deal with advertising and promotion as well as public relations.

Promotion does not stop short with advertising, marketing and public relations. The franchisor can also exploit the development of national accounts whose local business can be transacted with franchisees so that each franchisee benefits from obtaining business to which it would not have had access but for its membership of the franchise network.

Communications

Good communications in franchising are fundamental to a franchisor's success. The role of communications is dealt with in detail in Chapters 10 and 11.

Chapter 9
How to become a franchisee

SELF-EXAMINATION

Everyone who decides that he would like to have his own business should subject himself to a detailed self-examination of his attitudes, capabilities and long-term goals. Some factors in any such examination apply whether or not the business is a franchise, while some are specific to franchising.

Every prospective franchisee must:

- engage in this self-examination exercise;
- be completely frank with himself; and
- not delude himself into pursuing his original desires, regardless of what he knows to be the correct answers to the questions which he must ask himself.

Consideration should also be given to a factor to which no attention appears to be paid when franchisee failure is reported in the media. Franchisees can be the cause of their own downfall. It should be borne in mind that at least 50% of franchisees who experience failure are themselves responsible for their plight. The provision by the franchisor of his know-how, system and business format does not guarantee success. The franchisor provides a basic DIY business kit, but the success of the practical operation of this 'kit' depends greatly upon the franchisee's skill and ability in maximizing the opportunity which it presents.

This factor sometimes makes it difficult to ascertain the reason for failure, although there is now enough experience available to identify the characteristics which give rise to self-induced failure by franchisees.

Any potential franchisee who engages in critical self-examination should be aware of these characteristics in case he recognizes that he himself possesses one or more of them. What are these characteristics? They include the following. (The examples quoted have actually occurred and are not figments of the author's imagination.)

1. **The franchisee who has previously been in business for himself, and possibly in the same type of business as the franchise system.** Such a person may have entrenched ideas of his own and thus be less receptive to the ideas of the franchisor and the disciplines of the system. It is for this reason that many franchisors will not accept as franchisees those who have previous experience in that type of business. Life being what it is there are exceptions, and there are cases where previous market knowledge and experience are essential since they cannot be learned in an economically sensible time frame. However, the acceptance of the disciplines of the franchise system by the franchisee is fundamental.

2. **Franchisee complacency.** No franchisee can afford to be complacent. There have been cases in which franchisees have failed to make the necessary effort because, as they put it, 'I am now a boss and bosses don't work.' The boss syndrome can be quite dangerous. Franchisees who have this problem behave in the way *they think* bosses should behave, which they usually believe means spending without working and earning. There are very few who can succeed on that basis. If the prospective franchisee's expectations of business life as his own boss are along these lines he should avoid self-employment because if put into practice he will be doomed to failure.

3. **The franchisee who loses his nerve.** This takes two forms.
   (a) The franchisee who simply loses his nerve when, after opening, the responsibilities and magnitude of the task of being a self-employed businessman dawn upon him.
   (b) The franchisee who cannot live with the losses which many businesses make in the early days before they become established. This reaction occurs even in cases where the franchisees have been warned of what will happen and have been advised to arrange their finance on such a basis that they have the working capital to sustain them during the start-up period. A strong nerve is necessary to be able to cope with trading losses while building a business.

4. **The franchisee who does not follow the system.** This is a phenomenon which is more likely to occur after the franchisee has been in business for a period of time and has become successful. He

begins to believe that he and not the franchisor is the reason for his prosperity. In part, he will, of course, be contributing to his own success. Some franchisees are better than others and some are more prosperous than others because of their diligence and hard work. The danger arises where this leads to an arrogant belief by the franchisee that he knows best and where this in turn leads to a rejection of the franchisor's system or a desire to impose his will and change without authority.

5. **Interference from other family members, or well-intentioned but busy-body friends**. It is important that the franchisee should have the support of his family (particularly his spouse), but support is one thing and interference is another. It can be appreciated that a spouse will have the welfare of his (or her) partner at heart, but the spouse should not usurp the franchisor's function, or take on the franchisor on behalf of his (or her) spouse. That is a recipe for disaster. Many franchisors will wish to interview both husband and wife, even when only one is applying for a franchise, in order to make an assessment of the degree of support which is likely to be forthcoming, as well as the degree of interference. Busy-body friends should be avoided like the plague. They should be politely kept apart from the business, especially those who profess to have an expertise which they consider to be of vital benefit to the franchisee. A person who is easily led and finds it difficult to reach decisions independently will find self-employment a dangerous undertaking.

6. **The franchisee who expects too much to be done for him**. Some franchisees feel that the franchisor should be doing more for them on a day-to-day basis than is allowed for in the franchise system. The franchisee who previously had a job with a salary will have to accept that he is now dependent upon his own performance for his take-home pay. He cannot if the going gets tough expect the franchisor financially to bale him out. A franchisor does, of course, provide fall-back assistance to a franchisee with problems. He does not, however, offer a day-to-day presence, or the local involvement and initiative necessary to develop the business. That is the franchisee's contribution, and no prospective franchisee should enter into a franchise relationship if he believes that the franchisor should be involved on a day-to-day operational basis in the business. The only exceptions are those franchise systems which specifically provide such involvement. (An example would be where the franchisor operates a central booking or ordering facility, or accounting system.)

7. **The franchisee who does not have the right aptitude**. This type of franchisee falls into two categories. Firstly, there are those who are so blinded by the attractiveness of the franchise opportunity that they do not recognize their own inabilities and deficiencies. A franchisor

can never know as much about the franchisee as the franchisee knows about himself. The franchisee must be honest with himself and the franchisor. If, for example, the franchise system needs the franchisee to be an active salesman and he knows that this is something he would find difficult he should hesitate to become involved. On the other hand, a franchisee who likes meeting people and who feels that the franchise of his liking will involve him in stifling administrative duties should think again. In the second category are those who have perhaps been in employment at a senior management level and are not accustomed to rolling up their sleeves and working hard at the basics and at the sharp end of a business. The subsequent sale of a franchise business which has been taken over by a franchisee with the right attitude often proves how wrong was the predecessor's attitude.

These are the characteristics which signal problems for the prospective franchisee. Those who are counselling the franchisee, including the franchisor, should assist him in questioning whether he will fall within one or more of these categories. The characteristics should be kept in mind as a general background against which to proceed with the evaluation process.

Let us now consider a widely voiced statement, 'Franchising is safer than independently setting up in business on your own account.' This, broadly speaking, is correct, and it is certainly so in the USA, where it is borne out by statistics. In the UK the experience of members of the BFA as a whole, of reputable franchise companies and of the banks involved in franchise finance bears out this claim. The annual BFA survey sponsored by the National Westminster Bank (see Appendix A) also supports this claim.

It is popularly believed that while 90% of all new businesses fail within a 5-year period, the comparable percentage in the case of franchises is not more than 10%. This popular claim is a step in the right direction, but it is an overstatement of the position. The failure rate within 5 years of new businesses registered for VAT is approximately 37%, whereas the failure rate for franchised new businesses is in the region of 4–5%. The difference between these two figures still demonstrates that franchising is a safer method of entry into a new business than going it alone.

However, there are dangers in making claims about the high levels of success in franchising. The prospective franchisee may:

- drop his guard when evaluating a franchise because he has heard such claims and come to trust the system as a whole, regardless of what may be the position in the particular franchise which he is considering;
- be lulled into the false belief that all he needs to do to make a lot of easy money is to sign a franchise agreement; and
- ignore the fact that it is still necessary to select the right franchisor

who has properly prepared the franchise for the market-place and the franchisor who is right for the franchisee.

The lessons to be learnt are that each franchise must be considered on its own merits in the light (at the very least) of the guidance offered in this book and in the certain knowledge that franchising is not the easy way to quick riches. In life, nothing comes easily and this is certainly true of franchising. Most successful franchisees have worked very hard to achieve their success.

Franchising should, however, reduce the risks inherent in opening a new business. This is because one of its main attractions is that the franchisor is selling the benefit of the experience he has gained in running his own business (or his pilot operation) and has detected and solved the problems with which any new business is always faced. Franchising should, therefore, provide the franchisee with a business which has a proven record of success upon which he can build. No franchise should ever be offered, or be considered, as a work-free way of making money. If it is offered in this way, the prospective franchisee should be suspicious, and if he regards the opportunity in this way, he should stop being greedy and come to his senses.

It is surprising that there are a significant number of prospective franchisees who take proper advice before entering into a franchise contract but who fail to heed that advice because it was not what they wanted to hear. In other words, they have already made up their minds when they take advice and despite what they are told it makes no difference. This particularly applies with new franchise systems where the tendency is to believe that however badly structured and inadequately tested it is, getting in early is desirable because those in first make most. This attitude is really only a manifestation of greed which prevents rational thought. While those 'in early' in a well-structured and properly piloted franchise may do extremely well the risks are higher, as will be seen below, and the prospective franchisee must be prepared to take a deep breath, reconsider his position and say 'no' however much he is enamoured of the proposition *unless* objective investigation coupled with sound independent advice confirm the necessary quality of the franchisor and his proof, by spending his own money, that he indeed has a well-tried, tested and successful business format.

The factors discussed are all important in the process through which all prospective self-employed businessmen should go before taking the plunge. Indeed, the prospective franchisee must not lose sight of the fact that in deciding whether or not to go into a franchise he is also deciding to go into business on his own account, albeit in a particular type of business which has been structured in a certain type of way.

The following questions should be asked and answered honestly.

1. Do I understand franchising and what is involved?
2. Am I qualified physically and temperamentally for self-employment?

3. Will my age and health permit me to run the business long enough to recover my initial investment and to make the effort worthwhile? Conversely, am I too young to have the maturity to run my own business, and employ and direct people?

4. Do I possess sufficient financial resources to enable me to start a business, and survive while it is struggling to become established?

5. Do I have the nerve and force of will to survive expected losses while building up my business and to cope with any unexpected set-backs?

6. What are my natural aptitudes and skills? Does this franchise opportunity provide me with the right platform for me to exploit and maximize my strengths?

7. Am I at my best with mental or physical tasks?

8. Do I mix well with people?

9. Will I be able to handle staff?

10. Do I have the ability and commitment to work hard?

11. Am I prepared to work unsocial hours?

12. How will my family be affected by my decision and the calls which the business will make upon my time?

13. Do my family wholeheartedly support my proposed venture?

14. Will any of my family be able, available, and happy to help me?

15. Am I prepared to put whatever assets I now possess at risk? Can I stand the stress which may follow taking such a risk?

16. Am I able to raise sufficient finance?

17. What am I looking for, and can I achieve it:
    (a) job satisfaction?
    (b) capital gain?
    (c) lots of money?
    (d) an investment (absentee owner)?

18. Will the business be sufficiently challenging for me over a period of time?

19. Can I accept the disciplines of a franchise system?

20. Will I resent the franchisor's authority?

21. Do I possess sufficient ability to exercise initiative and to capitalize on the opportunities presented to me?

22. Would I be better off if I enter the ranks of the self-employed other than through the franchise route?

23. Finally, what do I want to achieve in life?

It is vital for the prospective franchisee to subject himself and his attitude to the closest possible scrutiny. He should be sure he knows himself and knows what it is that he is looking for. He should ensure in carrying out the self-assessment procedures which are recommended that his particular strengths and weaknesses are relevant to and will be effective if put to use in the particular proposition which he is considering and the demands it will make.

TYPE OF BUSINESS

The position of the franchise in the market in which it trades is a vital consideration. Not only should the particular franchised business be examined in relation to its own activities, but an assessment should also be made of the prospects for the overall industry or trade sector of which it forms a part. The franchise will either be dealing in goods or products, or the provision of services. Table 9.1 contains a comparison of the various considerations which should help in making an assessment.

Table 9.1   Comparison of considerations

	Goods or products	Services
1.	Are the products new? Have they distinctive advantages over their competitors?	Is the service to be provided a new one? Has it a distinctive advantage over competitors' services?
2.	Has the franchised business been thoroughly proven in practice to be successful?	Same
3.	Is this a product distributorship, or agency, which is not really a franchise but one which is promoted as a business format franchise and thus suspect?	Does this service have a novel or distinctive element about it which clearly distinguishes it from other similar and competitive businesses?
4.	Does it have staying power?	Same
5.	Is it in a market area which is in a decline?	Same
6.	Is it in a growth market?	Same
7.	Is it exploiting a fad or a current fashion which is transient and short-lived?	Same
8.	How competitive is the market for the particular products?	How competitive is the market for the provision of these services?

9.	How competitive is the price of the products?	How competitive is the price at which the services are to be offered?
10.	Can this competitiveness be maintained?	Same
11.	What is the source of supply of the products?	Not applicable
12.	How certain is it that the source will be available for the future?	Not applicable
13.	Are alternative sources of products of comparable quality and price available?	Not applicable
14.	Are the products based upon a trademark?	Is there a strong, distinctive trade name or service mark associated with the provision of the services? If a celebrity name is used, remember that celebrities and their reputations come and go, and so too can any related franchise.
15.	Are the products produced by a patented invention?	Not strictly applicable, although it is possible for a patented product to be featured in a service business so this could still be relevant. Is the service based on an exclusive process?
16.	Does the franchisor have his lines of supply properly tied up?	Not applicable
17.	Is there adequate back-up in terms of guarantees and service facilities?	Not applicable
18.	Could the manufacturer or supplier easily bypass the franchisor and you, and set up his own competitive franchise?	Not applicable

19.	What is the reputation of the product?	What is the reputation of the service, or process?
20.	What is the reputation of the supplier?	Not applicable
21.	If it is a successful franchise newly imported from another country will it hold a similar appeal in the UK market? Has it been market tested in the UK by careful and thorough pilot testing?	Same

Do not underestimate the importance of the questions in Table 9.1. Make sure that the proposition has been well enough tested and for a long enough period of time for one to be satisfied that the market really exists and has long-term prospects.

Please do remember, and there is no apology for the repetition, one must not enter into self-employment and franchising if one is not prepared to risk losing all! No prospective franchisee should delude himself into believing that any franchisor guarantees his success and that he will underwrite a franchisee's failure. The business risk the franchisee runs is his. That risk must be fully understood and appreciated.

ASSESSING THE FRANCHISOR

The assessment of the franchisor is a very important part of the process of making up one's mind about whether or not to take up a franchise and if so which to choose.

Do not assume that just because someone calls himself a franchisor, it means that he really is one. Many who perpetrate frauds will often try to lull the unsuspecting into believing that what they offer is a franchise when it is not. One should not allow oneself to be misled, particularly by these pro-moters of spurious schemes who suggest that disproportionately high rewards will follow.

It is quite common for a person with a business to be approached by someone who feels that he would like to become a franchisee of that business. This is very often the first time that the owner of the business has heard of franchising and in such a situation he is totally unprepared and quite incapable of offering a viable franchise. Frequently, the response by the owner of the business is to rush out and ask his solicitor for a franchise contract.

There is, of course, more to franchising than a contract. That, in a sense, comes last after the commercial viability of the business as a franchise has been properly structured and established. So do not make the mistake of trying to rush the owner of an existing but non-franchised business into selling a franchise. There have been cases where an approach from a prospective franchisee has acted as catalyst for the creation of a new franchise. But from the planting of an idea to the establishment of a viable franchise can take a considerable amount of time. Indeed, very few properly structured and piloted franchised systems can be ready for marketing in less than 2 years from the time the idea is first conceived.

If you, as a prospective franchisee, believe that the business is attractive you must be patient and wait until the owner has had the opportunity to develop a proper franchise system in which it would be safe for you to invest. Otherwise, you may well be contributing to your own downfall.

Most of the franchise systems on the market are likely to be at different stages in the development and maturity of their franchise. The more franchisees that there are, the easier will be the task of assessment because there will be many franchisees to talk to about what the franchise and the franchisor have done for them.

In situations where the franchisor is just getting off the ground, greater care is needed in making a choice, but this does not mean that one should not take up such a franchise. New franchises can and do provide splendid opportunities for those who take the trouble to investigate them properly and choose wisely. Table 9.2 illustrates the different stages in the development of a franchise system and the problems which can arise at each stage.

Table 9.2   Stages of development

Number of franchisees	Comments
1–10	The franchisor at this stage is still feeling his way. This is when he will be discovering whether he has been sufficiently thorough in pilot testing his concept. Has his pilot testing been wide enough, or conducted over a sufficiently long period?
	He is very vulnerable at this stage to his inexperience in selecting franchisees. He will also be feeling impatient because he has invested his resources in preparing to market his franchise and he will want to get on with selling his franchises in order to develop some cash flow.

11–40 The franchisor has now overcome his first hurdle, but he may be facing the problem of having among his first 10 franchisees four or five who are unsatisfactory. The unsatisfactory nature of these franchisees may not yet be apparent, but they could already be taking up a disproportionate amount of the franchisor's time. At this stage, if the franchise has not been properly structured, various stresses and strains will emerge.

The franchisor will at this point be developing his organizational infrastructure to cope with a hoped-for increasing number of franchisees and the growth of his business. Care must be taken to ensure that the growth rate does not outstrip the resources and capacity of the franchisor.

41–100 By now the franchise is relatively mature. The franchisor should be well organized and enjoying a reasonable return from his activities. He will now be turning his attention to laying the foundations for substantial expansion.

He will also be at the phase at which he will need to evaluate what is happening within the franchise. Does it need a fresh approach? Does it fulfil its function?

Certainly, he will be a very different franchisor from the one at stage 1–10. It should now be possible to see how capable the franchisor is at adapting to progress and change and how well he has serviced his franchisees.

Over 100 The franchisor will now have reached maturity and all the relevant information with which to assess the franchise should be readily available. The existing franchisees will provide a valuable source of information about the quality of the franchisor as well as the franchise system and the relationship which exists between them. The ability of the franchisor successfully to adapt to change and respond to developments and opportunities in the market-place should also be apparent.

In order to place the transaction in perspective it is sensible to compare buying a franchise with buying any non-franchised business. In buying a non-franchised business one makes an investigation of the business, examines the accounts, takes advice, negotiates the contract and completes the sale. The vendor may allow the purchaser into the business to work alongside him for a while to familiarize himself with the business or the vendor may stay for a day or two following completion. After that the purchaser is on his own and runs the business entirely as he thinks fit, making his own decisions good or bad on which his success depends.

How does this differ from taking up a franchise? In many respects there are similarities and in some vital respects there are not. The vital differences all stem from the fact that with a franchise one is not only setting up a business but is:

- accepting the use of the franchisor's name and branding;
- adopting the franchisor's system methods and know-how;
- relying on the ability of the franchisor:
  (a) in helping the franchisee into business; and
  (b) in continuing to support the franchisee during the life of the franchise relationship; and
  (c) to develop and maintain the business which is the subject of the franchise; and
  (d) to operate an honest, ethical business.

It is therefore necessary for the franchisee's enquiries to be directed at investigating the quality of the franchisor so far as is possible.

The questions which follow are designed to provide a prospective franchisee with the range of questions to which his enquiries should be directed so as to result in the relevant information being available to him before a decision is made about whether or not to enter into a franchise contract with any particular franchisor.

Fundamental questions

What qualifies the franchisor to be a franchisor? What is his background? How well has he prepared his scheme? What is there to suggest that he is able to discharge his promises and obligations?

To answer these important questions, the franchisor should be asked to provide the following information:

1. What is your business background and experience and that of your directors and principal shareholders (or partners)?
2. A detailed history of the development of the business to date.
3. What steps have you taken to prepare your business for franchising? (This and questions 4–8 are particularly appropriate for a franchise which is in the early stages of development and will become less relevant as the size of the franchisor's network grows.)
4. What knowledge or experience do you have of franchising and how did you acquire it?
5. How many pilot franchise operations did you establish before you began to offer franchises for sale?

6. How much of your own cash did you invest in establishing that your business was franchisable?

7. How can I be sure that you have adequately investigated the market-place and that you have acquired sufficient knowledge so that I can be satisfied that I am investing in a thoroughly tested business which has had the experience of confronting and solving the daily problems which arise? Please provide details of the performance achieved by your pilot operations. Please explain why you consider that the number of pilot operations which you conducted was sufficient in numbers and range of location or area of operations to prove that the concept works and that you are justified in commencing franchising operations.

8. Why did you decide to franchise rather than develop your business by the expansion of your own operations?

9. What is the growth rate you are planning over the next 5 years?

10. What is your corporate structure? How well can it cope with the growth of your franchise network and what plans do you have for the expansion of your support staff and the development of your infrastructure?

11. Who are the senior executives who will be influencing and planning the growth and development of the franchise network and dealing with the franchisees?

12. Can you confirm that none of these senior executives has ever been:
    (a) involved as principal, shareholder or executive in a company which has gone into receivership or liquidation, or had an administrative receiver appointed or an administration order made against it?
    (b) bankrupt or made an arrangement with his creditors?
    (c) involved in a franchise company which has experienced business failure?
    (d) unsuccessfully involved in business as a franchisee?
    (e) convicted of a criminal offence (other than a motoring offence not involving imprisonment)?

13. Please provide details of the following.
    (a) How many franchisees do you presently have? May I have their names and addresses?
    (b) How many franchisees did you have 12 months ago?
    (c) How many franchisees, within the last 2 years, have:
        (i) had their contracts terminated by you?
        (ii) terminated their contract with you?
        (iii) mutually agreed with you to terminate their contract?
             Please explain the circumstances.

14. How selective are you in choosing franchisees? Explain your approach.

15. Please provide a copy of your latest audited accounts.
16. Can you confirm that there has not been any deterioration in your financial position since such accounts were prepared? If confirmation cannot be given, please explain why not.
17. Please confirm that you have made arrangements adequately to finance your activities during at least the ensuing year.
18. Are you a member of the BFA? If so, which category of membership?
19. Have you applied for membership of the BFA and been refused?
20. Who are your bankers? May I take up a reference from the bank for at least the level of my proposed investment?
21. Do you have any franchisee finance schemes with any of the banks? If so, with which and may I have details?
22. Please provide at least two financial and business references, other than your bankers.

The views of existing franchisees and the experience they have had with their franchisor are always very important. However, and particularly (but not exclusively) in the case of early franchisees, beware of any franchisees who may have caused, or largely contributed to, the problems of which they complain. This possibility has been referred to above.

Advice should be taken from a solicitor and accountant and they will help you place the replies you receive in perspective. But whatever the replies and advice you receive, you must satisfy yourself that the franchisor whose system you decide to join is one who will provide you with a long-term business relationship and one on whose judgement you feel that you can rely.

ASSESSING THE BUSINESS PROPOSITION

The business of the franchisor has to be investigated. This investigation should be concerned with securing answers to the following issues.

1. How is the business structured?
2. What will the franchisor do to assist the franchisee into business?
3. What are the operational factors which are relevant and have to be considered?
4. What are the details of getting into the franchise?
5. What are the ongoing services and how will they be provided?

At this point of the investigation the franchisee should be trying to ascertain the 'nuts and bolts' of the franchisor's operational system and his methods of working.

In most cases, the franchisor will provide the franchisee with the services mentioned in Chapter 8 in order to assist the franchisee in obtaining his premises and preparing them for the opening. However, there can be cases in which the franchisor offers what is called a 'turnkey' operation. This means that the franchisor obtains the site and fully refurbishes, shopfits and stocks the store before handing the franchisee the 'key' against payment of the cost. In a turnkey operation, the franchisee, who will receive his training whilst his shop is being prepared, does not get involved in any way in the construction and fitting-out work, although the franchisor will keep in close contact with him during construction and will keep him in the picture and consult with him about what is being done. The franchisee will, of course, be responsible for the cost of fitting out, equipping and stocking of the business.

The following questions should be asked.

1. What is the total cost of establishing a business under your franchise?
2. What does this cost include?
3. What capital or other costs will be incurred by me in addition to the cost of establishing the business?
4. Do I have to pay a deposit? If so, on what terms? Are there any circumstances in which, if I do not proceed, I will lose my deposit, or any part of it? If so, please explain.
5. What initial franchise fee do I have to pay?
6. How much working capital do I need? What is the basis for your calculation of this requirement?
7. How long will it take to set up the business before it actually opens from the time we sign a contract?
8. What initial services do you offer?
9. What training facilities are there and where do you provide them? How long will the training last and what will it include?
10. Who pays for the training? Who pays the expenses I incur in attending the training, including fares and hotel accommodation?
11. Do you provide training facilities for my staff? If so, on what terms? If not, who trains them, and if I have to do so how am I provided with the means to do so?
12. What level of gross profit margin should I expect to achieve? Please itemize the expenses which I shall expect to incur. What level of turnover do I need to achieve to break even and how long should it take to reach that level?
13. May I see actual accounts which confirm, or fail to confirm, your projections? Can they be relied upon? Or are they merely illustrations?
14. What financing arrangements are available and what terms for repayment will there be? What rate of interest will be required and will the bank or finance company want security?

(Note: The questions which relate to financial performance will probably be answered in a qualified way. Very few franchisors will be prepared to make representations or give warranties of what financial performance will be achieved. Any franchisor who is prepared to give firm representations or warranties in regard to likely financial performance should be viewed with suspicion. A franchisor should be prepared to disclose actual figures which have been achieved, although he should not identify any franchisee who achieved the figures without that franchisee's consent. No franchisee should ever rely upon the financial projections as being a guarantee that they will be achieved. There can be many reasons why they are not achieved including market trends and economic factors affecting business as a whole as well as the franchisee's own deficiencies.

15. Is the business seasonal? In the case of a relatively new franchise involving a seasonal business, particular attention should be paid to whether the pilot testing was of a sufficiently long-term nature to be certain that seasonal factors have been taken into account. In the case of a longer-established franchise, the position should be more clear.
16. What opening support staff do you provide?
17. Do you provide an opening launch of the business? If so, what does it consist of?
18. How do you make your money?
19. Do you charge on-going franchise fees? What are they and how are they calculated?
20. Do you make a mark-up on product sales to your franchisees?
21. If so, how much and what sort of protection do I have against unfair and unjustified increases?
22. Do you take any commission from suppliers of goods or materials to a franchisee? If so, please provide details.
23. Do you receive any other income or commissions from any other source based upon that source's business dealings with your franchisees? If so, please provide details.
24. Will I be obliged to maintain a minimum continuing franchise fee, or to purchase a minimum amount of goods? What happens if I fail to meet this commitment? How do you calculate these minimum commitments?
25. What advertising and promotional support do you provide?
26. Do I have to contribute to advertising and promotional expenditure which you incur? If so, how much? Do you provide an auditor's certificate or other proof that the sums you receive for advertising and promotional expenditure have been spent for that purpose?
27. What point-of-sale and promotional literature do you supply, and what do I have to pay for it?
28. What help will I receive in local advertising and promotions? What will it cost me?

29. Will I be able to obtain and motivate a sufficient number of competent staff? Will they require specialist skills and are such people readily available?
30. Which of the following continuing services will you provide after the business has commenced:
    (a) research and development;
    (b) market testing;
    (c) negotiation of bulk purchasing terms for the benefit of franchisees;
    (d) field support;
    (e) performance monitoring;
    (f) general business advice;
    (g) advertising, marketing and promotion.
31. Are there any other continuing services provided by you? If so, please provide details.
32. Which of your field support staff will be my link with you after I have opened the business?
33. Can I meet him/her?
34. Can I meet some of your other field support staff?
35. Can I meet your head office team?
36. How long have they each been with you and do they have a service contract which will ensure continuity?
37. Please explain the procedure which you will adopt to get me ready to open your business.
38. Will you find me a site, or do I have to find it myself?
39. What will be the opening hours of my business?
40. Will I own the equipment necessary to operate the business?
41. How soon will I have to spend money on replacing equipment or remodelling my premises?
42. How many times in the past and at what expense to franchisees have you required re-equipping or remodelling to take place?
43. What systems do you have for keeping franchisees in touch with you and each other?
44. Do you publish a newsletter?
45. Do you hold seminars?
46. Is there a franchisee association within your network?
47. How will I cope with my accounting and record keeping?
48. What restrictions will there be on what products I can sell?
49. Do you provide instructional and operational manuals?
50. What will you do if by a clear mistake you misjudge my site, and it does not produce the anticipated figures, resulting in a loss?
51. What would happen if I ran into operational problems which I was unable to solve? What help would I get?
52. How can I be sure you will do what you promise?

WHAT HAPPENS IF THE FRANCHISOR FAILS?

Fortunately, there are not many examples in practice of a franchisor becoming bankrupt or going into liquidation. Nonetheless, the subject is important since there have been failures and there certainly will be more in the future. In making a decision to take up a franchise the possibility must be borne in mind as well as the consequences. The fact that someone sets himself up as a franchisor does not mean that he is thereby invested with an aura of invincibility and cannot fail.

A franchisor may fail for a number of different reasons.

1. There may have been a deliberate fraud.
2. There may have been a badly structured franchise.
3. The business which is being franchised may not have been sufficiently well market tested.
4. The franchisor may be under-capitalized, particularly in crucial early years.
5. There may be a good franchise system but the franchisor runs his end of the business badly.
6. The franchisor may make bad policy decisions.
7. The franchise scheme may fall foul of the law.
8. The franchisor may make poor selection of franchisees.
9. There may be over-rapid expansion leading to lack of adequate support for franchisees.
10. There may be a lack of management ability in the franchisor's organization.

In some of these cases the collapse of the franchisor may cause irretrievable loss, and in this connection one has in mind those losses referred to in (1), (2), (3) and (7), the first three having been avoidable and the last perhaps avoidable or perhaps unforeseeable. In such cases the franchisee will probably be left with little except a financial loss and a large headache. He may have some sort of business still left which, with imagination and hard work, he can work up sufficiently to reduce his losses. It may be that what he is left with cannot be worked upon at all and he has to cut his losses and close up as soon as possible. It could also be that the franchisee has so little past experience and training that he is not capable of continuing without a franchisor's support.

It is of little comfort to one who finds himself in that position to be told that he should not have gone into the franchise at all since the weaknesses would have been apparent had proper enquiries been made. In one respect a potential franchisee is now far better placed to judge the good, the bad and the fraudulent than he ever had been in the past. A higher level of expertise is developing in the legal and accountancy professions, and the government business advisory services and centres are a useful source of advice. The banks involved in franchising provide an additional source of informed advice which should not be ignored. The BFA runs educational programmes and sells a franchisee information pack to prospective franchisees. The implications of BFA membership are dealt with in Chapter 17.

All may not be lost for the franchisee since there are possibilities. The franchisor will be the proprietor of:

- the system under which the franchised business is operated;
- the know-how associated with it;
- trade secrets;
- trademarks and/or trade names with associated goodwill; and
- copyright material.

None of these will disappear with the franchisor's business failure. They will be assets of the business with which a liquidator or receiver will have to deal, but subject to the rights granted in respect thereof to the franchisees.

The liquidator or receiver will be seeking to obtain whatever is the market price for these assets but, since the rights granted will also be subject to the provision of a franchisor's services, it may not be easy to dispose of them. The value of the assets of which the liquidator or receiver will be seeking to dispose will be enhanced by the potential income from the franchisees under the franchise agreements.

There are two potential purchasers of these assets. First, a competitor of the franchisor who may or may not already be a franchisor himself. If he is a franchisor he may have reservations about whether the former competitor's disgruntled franchisees could fit in. The risks for him would be very high. Undoubtedly he would insist on meeting all the franchisees to see whether a working relationship would have any prospect of success. If he is not yet a franchisor the opportunity presented to him may have the effect of triggering his entry into the field with a ready-made network. He would, however, have to be very sure of his own franchising ideas and of his ability to develop the right sort of relationship with the franchisees, who may resent the intrusion presented by new ideas. Second, the franchisees themselves. It is unlikely that the franchisor will have become bankrupt or gone into liquidation without some warning signs having been apparent for some time. The warning signs should not be ignored.

The franchisor will usually have contractual obligations to:

- provide management back-up;
- provide advertising;
- maintain standards;
- provide continuing development;
- supply and/or arrange the supply of products, etc.

As his financial resources become stretched his ability to finance the provision of these services will be impaired. His franchisees will notice the deterioration of, or decline in, provision of services and undoubtedly will be complaining. Some franchisees may add to the franchisor's cash-flow problems by stopping the payment of franchise fees in retaliation for the failure to provide services. This could be a dangerous course for the franchisee to follow since it would probably ensure that they are in breach of their contractual obligations.

Additionally, some franchisees may take steps to terminate the franchise agreement for the breach of its provisions by the franchisor and make damages claims. These claims will probably be worth little in view of the franchisor's lack of financial resources. The consequence for a franchisee who terminates or whose agreement is terminated for his breach of contract will, in all probability, mean that he is prohibited thereafter from using the franchisor's:

- system
- know-how
- trade secrets
- trademark/trade name and goodwill
- copyright material

and also limited in his future activities by a restrictive covenant. Termination may not be the best step to take. However, it should also be borne in mind that there may be some bargaining power available to a franchisee who does not terminate and is in a position to make a claim in dealing with a liquidator or receiver.

Depending upon the maturity of the franchise system there may exist a Franchisee Advisory Committee or some informal liaison between franchisees. In any event it is quite likely, with the franchisor labouring noticeably under the strain of a lack of cash, that the franchisees will get together to discuss their common problem with a common approach to the franchisor. In the author's view, therein lies the best course which franchisees can take in these circumstances. Again, there may be different views on what to do and on the degree of involvement which some wish to have. However, the best prospect they have is that the franchise system is kept in existence.

In most franchise chains the franchisees have varying degrees of ability and the most able may well have been involved for a sufficiently long time to be capable of providing many of the franchisor's services and of organizing the employment or involvement of others with the requisite specialized skills. The franchisees in this predicament should therefore organize themselves, or such of them as wish to be involved, so that they can negotiate to acquire the assets which can be taken into a joint company which those concerned can own. Some thought will have to be given to the structure in that company and the rights to dispose of shares. The company will then have to be organized—it may be that one of the more able and successful franchisees could successfully take over this responsibility. Such a group would be able to deal with suppliers of goods and products who may be disenchanted by having been let down by the franchisor but who may be persuaded by the number of franchisees involved and their determined attitude to continue supplying on a favourable basis.

If it is not possible to negotiate such a purchase of the assets the franchisees may wish to go their separate ways using different names. Some may wish to, even if the assets can be acquired. Others may be nervous about breaking free. It may be possible to compromise any claim for damages which franchisees may have against the franchisor by acquiring the right, for a significant period, to continue using the trademarks/trade names, goodwill and system for a nominal charge free from post-termination restrictions until the franchisee can reorganize his business or the franchisor's business is restructured and perhaps able successfully to re-establish its former activities. The franchisees will have a role to play and should consider whether their most prudent course would be to embark upon a programme of constructive co-operation with the franchisor.

If the franchisees are able to continue to use the trademarks, trade names and system there will be merit in co-operative effort, at least to ensure the pooling of advertising and promotional resources and the bargaining power which gives advantage to a group compared with a number of individuals.

FINAL STEPS

The prospective franchisee must weigh up and consider the advantages and disadvantages of franchising described in this book as well as the replies to the questions suggested, before making the decision on whether or not to enter into any specific franchised business venture. A decision must also be made as to whether the advantages, such as the established business format, training and support provided by the franchisor, are worth having in return for surrendering some independence and submitting to the degree of outside control which is inherent in a franchise transaction.

The prospective franchisee must decide whether the particular franchisor is the right person with whom to do business. Also, he must decide whether he is personally and temperamentally suitable for this type of relationship. The prospective franchisee may also consider the advice of his local bank manager, or a businessman whose judgement he respects. He should certainly discuss the matter with his immediate family.

When all these relevant factors have been weighed up, the legal issues and the franchise contract considered (Chapter 12), and proper professional advice has been taken, then the prospective franchisee has to make his final decision. If he is not able to make his decision with confidence, after having heard all his advisers have to say, he should consider whether he is indeed capable of running his own business, whether franchising is right for him, whether the particular franchisor is right for him and whether the particular business is the right one for him.

Chapter 10

Franchisor–franchisee relations

THE FOUNDATION

In this chapter we examine the relationship between the franchisor and franchisee from the moment of first contact through to the development of a mature network. As will be seen the relationship changes as the franchisee moves from a state of ignorance about the way in which to conduct the franchised business and almost total dependence, to being a confident, successful operator of that business. In some cases the franchisee may not be successful but may experience difficulties for various reasons, which may include:

- factors outside the control of both parties, e.g. general economic conditions;
- some deficiencies in the franchisor, his system or his support services;
- some deficiencies in the franchisee's attitude or execution of the lessons learned from the franchisor.

Many of the issues which are identified in this chapter as having a bearing on franchisor–franchisee relations are dealt with elsewhere in this book in the appropriate chapters. The relationship between franchisor and franchisee is a very special one and is different from most business relationships. There is an analogy to be drawn between parent–child relations on the one hand and franchisor–franchisee relations on the other. In the franchise's early stages the franchisee, like a child with a parent, is dependent upon the franchisor for his sources of information and the understanding of how to apply the knowledge acquired. As the franchisee gains practical experience he becomes less dependent, and in some cases positively independent to the point that he no longer sees the value in his association with the franchisor, or at least a diminished role for the franchisor. He regards himself as being totally responsible for his success and he resents the payments he is making to the franchisor and the controls to which he is subjected. Furthermore, he may see no need to continue to be supplied with any services by the franchisor.

This is similar to the developing parent–child relationship—as the child grows older so it becomes less dependent and more fiercely independent. The child has its own ideas, cannot see the need for parental control and rejects parental influence. So both the franchisor and parent face a similar problem. It is the recognition of, and response to, the changing and evolving nature of the relationship which is an essential element in the skill of both franchisor and parent. Those who deal with this problem best are the most successful in practice.

There is also a vital difference, for when the child becomes an adult it is free to do whatever it wants to do. Respect for parental feelings and guidance may or may not be considered, but even so it is the child's final choice of career and the country in which it wishes to pursue that career which dictate events. The franchisee, however, is locked into the franchise relationship throughout the term of the contract (and any renewals) or until he sells his business. That he is a mature franchisee with years in the business behind him will give him no greater freedom to run his business than the newest recruit to the system. That is fundamental to the franchisee method. The fact that the intelligent, ambitious, entrepreneurial franchisee does well and applies himself diligently to the development of the franchised business has to be recognized. His input should be encouraged and he should be treated with respect as should the ideas which he can contribute. However, the franchisor cannot allow the franchisees to take over the control of the franchise system and its development. The fundamentals remain true at whatever stage one finds oneself. The franchisees operate the franchisor's system using the franchisor's names and trademarks and the franchisor must have the final word on what can and cannot be permitted. Indeed, without centralized control the franchise system and network could rapidly lose its corporate identity and uniformity of branding produce and service.

It may be said that franchising involves the development of a multiple chain of outlets in multiple ownership. What it does not involve is multiple ownership of a multiplicity of subtly different outlets. It is for such a reason that the controls which appear in a franchise agreement to be rigid cannot be qualified as so many franchisees would like by the insertion of the word 'reasonable'. The prospect that in a mature network of say more than 50 franchisees, a franchisor may have to cope with 'reasonable' but different requests from each franchisee is not only difficult to cope with but is incompatible with the maintenance of uniformity. Uniformity cannot be maintained if a 'reasonableness test' has to be applied to each request by a franchisee to initiate change or vary existing procedures. The recording of what is or what is not permitted in each individual case will become a burden and create endless opportunities for conflict. Furthermore, the task of field support staff in educating themselves in the differences will be considerable, as will the opportunities for dispute.

Lastly, and not least in significance, it will become impossible to know what is the franchisor's system and know-how. This will make the protection of the vital property rights of the franchisor very difficult, with adverse repercussions for both franchisor and the network of franchisees. In addition, the provisions of the European Community block exemption regulation for categories of franchise agreements may not be complied with since it may not be possible for the franchisor's know-how to be identified as required by the regulation.

From these issues we learn that there must be:

- respect by both franchisor and franchisee for the basic principles upon which the franchise system of marketing is based which are the foundations of its success;
- respect by the franchisee for the achievements and guidance which the franchisor provides. Not respect so blind that the franchisee does not see when the franchisor should be questioned and challenged, but respect for the ownership of the name, system know-how and practical experience upon which the franchise is based and all that such ownership implies;
- respect by the franchisor for the achievements of the franchisees and the contribution to the system which each franchisee can make, gained from his experience in running an operational unit.

This assumes all is well with the system, franchisor and franchisee, and that all the plans, hopes and expectations fall into place. Even if this Utopian state of affairs could exist it would not last for long if all parties did not put a great deal of effort into the maintenance of the franchisor–franchisee relationship. The relationship does not end with the signing of the contract any more than a parent's duties and obligations end with the birth of the child. The vagaries of the relationship, the strains and the stresses all combine to provide the parties with great challenges in an endeavour to ensure success.

There are many areas which can give rise to stress in the relationship.

1. The franchisee is not suited to self-employment.
2. The franchisee does not have the right aptitude for the particular franchise operation.
3. The franchisee may feel let down by what he expected not being matched by the reality.

4. The franchise is in an early stage of development and the franchisee does not consider that the franchisor has conducted sufficiently comprehensive pilot testing of the operations.
5. The franchisor may feel that the franchisee is not putting in the right level of effort.
6. The franchisee is dissatisfied with the up-front franchisor services.
7. The franchisee fails to make payments and/or reports on time.
8. The franchisee fails to maintain operating standards.
9. The franchisee seeks to break away from the system.
10. There are problems with the quality (or lack of quality) of the location.
11. Difficulties arise over the sale of the franchisee's business.
12. There are personality clashes between the franchisor's staff and the franchisee.
13. There are failures of communication.
14. The franchisor behaves too autocratically.
15. The franchisees resist change and improvement.
16. The franchisees are dissatisfied with the franchisor's promotional and advertising activities.
17. The franchisee's business is not as successful as the franchisee thinks it should be.
18. The franchisee's business is not as successful as the franchisor thinks it should be.
19. The franchisor does not provide the right level of back-up with field support staff.
20. The franchisee takes niggling liberties in his operation of the system.
21. The franchisor is not understood and seen by franchisees to be implementing research and development programmes to maintain and/or improve the franchise network's competitiveness in the market-place.

THE PARTIES' RESPONSIBILITIES

The franchise relationship will come into existence as a result of the efforts of the franchisor to recruit franchisees and the interest of the franchisee in becoming a franchisee. Before either of them reach that stage of their development the franchisor will have prepared his franchise for the market-place or may have been established for some period of time. The franchisee will have concluded that he wishes to own and operate his own business.

As emphasized in other chapters of this book, the franchisor should have done his homework properly, as should the franchisee. There is always and quite properly a great emphasis placed upon the franchisor's obligations to a franchisee.

1. Properly to pilot test and prove that the business is profitable.
2. Honestly to present the facts to the franchisee to enable the franchisee to make an informed decision.
3. To provide a proper effective and efficient range of initial services to assist the franchisee in establishing his business.
4. To establish the skilled range of continuing support services which will include:
    (a) operational back-up;
    (b) updating of the operational manual;
    (c) marketing and promotional support;
    (d) advertising on a national or regional basis with funds contributed by franchisees;
    (e) standards and performance monitoring;
    (f) research and development; and
    (g) the benefits of the bulk purchasing power which the network commands.

The franchisor is also regarded as having a responsibility to exercise care in his choice of franchisees. He should not accept as a franchisee anyone who applies and has the money. There is much more to making a choice than that. The British Franchise Association Code of Ethics deals with the issue in the following terms:

> A franchisor shall select and accept only those franchisees who, upon reasonable investigation, possess the basic skills, education, personal qualities and adequate capital to succeed. There shall be no discrimination based on rank, colour, religion, national origin or sex.

By becoming a member of the BFA a franchisor accepts the obligation to work within the framework established by the Code of Ethics.

There does not exist any similar framework within which franchisees should operate. The process of franchisee selection by a franchisor is not the one-sided exercise which perhaps some franchisors would suggest it is. The entry into the contract and the establishment of the franchise relationship is very much a combined effort. Both parties have to be right for each other, and in addition the franchisee has to be able to:

- cope with the stress and strain of self-employment; and
- demonstrate the qualities which the business which is franchised requires of those who run outlets.

The franchisee, although he owns the business, has to accept the constraints which franchising will impose upon him and his freedom to do exactly what he pleases.

Apart from the obligation which the franchisee has to be honest with the franchisor he also has obligations to himself and his family.

1. He must be honest with himself over the issue of whether he has the qualities which equip him to cope with self-employment; is he and are his family prepared to live with the disruption to life which self-employment can bring with it? Searching self-examination is very necessary at this stage.

2. He must, whatever the temptations, be totally objective in his evaluation of the franchise opportunities which interest him. There are far too many franchisees who become so 'taken' with a proposition that all normal danger signals are ignored. Advice is not listened to because it does not confirm what the franchisee wanted to hear. Thus one finds a significant number of people signing up to become franchisees where the franchisor has not properly market tested his operations, where the franchisor's financial situation is clearly unsatisfactory, and where the franchisor's contractual arrangements place the franchisee at a severe disadvantage in relation to such matters as product supply and price, terms of transfer of business and renewal rights which are easy to defeat and/or which cost unreasonable sums to exercise. Any would-be franchisee who cannot be totally objective and who ignores obvious danger signals will find that not only will franchisor–franchisee relations be poor but the franchisor may not survive.

    Another danger is that even if the franchisor is a good franchisor with a well-developed system, the franchisee may by lacking in objectivity take on a franchise which does not suit him and his capabilities.

3. The franchisee must not allow anyone else to sort out a 'short list' of prospective franchise opportunities for him. He should personally meet and discuss the opportunities available with as many franchisors as will be prepared to meet him. Both parties will benefit enormously from this, particularly the franchisee. Both parties will be making a very important decision; the more prospective franchisees a franchisor can interview the more experience obtained and the better will be the quality of those who enter into the franchise; the more franchisors the prospective franchisee can meet the more he will learn about franchisors and the opportunities on offer. The greater the franchisee's experience in meeting and discussing opportunities with franchisors the more likely he is to make the right choice when exercising an *objective* judgement. These meetings and particularly those with the franchisor with whom the franchisee will enter into an agreement will be laying the foundations of the future franchisor–franchisee relationship.

4. The franchisee must be completely honest and open in his dealings with the franchisor. This is the approach he expects of the franchisor, so he must divulge all that is relevant to enable the franchisor to reach an informed conclusion about the franchisee. A franchisee who feels let down when he discovers that what the franchisor told him was not the whole or the right story should understand that a franchisor will feel let down if the franchisee withholds material information from him. Either way the trust which each must have in the other is damaged or even destroyed and the relationship will at best be difficult if not impossible.

It must therefore be appreciated by both franchisor and franchisee that their pre-contract meetings and discussions are laying the foundations for a possible long-term future relationship. It is in the interests of both parties that the ground rules for the relationship are clearly explained and established.

The main areas which give rise to stress in the relationship are listed above; some of these can be taken into account at this early stage of discussion. If each of the parties is aware of these potential problem areas they can and should feature in the pre-contract discussions so that each can judge the other's reaction and take a view for the future.

At this stage in the discussions the franchisor should reveal to the franchisee all sources of income which the franchisor derives from the operation of the franchised network. No franchisor should have any source of income which the franchisees do not know about and the franchisor must not make any secret profits. The relationship will suffer considerably in terms of loss of trust or respect if franchisees find that the franchisor is profiting at their expense from a source of which they are not aware.

It is also important that the franchisor does not do 'special deals' with any individual franchisees. Special deals create problems in the relationship:

1. The franchisee who is given a special deal always regards himself as a special case and will always expect privileges.
2. Other franchisees who do not have such special deals will resent those who do and the franchisor for not having given them the same deal.

The franchisor should ensure that the franchisee understands what the franchising method of marketing is and how it works in practice. It is crucial that the franchisee understands the nature and scope of the relationship and what is expected of a franchisor and a franchisee. The franchisee must be made aware of what will later be:

- provided to him by the franchisor as continuing services and how these services will be provided; and

- expected of him in terms of standards, operating procedures and likely expenditures on keeping the image fresh and the business up to date.

The quality of the franchisor's training is a key factor in ensuring that these foundations for the future are properly explained and will provide the introduction to the franchisor's operational manuals and the day-to-day operation of the franchised business. The franchisor should be capable of explaining and indeed should explain to the franchisees the reasons for the operational requirements and the individual provisions in the franchise agreement. A franchisee who can be given a proper perspective and understanding of the way in which the operational and legal obligations are brought together will find it easier to come to terms with the one-sided nature of the arrangement which is essential if the franchisor is to be capable of maintaining the standards and the integrity of his name, goodwill and operating system. These requirements place the art of communications high on the list of skills which the franchisor must possess. Whatever he promises and demands should not only be in the contract and manual but should be represented by daily reality in his dealings with franchisees. These early dealings between franchisor and franchisee are crucial as they set the tone for what will follow; what follows must involve the delivery by both the franchisor and franchisee to each other of what is expected, undertaken and promised.

Above all, both parties *must* appreciate that they are laying the foundation for what needs to be a harmonious positive 'partnership' (not in the legal sense) for their mutual advantage. What they should not be doing is laying down the foundations for conflict within a legal arena. Once any of the parties reaches for the contract the relationship has failed. If both parties can always bear in mind that they are better off if they perform their obligations and conduct their relations with each other on the basis that the contract should never be looked at after it is signed until it needs to be renewed that will be a good start. Good franchisor–franchisee relations do not happen; they have to be worked at.

THE CONTINUING RELATIONSHIP

We now move on to the stage in the relationship when the franchisee has signed his contract and undergone training. The franchisor should now be delivering the services to the franchisee which should result in a successful opening of the franchisee's business. This will be at a time when the relationship between the parties should not be tainted by any ill feelings, rather there should prevail a spirit of willing co-operation. That is not to say that this will always be the case for, even at this early stage in the relationship, there is no guarantee that some franchisees will not be testing the franchisor's resolve by attempting to cut corners and save money by seeking to get by with a lower level of specification than the franchisor requires. Such an attitude on the part of an individual franchisee could be an indication that there may be long-term problems with that particular individual. This attitude at such an early stage may be a warning that if not brought under control this franchisee will always challenge the franchisor's system, methods and authority.

In the early stages of the development of a franchise the franchisor is far more likely to take on, as franchisees, persons who are unsuitable. There are two reasons for this. Firstly, the franchisor is inexperienced at the task of assessing and evaluating the suitability of prospective franchisees and has not yet developed the art of knowing and recognizing the relevant qualities which a franchisee of his network should possess. Secondly, the franchisor will be anxious to embark upon his programme of selling franchises so that his initial investment in pilot operations and the franchising infrastructure of his business can be rewarded. This anxiety is often translated into a loss of objectivity coupled with impatience which results in the recruitment of franchisees who apparently have the requisite basic qualities but who may be temperamentally and by nature unsuited for the relationship with the particular franchisor or to bring the right skills to the network's operations. For example, the franchisee may lack ability as a salesman where sales ability is a crucial feature of the franchise system.

These two factors combine to provide the foundation for problems which may not be capable of resolution by even the best possible franchisor–franchisee relation programme of the franchisor. It is common to many franchise networks that of the first 12 or so franchisees there will be more difficulties to contend with than with those who subsequently join the network. Apart from the fact that the existence of these 'difficult' franchisees will make disproportionate demands upon the franchisor's resources there will also be difficulties in recruitment as well as resentment by other franchisees of the problems which can affect the network as a whole. Normally a good franchise will sell itself but no matter how good the franchise, bad news from early entrants, whatever the cause, can only inhibit growth as prospective franchisees are deterred by their contact with those franchisees. It is also a feature found in mature networks that some of the early 'difficult' franchisees later become active organizers of franchisee dissent, again causing disruption to a network and a diversion of franchisor and franchisee resources from their normal business activities.

Franchisors should recognize that it is vitally important to ensure the correct selection of all franchisees to the system but particularly the first 12 in order to avoid the potential future problems which can arise. Patience and the ability to say 'no' when needed are essential. Great care should be taken to ensure that franchisees have the requisite skills and are not likely to find the day-to-day requirements of their business alien to their nature.

I emphasize these factors since if the foundation, which comprises the initial franchisees, is not sound the task of fostering and maintaining good franchisor–franchisee relations becomes that much more difficult.

The responsibility for good franchisor–franchisee relations is shared by franchisor and franchisee but undoubtedly it is the franchisor who must take the initiative in establishing their tone and quality. The franchisor and franchisee must *not* take each other for granted. If they do the franchisor will be neglecting his responsibilities and the franchisee will be failing to develop as an independent businessman to the full extent of his entrepreneurial abilities. The franchisor should be seeking to create a climate in which the franchisee feels that he is being encouraged to develop his business and apply his entrepreneurial skills. He should be made to feel a member of the 'family' and be encouraged to provide his input, based upon his experience, for the good of the network of which he is a member. Many innovations in franchised networks are prompted by suggestions which originate with franchisees.

Good franchisor–franchisee relations do not occur spontaneously, they flow from a conscious effort on the part of both parties to work at enhancing the relationship. It can be easy for a franchisor to take advantage of his franchisees. Many franchisees join systems because they have a strong belief in the basic business and their prospects for success. Their first feelings if the franchisor is, to their mind, underperforming are of disappointment and frustration coupled with a strong wish to try to get the franchisor properly to perform his obligations. Apart from the fact that no franchisor should allow any franchisees to be able to claim underperformance, the perception (even if unjustified) that the franchisor is underperforming is a clear indication that the franchisor is failing properly to communicate with his franchisees and is not concentrating his efforts sufficiently well on the franchisor–franchisee relationship. In seeking to maintain the relationship at the right level the franchisor should understand that the franchisee's perception of his role and performance are very important and channels of communication must be kept wide open and thoughtfully used to ensure that the franchisees' perception of the franchisor's abilities are accurate. Before dealing with channels of communication there are a few other points worthy of consideration.

The franchisee's contribution to good relations with the franchisor requires that the franchisee should work at doing his job properly and wholeheartedly. The operational standards must be complied with; the franchisee should work hard to make a success of his business—no clock watching!; reporting requirements and financial obligations should promptly be met— nothing could be calculated to do more harm than failure to provide what the franchisor will regard as vital information and to pay monies due; the franchisee should participate in events organized by the franchisor, e.g. annual regional franchise meetings, contributions to franchise network newsletters.

For his part the franchisor must concentrate on maintaining and improving the quality of his services. In short the franchisor should deliver what he promised he would. The ongoing back-up, demonstrating an interest in the franchisees and the development of their business, is important. Also important is the maintenance for research and development and the processing and evaluation of new ideas. Demonstration by the franchisor of his ability and will to introduce new ideas, adapt the system, modernize the image and introduce new product lines or services so that the business remains competitive will provide welcome comfort to a franchisee and enhance the relationship.

The franchisor should ensure that not only does he give the franchisee value for money in the provision of continuing services but the franchisee perceives that he is getting value for money. This requires the introduction and maintenance of excellent means of communication between franchisor and franchisee. The franchisor should take trouble to ensure that written communications are not only received but read, assimilated and acted upon. The role of field support staff in ensuring that this occurs is very important. Field support staff are the eyes and ears of the franchisor; they must be receptive and not hostile to what the franchisees have to say. Field support staff should be trained to look out for the early warning signs that something is amiss. Any such signs should be acted upon, for even if there is no logical or apparently justified ground for complaint, the fact that the franchisee is unhappy should be sufficient to raise the alarm that something needs to be done.

The franchisor must have a system for dealing with the stresses and strains which will always arise in any network no matter how well it is run. In the final analysis the managing director and/or chairman of the franchisor company must be prepared to become involved to ensure that the right outcome results.

It is suggested that the franchisor should ensure that all his staff understand the importance of the highest possible quality of franchisor–franchisee relations. Staff training should ensure that the emphasis is placed upon the quality of good relations and how they can be achieved and maintained. The franchisor should appoint a senior member of staff backed by and reporting to the chairman or managing director to have responsibility for ensuring that these policies are effectively maintained.

Chapter 11

Channels of communication: franchisee advisory associations

None of the efforts which franchisor and franchisee make to enhance their relationship will be effective unless there is a programme in place to ensure good and effective channels of communication between them. It will be appreciated from Chapter 10 that communications are a two-way process. The franchisee cannot respond to the franchisor unless the franchisor has made his point clearly and effectively and the franchisor cannot know what concerns the franchisee unless the franchisee opens up to the franchisor. Whatever frustrations either party may feel about the actions or non-actions of the other, communications must not be conducted on a background of hostility; they must always be constructive with a view to resolving problems to the mutual advantage of franchisor and franchisee. Hostile action tends to bring hostile reaction and a deterioration in relations which can not only usually be avoided but which will inevitably be counter-productive and result in a situation which helps no one.

One may summarize the areas to which efforts should be concentrated in order to enhance good relations.

PERSONAL CONTACT

Personal contact is an important feature of the relationship and must never be neglected. Even successful franchisees require personal contact with the franchisor; their success should not result in their neglect by the franchisor. They may not need so much personal contact or attention as the unsuccessful nor will they need the same level of input. Dialogue with successful franchisees not only keeps high their level of awareness that they belong to the network, it also assists in the perpetuation of their belief that membership of its network is worthwhile. Their very success, of which they will be proud, has to be recognized and encouraged. They may well also prove capable of providing the franchisor with a valuable input which can assist in developing new ideas and product (or service) lines.

Personal contact will be provided in most cases by specialist staff at the franchisor's office and the franchisor's field support staff. However the franchisor organizes his resources he should ensure that all his staff recognize that each franchisee is special to the franchisor and respond to each of them on a personal basis. Each franchisee must be dealt with on the basis that his role and importance are recognized and that he feels that the franchisor really cares about him, his problems and his success.

All visits by the franchisor to the franchisee's operational unit should be recorded on a form containing a check-list to verify compliance by the franchisee with operational standards and contractual obligations. The franchisor's representative *must* discuss the report with the franchisee to ensure that the franchisee knows and understands in what respect he is not regarded as performing correctly. He may have explanations which he must be given an opportunity to provide. Nothing could be worse than to have a franchisee think that unjustified secret reports are being made about him and his operations. Apart from monitoring compliance the franchisor should be using the information to help the franchisee improve his standards and performance.

WRITTEN COMMUNICATIONS

It is likely that in many cases written communication from franchisors will be more frequent than personal contact. Because of the more impersonal nature of written communications it is more important to get the right message to the franchisee in an unambiguous way. In face-to-face contact misunderstandings can be discussed and resolved. A written communication which is capable of being misunderstood is like a festering sore which left unattended can become a major problem; what is worse is that the franchisor may not even realize the havoc his misunderstood communication has caused until the franchisee explodes into reaction. Even unintended carelessness can create the wrong impression, which underlines the need for extreme care in the preparation by a franchisor of written communications. The methods of written communication can vary from case to case but it is likely that there will be four basic categories of written communication:

- normal correspondence
- newsletters
- updates of manuals

- field visit reports

It is clear that the authors of these various communications will differ. There will probably be more than one author of letters, which could be written by any member of the franchisor's team; this will also probably be the case with updates of manuals where the authorship will depend upon the segment of the manual which is being updated. The franchisor should have some system for checking that all authors of its written material appreciate the need for accurate, unambiguous communication and should introduce some internal method of checking material before it is dispatched. Checking is more difficult with normal correspondence without impairing efficient operations but franchisors must take care because it is so easy to cause unnecessary offence with a thoughtless comment.

FRANCHISE MEETINGS

Many franchisors take the trouble to organize meetings between themselves and groups of franchisees as well as the whole network. Regional and national meetings can be a very effective means of keeping in touch with franchisees, their feelings, doubts, fears, ideas and complaints. These meetings also enable the franchisor to make presentations indicating how franchisees can improve performance, what new ideas are to be introduced, what is under research and development and what promotional and marketing activities are proposed. Franchisees rightly expect to be kept informed and if the right climate of co-operation can be created many ideas and suggestions from franchisees can be useful and make a positive contribution to the development of the network.

FRANCHISEE ASSOCIATIONS

There are two types of franchisee association. There are those born out of the frustration and dissatisfaction of the franchisees and which adopt a hostile adversary position with the franchisor. This must be avoided at all costs. For an association to be set up in these circumstances must mean that the franchisor has failed in some of the following areas:

- adequately to communicate with his franchisees;
- to be receptive to his franchisees' ideas;
- to be supportive;
- to provide the right field support between the franchisee and franchisor;
- in his marketing programmes;

- in his innovative functions—he has not kept the system and image up to date with market trends;
- to organize advantageous purchasing arrangements;
- to develop and maintain the feeling in the network of mutual trust and interdependence between franchisor and franchisees which is so vital—the franchisor may have become overbearing or, by contrast, appear disinterested;
- in other material respects to discharge his obligations to his franchisees.

A franchisee association which develops in these circumstances is symptomatic of the problems; it will not solve them; it is an indictment of the franchisor. The franchise system will be attacked and the franchisor will find himself with either a combined legal action or tremendous pressure which could lead to the dismantling of his franchise system. Alternatively, the franchisees will try to lead the franchisor back along what they regard as the path of franchise righteousness.

In any event, all parties will have suffered traumatically in terms of personal relationship, confidence and undoubtedly financially. The amount of time and effort which franchisees and franchisor will have to spend on the areas of dispute will divert resources from their respective basic businesses, resulting in a downward spiral which will exacerbate the difficulties.

Concerted actions by franchisees on such a basis have a tendency to run into difficulties. Human nature being what it is there will inevitably be ringleaders (some of whom may be early unsatisfactory franchisees) and those who will respond to peer pressure. Experience shows that when serious action is proposed many franchisees lose enthusiasm—those who responded to peer pressure step back and those who fear a loss of their business investment are not prepared to run the risk. Furthermore, since each franchisee's case and circumstances are different, a group of this nature can result in inter-franchisee disputes and differences which harm the whole network and can sour the atmosphere.

The franchisor will always, and quite rightly, take the view that he has a direct contractual relationship with each franchisee and that he will only deal with each franchisee on a one-to-one basis in resolving any problems or issues which the franchisee may wish to discuss. It is for the franchisor to evaluate what his franchisees provide as input, to balance the diverse issues which not surprisingly are likely to be based upon personal self-interest, and to produce solutions which are in the best interests of the entire network. Franchisees must accept that they are part of a team and like all teams there is a leader—in this case the franchisor.

Getting the attention of the franchisor is all well and good up to a point but franchisees who contemplate the route of establishing the 'trade union' type of association should give very considerable thought as to whether or not to adopt this approach rather than a more constructive and less confrontational route—the risks can be significant.

The other type of association is that which is formed either on the sole initiative of the franchisor or jointly by franchisor and franchisees as a means of improving communications and acting as a means of liaison when problems arise or to ensure that problems are avoided. It is difficult to state when would be the right point in time in the development of any individual franchise to introduce such an association. Obviously in the early stages it will not be necessary or appropriate, but once the franchisor is established with some experienced franchisees in the field the advantages will become apparent. The association which is created in a spirit of goodwill with mutual advantage as its objective extends the climate of understanding which should exist into a practical reality, thus providing a strong weapon in cementing the franchisor and franchisees together in a powerful business alliance. It acts as a positive synthesis of the franchisor's and franchisee's entrepreneurial talents for their mutual benefit.

There are those who do not believe that franchisee associations are the answer to the communications problem. There have been attempts by franchisors to establish associations which have failed owing to the apathy displayed by franchisees. One is inclined to wonder whether the reason for the lack of interest was that the franchisor's system for conducting relations with franchisees was so effective that an association was not felt necessary by franchisees. If a franchisor can devise a system which achieves that result an association may not be necessary. As with most techniques which are available there is no dogmatic rule that one should or should not have a franchise association. It may be a helpful business tool but it is only one of the options available to a franchisor and certainly does not, and cannot, replace direct personal face-to-face contact between franchisor and individual franchisees. If it is intended to result in, or does result in, a reduced level of such personal contact it is a misuse of the technique.

In considering the areas of activity for an association which follow it must be understood by franchisees (as explained in Chapter 10) that the franchisor owns the name under which the network trades and the system which it employs in doing so. The franchisor must inevitably take the final decision on all system and system management changes in the interests of all. The existence of an association is merely a method of informing and consulting with the network to ensure that the franchisor has available to him the maximum relevant information in his decision-taking process.

The areas of activity in which such a association can operate effectively are given below.

1. Communications. Practical difficulties and problems can be identified and discussed between the association and the franchisor. Style and content of communications can be discussed and improved. The

franchisor can find out at first hand, and with constructive rather than destructive criticism, why his communications fail to achieve their objective. It may be that the association feels that the franchisor could introduce (if one is not already available) or improve a regular newsletter and make suggestions for topics to be included.

2. Franchisee experience in the field can be passed on to the franchisor and methods of coping with problems discussed. There is often a wealth of experience and ability among franchisees which the franchisor would be wise to tap. A limited size of group participating can make the discussion more fruitful than if all franchisees were present. One would hope that the franchisee representatives in the association will present a filtered distillation of their fellow franchisees' ideas and suggestions.

3. New ideas can be introduced by the franchisor for the association's considered views and reactions. The franchisor can either discuss the franchisees' views before market testing in company-owned stores or operations or report the experience in practice after pilot testing has taken place. This would of course include innovations in products and services.

4. Suggestions can be made for the improvement of operational manuals if franchisees find that the explanations contained in them are not adequate or that there are areas which have been neglected. The manuals may also be expanded by the introduction of additional material to improve the range and scope of the available guidance.

5. Training or retraining procedures and facilities can be discussed by the franchisor with franchisees who are, of course, past 'pupils' of the franchisor's training facilities.

6. Discussion of detailed problems arising from the failure or inadequacy of field support staff procedures or the franchisor's other operational and support services.

7. Difficulties which may arise with regard to accounting and reporting procedures can be investigated and any remedial steps taken. Many franchisors are finding that the availability of computer systems which cope with the ever-increasing volume of accounting information with which they and their franchisees have to contend can be introduced to a network with cost-effective benefits to both franchisor and franchisees. In such cases, and often with little ongoing additional expense, a full accounting and information service can be produced and made available to franchisees. The introduction of such a service, its scope and cost, can be discussed with a franchisee advisory association and a scheme acceptable in its details can be agreed.

8. Proposals by the franchisor for the introduction of contractual changes. The reasons for such changes can be explained. The

franchisor may wish to introduce new provisions to fill gaps revealed by experience or to adjust to changes in laws which must be reflected in the system. For example, some franchisors historically either have little or no provision in the franchise agreement for realistic advertising and marketing programmes. The development and introduction of contract changes to enable a viable programme to be introduced is an ideal subject for discussion between a franchisor and a franchisee advisory association.

9. Most franchisees contribute in one way or another towards funding the cost of national advertising, local advertising, point-of-sale material, promotional activities and public relations. Invariably they are keenly interested to know how, where and when the funds will be spent and how much these activities will help each of them. Each year's proposed activities can be discussed with franchisees through the association. Frequently a franchisee will have a valid contribution to make because he will be looking at the proposals with his narrow self-interest in mind. This sort of grass-roots detail can escape the attention of the franchisor and his marketing, advertising and promotional advisers. Promotional activities, in the planning of which the franchisees have participated, will be greeted far more enthusiastically and with greater prospect of success than would be the case if they were forced upon the franchisees. It will also be possible to discuss such details as how long before the promotion starts does the franchisee receive;

(a) point-of-sale material;

(b) any special range of stock, and so on, and on what basis.

10. There should always be continuing new product or service research and development which will necessitate market research and surveys. Franchisees through the association have a contribution to make in providing information for such research and surveys. Franchisees have in many cases introduced ideas for research and development of new ideas. In the course of discussion about the introduction of the research and surveys franchisees could assist in the compilation of the terms of reference and the scope of the enquiries which may involve some of their members.

11. By liaison with a franchisee advisory association a franchisor can organize selective trials by franchisees willing to participate, of new products or services to assist in their research and development.

12. Franchisees should also be given the opportunity to raise topics of concern or interest to them. Care should be taken to ensure that the association only deals with matters of concern affecting franchisees as a whole. It should not allow itself to be used as a vehicle for the promotion of any individual dissatisfied franchisee's complaints. It cannot act as advocate judge and jury in what would inevitably be a

two-sided story. The quality of the relationship between the committee and franchisor should not be placed in jeopardy for the sake of individual problems or disputes. If the franchisee representatives in such an association try to become involved in such matters it will undoubtedly sour the atmosphere and is likely to lead to the dissolution of the association.

Concerning the organization of the association, it should be understood at the outset that while the association will be an association primarily comprising franchisees, the object will be to:

- improve communications between the franchisor and franchisee;
- provide a forum for the discussion of mutual problems;
- create a climate for improved liaison between the parties to the franchise transaction.

The franchisor must also be represented.

It is possible to establish a formally constituted association with a limited company or an unincorporated association. Whichever is required, the franchisor should incur the expense and organize the franchisee advisory association. Most of the franchisee advisory associations which exist in the UK at this time, at the very least, have an informal constitution.

The document establishing the advisory committee should deal with the following matters.

The terms of reference

The terms of reference of the association can include all or some of the points already discussed above. Consideration should be given to whether one should establish more than one association or subcommittees in the association to deal with different aspects; for example, there could be an association which focuses on marketing and advertising and another which focuses on operational issues and so on. The number of franchisees in the network will have some influence on the desirability of more than one association or the establishment of subcommittees.

Membership

Membership should be open to all current franchisees.

How it should be managed

Normally one would expect to see some sort of representative committee which is kept to a manageable size. A large and unwieldy committee would

be counter-productive. It is best to organize some form of regional representation so that each committee member can consult with the other franchisees
within his region. Assuming that there is a nationwide network, one might
contemplate the following regional representations:

- Scotland
- Wales
- Northern England
- Midlands
- South-east England
- South-west England
- Northern Ireland

There may be one representative from the smaller (in terms of numbers of
franchisees) regions and two from the larger. When the differences in
numbers are not so significant, one representative from each region would
probably be enough. Each region should select its own representative(s). A
nominee (who should be another franchisee from within the same region)
should attend if the selected representative is for some reason not able to
attend any particular meeting.

Meetings

It should be sufficient to have three meetings each year with an agenda
established by consultation with the franchisor. In that way all the subjects
with which franchisor and franchisees wish to deal, or raise, can be discussed.
One of the meetings could coincide with any national franchisee convention
which the franchisor may organize. The franchisor should be represented at
all meetings by senior staff relevant to the topics to be discussed.

Secretariat

The franchisor should provide and cover the expenses of the secretariat for
the association. The individual franchisee representatives will be responsible
for keeping in touch with the franchisees in the region which he represents so
that they are effectively informed of the association's discussions.

Finances

There should be little expense incurred in running the association. Mention
has already been made of the franchisor funding the costs of establishing the
association and of the secretariat. There will also be the cost to franchisee
representatives of travelling to and attending meetings. This cost should be

borne either by the representatives or collectively for each representative by the franchisees in his region.

It is essential to bear in mind that the objectives of any franchisee association should be to work for the mutual benefit of all who participate in the franchise network by creating a harmonious atmosphere in which problems are dealt with quickly and new ideas are encouraged.

Chapter 12

The franchise contract and legal aspects

The franchise contract is a very important document. It is the moment of truth. It is the occasion when the franchisor's promises have to be presented to the franchisee in writing and be subjected to careful scrutiny.

The contract is a legal commitment which is binding on both parties. The franchisee must therefore at this stage take competent legal advice as to the meaning and effect of the contract. In consultation with his solicitor he will check to see whether the contract confirms what he has been told. The franchisee should realize that the extent of the advice he is given is limited to the meaning and effect of the contract. It is the decision of the franchisee, and the franchisee alone, whether or not to proceed with any particular franchise opportunity. Decision making is an essential part of his role as a businessman.

In this chapter account will be taken of the European Code of Ethics ('the Code') adopted by the British Franchise Association (BFA) in 1990. The Code is set out in full in Appendix B. The BFA has also published guidelines in a booklet entitled *The Ethics of Franchising* to what it considers to be compliance or non-compliance with the ethical principles of the Code. These guidelines are also taken into account in this chapter. A franchise contract has to take into account a number of different considerations. These may be examined under a number of separate headings.

1. Although basically a contractual relationship between the franchisor and the franchisee, the franchise contract involves two other parties who are not joined as parties to the contract. The other parties are, firstly, all other franchisees within the network and, secondly,

members of the public, the consumer, and it is to both of these parties that the franchisor and the franchisee owe considerable responsibilities. It is simple to see how this arises. Each franchisee within the chain will be affected for good or bad by the actions of his fellow franchisees. If a franchisee runs his operation in a manner which is inconsistent with the standards associated with the franchisor's brand and image, it will damage the goodwill associated with them, thereby adversely affecting the business prospects of other franchisees. So each franchisee owes a heavy responsibility to the other franchisees and should therefore look on the restrictive provisions of the agreement, which are concerned with the maintenance of the standards and the correct operation of the franchised business, not merely as a tiresome chore, but as a duty and responsibility which he owes to himself and his fellow franchisees to ensure that the reputation and integrity of the franchise chain is always maintained.

The consumer features in this, of course, because the consumer is not concerned with whether or not an outlet is franchised. A consumer is merely concerned with the brand image. A consumer will frequent a business which has given satisfaction in the past and will regard franchised businesses as being branches of a larger chain. If the franchisee does not do his job properly the consumer will not accept as an explanation 'but this was operated under franchise and unfortunately we have problems with that franchisee'. All the consumer is concerned with is that when he goes into the store he receives the same standards of products and service which he has been led to believe he can expect from that particular 'branded' business. Consumers are becoming increasingly aware of franchising and its place in the business community because of the publicity which franchise systems are receiving. This, coupled with the increasing tendency for legal reasons to identify franchised outlets as being operated under franchise, results in the consumer knowing the identity of the trader with whom he is dealing. Franchisees therefore owe a great responsibility in the maintenance of these standards to ensure that the consumer is not misled and that, whichever outlet within the franchise chain the consumer patronizes, he is provided with the quality product and service he had reason to expect he would receive.

2. It has already been explained that the franchisor in a business format franchise will be contributing his 'blueprint' which embraces a package comprising trade secrets, methods of operation, use of trademarks, trade names, and many of the other features previously mentioned. The franchisor will be concerned in his agreement to ensure that provision is made for the franchisee (a) to use the

'blueprint', methods of operation, trademarks, trade names, etc., and (b) to preserve the element of trade secrecy which is associated with the franchisor's particular methods and 'blueprint'. The agreement, in essence, is a licence permitting the franchisee to run the business *only* according to the blueprint. If the franchisee wants the freedom to do only as he pleases then franchising is not for him.

3. It is inherent in discharging the four-way obligations outlined in item 1 above that consideration is given to the establishment of standards, the manner in which those standards are imposed upon the franchisee, and what provision should be made to enforce them.

4. The term of the agreement has to be considered. As a basic principle one should expect the franchise relationship to be capable of subsisting in the long term. The Code provides that the 'duration of the agreement . . . should be long enough to allow the individual franchisee to amortise his initial franchise investment'. This ethical principle, which is vague and anomalous in many respects, is thankfully expanded upon by the BFA in an 'Extension and Interpretation' attached to and incorporated in the Code which states: 'it is recognized

    (a) that franchise contracts are ordinarily offered for a uniform term within a network;

    (b) that for a minority of the largest franchise opportunities amortising the initial investment may not be a primary objective for the franchisee. In such cases the objective should be to adopt a contract period which reasonably balances the interests of the parties to the contract;

    (c) that this section could be subject to national laws concerning the restraint of trade and may need to be met through renewal clauses.'

    There may be legal reasons in some cases in the UK why the initial term should not exceed 5 years. In these cases the franchisee should ideally be given an option to renew the agreement. It is a requirement of the Code that the agreement should contain 'the basis for any renewal of the agreement'.

    Some franchisors do not like to grant too long a term on the belief that there may be developments in the law to which they would like to have the opportunity to respond sooner rather than later. In any event it is the invariable practice to grant franchisees an option to renew provided the franchisee has performed his obligations under the agreement, updates, refurbishes and requips the franchised unit, and enters into a new agreement in the form of the franchisor's then current agreement.

    However, there is a detectable trend for some franchisors to use renewal to impose wider conditions.

(a) A 'revamp' clause, which could involve the franchisee in going back to the shell of his shop and completely refitting it out to accommodate a new presentation with costs perhaps equal to or greater than those incurred when he originally set up; the franchisee can of course decide that he will not renew on those terms, maybe because the franchisor cannot demonstrate that the required capital investment is cost-effective for the franchisee; the franchisee may not be able to raise the money from the banks, who are equally uncertain about financial viability; the franchisor, who will benefit from the possibly increased turnover in the form of product mark-up or franchise fees based upon gross sales regardless of the effect on the franchisee's net return, has a conflicting interest at this point in time. Such a revamp clause may be necessary in order for a franchisor to keep his business competitive and up to date.

The presence of such a clause in itself is not unfair but the way in which it is enforced can be. A franchisor who has such a provision should observe the following requirements. These requirements bear in mind the BFA membership criterion that pilot testing must be carried out. A revamp is analogous to opening a new operation in many significant respects.

    (i)   The 'revamp' should be previously tested by the franchisor in practice, who should be able to demonstrate the effect which it has on the financial performance of the units where it has been tested.

    (ii)   The testing should be in a sufficient number of representative operational units to ensure that there are sufficient comparables to enable an informed decision to be made by franchisees. The franchisor should make the decision as to the sufficiency of the number of units at which testing should take place.

    (iii)   The franchisor should be prepared to assist his franchisees in making arrangements with their banks for the financing or refinancing which they require for the purpose of revamping.

    (iv)   Revamps should not be required so often that a franchisee cannot reap the financial rewards for the expenditure he has made both in terms of recovery of investment but also increased profitability over a reasonable period.

(b) A 'relocation' clause, where the franchisor will make it a condition of renewal that a franchisee should close down at his present premises and move to fresh premises which the franchisor may decide offer a better trading opportunity or larger accommodation into which to fit the franchisor's new ideas. This is in essence requiring the franchisee to set up an entirely new business with all the inherent risks and considerable expenses plus the cost of the existing premises until they can be disposed of and the cost, which may be at a loss, of disposal.

This highlights a problem which can arise where a franchisor decides that a completely fresh approach is necessary. The franchisor may well be completely right and the changes essential but there are ways in which such issues can be handled properly. The following considerations should be applied in the circumstances.

(i) Is it really necessary for the franchisee to be required to move? Is it possible for the 'old' and the 'new' to live alongside each other? A franchisee required to relocate may not be able to afford to do so and the franchisor does have a responsibility to him. The franchisee may well have a successful operation earning good profits for him and a good flow of franchise fees for the franchisor. A franchisor must in these circumstances exercise the utmost good faith consistent with his responsibilities, and should be prepared to demonstrate that the need exists in terms of future competitiveness and updating of the system.

(ii) The franchisor must be able to demonstrate that the relocation is likely to be cost-effective for the franchisee from previous and adequate pilot testing by the franchisor.

(iii) The franchisor should be prepared to assist the franchisee in making his financing arrangements with his bankers.

(iv) In no circumstances should a franchisor use revamping or relocation as an excuse for unfairly ridding himself of any franchisee. His motive should be to enhance and promote the franchise system and its profitability equitably for both franchisor and franchisee.

5. Quite apart from the position on renewal of the agreement it will also be advisable that over the passage of years the freshness of the image appeal to the consumer and comprehensiveness in the market place are maintained. It will be necessary to ensure that provision is made in the contract to require the franchisee to make provision, by setting amounts aside periodically, for investment in the modernization and the upgrading of the premises and equipment employed therein so that with the passage of time the appeal of the business and its attractiveness to the consumer does not fade.

6. In these days of rapid technological progress many franchisors have to consider the possibility that some new technology will have to be introduced in the future. The most common area in which this is likely to arise is where it is desired to introduce computerized tills

which fulfil many functions, such as stock control, recording of gross income and categories of income. There is often a link with the Head Office computer, which can then provide franchisees with monthly P&L and stock order lists. These are undoubtedly the sorts of service a franchisor should provide and they are welcomed by franchisees if part of the original package. However, if a franchisor wishes to have the right subsequently to introduce such a system he will also need to reserve the right to require the franchisee to spend whatever is necessary to install and run the system regardless of the benefits. This clearly is untenable since the franchisee would be exposed to an obligation, unilaterally imposed, to spend without limit. This means that the franchisor will have to be precise in his plan and proposals. One method of overcoming the problem is for the franchisor to delineate the scope of the planned requirements and to indicate limits of capital and running costs so that the franchisee can make an informed decision before undertaking a commitment.

7. The method by which the franchisor obtains his income and secures payment with the minimum opportunity for avoidance of the true extent of the franchisee's liability. Since the franchisor's gross revenue will largely, and in some cases wholly, be dependent upon the payment of franchise fees and/or management services fees by the franchisees, franchisors will be concerned to protect themselves against the franchisee not making full disclosure of all his income against which the management service fees are calculated. Obviously, there will always be those franchisees who see the payment of fees calculated by reference to gross income as a challenge but in franchising there is an overall structure which puts the cheat at a disadvantage.

The structure contains a number of features which will inevitably be reflected in the contract and the system which has been developed by the franchisor and is operated by the franchisees.

(a) The franchisor, in establishing the system by his experience in the market-place, will have laid down the guidelines for financial achievement. He will be illustrating to franchisees, when training them and in setting them up in business, what their gross and net margins should be at given levels of turnover and the percentage which each group of expense items should bear to turnover. A concealment of gross income would inevitably distort those margins. The margins could, of course, also be distorted by incompetence or by leakage attributable to staff or customer theft but, if that is the case, the franchisor should quickly be able to assist the franchisee in identifying the cause and advise or initiate appropriate remedial action.

(b) The franchisor will establish standard form accounting systems and reporting procedures in order that he can be informed about the performance of each franchisee's business.

(c) The franchisor will require the right to do spot audits of the franchisee's financial record without prior warning being given.

(d) The accounting system and reporting procedures will enable the franchisor to monitor the franchisee's performance and to detect warning signs if all is not well.

(e) The franchisor's field support staff, who provide back-up to franchisees by regular visits, will have the opportunity of discussing performance with franchisees and making spot checks on stocks, books and other records to verify the accuracy of the information which the franchisee is reporting to the franchisor. These checks are part of the support which a franchisor provides since inaccurate information, whether intentionally or unintentionally provided, hampers the franchisor's ability to provide assistance and guidance.

(f) The franchisor in collecting and collating the information from each franchisee is building up a record of each franchisee's performance and is able to establish an average for the whole network's results. Any franchisee whose achievements are markedly below average will be a candidate for special attention so that the cause may be identified and remedial action taken.

(g) The franchisee will be required to make a return of gross revenue to the Customs and Excise authorities for Value Added Tax purposes. Copies of these returns and any assessments to VAT made by Customs and Excise should be obtained by the franchisor and compared with the figures submitted to him.

(h) The franchisor will have access to the franchisee's supply sources. If he knows what the franchisee is buying he will have a very good idea of what his gross sales figures should be if the business is operated properly. The field support staff visits should reveal if the franchisee is purchasing products from non-approved sources which if not put through the system could provide the opportunity to falsify figures as well as distort the performance of the outlet.

(i) In some cases the franchisor may be able to obtain information from large customers of the network with whom arrangements have been made for the supply of goods and/or services by the network.

8. Consideration will have to be given to the question of the circumstances in which the franchise agreement can be terminated. In doing so, the position of the franchisee must be considered responsibly so that the franchise cannot be terminated capriciously. The Code requires franchisors to give written notice to franchisees of

breaches and to allow a reasonable time for the breach to be remedied. Consequences of termination also have to be clearly thought out in order that the franchisor's property rights are properly protected.

9. Of prime concern to franchisees will be the way in which a sale of the franchisee's business might be achieved. Obviously in a franchise which requires the franchisee to be trained, as most do, or which may require a specialized area of knowledge or the application of particular processes, a franchisee can never be permitted freely to assign his franchise agreement when disposing of his business. Safeguards have to be built in to ensure that the new franchisee will accept the responsibilities, will undergo any necessary training, and provide the same standards of service and product as if, in fact, there had been no change of franchisee. Indeed, the new franchisee has to be as acceptable to the franchisor as if he had applied direct to the franchisor. The identification by a franchisee of a prospective purchaser of his business is the only occasion when a franchisee is recruited by someone other than the franchisor. It is usual therefore to demand the same qualifications and standards for acceptance of a purchaser of the franchisee's business as are being applied to direct applicants to the franchisor for a franchise.

10. Thought has to be given as to what will happen if the franchisee, being an individual, or if the principal shareholder and director of the franchisee, if it is a limited company, dies? Most franchise agreements make provision to deal with these circumstances although not all are satisfactory. There are some which make no provision at all. Clearly, it is an area of serious concern for both franchisor and franchisee that the right balance is struck so that the dependants of the franchisee are permitted (if they can satisfy the franchisor's criteria and pass any training course satisfactorily) either to continue the business formerly carried on by the deceased or, alternatively, are able to turn the business to account by selling and receiving the capital value of the business.

11. The franchisee's expectations cannot be ignored. Quite apart from the consideration which is given to the franchisee's point of view in the aspects already dealt with, the franchisee must be satisfied that the contract offers him exactly what he has been led to believe he would receive. He should not leave anything to trust; he should ask the franchisor to write into the agreement, or perhaps as an amendment to the agreement, confirmation of all the obligations undertaken. Nothing should be left to implication. Most franchisors will not normally (and quite properly) accept amendments to their standard form so they will only have their own lack of foresight to blame if they encounter difficulties where their promises are not reflected in

their contract. Furthermore, although the tendency exists for a successful franchisee to forget what he owes to the franchisor for his success, the franchisor will invariably always know just that little bit more about the business than any one individual franchisee. In such a case the franchisor must be able to contain the franchisee within the scope of the franchise scheme by appropriate contractual provisions.

12. There is an increasing tendency for franchisors to become involved in the property aspects of the transaction. This arises for a number of reasons.

    (a) The franchisor may already be a multiple outlet operator who is converting some of an existing chain to franchising. He is involved as a freeholder or lessee of the premises which are occupied for the purpose of his business. In granting the franchise he will grant a lease or sublease to the franchisee. He may, of course, decide to assign the lease to the franchisee.

    (b) The franchisor may decide, as a matter of policy, that in securing sites for outlets for the network he wishes to buy the freehold or become the leaseholder and grant a lease or sublease to the franchisee.

    (c) The franchisor may be more selective and only become involved in a property if it comes into the 'flagship' or 'irreplaceable' category. Into this heading would come scarce sites, such as existing light industrial uses close to residential areas, where, if the franchisee leaves the network, the franchisor may find it difficult (if at all possible) to obtain any suitable alternative from which to trade or in which to establish an attractive franchise.

    (d) The franchisor may decide that he will use the value of his covenant to obtain sites for the network which franchisees may not otherwise be able to secure at all.

    (e) The franchisor may find that he is forced into giving his covenant in order to secure a site since the landlord or his agent realizes that the franchisor's covenant may be worth having while that of the franchisee is not.

Each franchisor will formulate his own policy regarding involvement with property; but if he does get involved, the lease and franchise agreement will have to be linked with each other so that termination and/or renewal of one will result in the same treatment of the other. The rights given to tenants of business premises under the Landlord and Tenant Act 1954 (as subsequently amended) have to be considered in the formulation of a property policy. If the franchisor does become involved in property, the franchisee should be no worse off upon termination of the agreement than he would be if the franchisor were not his landlord.

13. On 30 November 1988 the European Commission adopted a block

exemption regulation for categories of franchise agreements which, subject to compliance with its terms, exempts franchise agreements from the competition laws of the European Community which are contained in Article 85 of the EC Treaty. The UK has its own competition laws which can apply to franchise agreements particularly where exclusive territorial rights are given to franchisees. The UK government has published a White Paper indicating an intention to change the UK competition laws to a system similar to that which is imposed by the EC Treaty. If these laws are introduced, then according to the White Paper, compliance with the EC Regulation will give exemption from the new UK laws. In addition to this the existing UK system which, if the law applies, requires the furnishing of particulars of the agreement to the Director General of Fair Trading is unlikely to give rise to any difficulties if the EC Regulation is complied with. Before considering the structure of the franchise contractual arrangements it is necessary to understand the requirements of the Regulation since its provisions will clearly have a wide impact on franchise agreements. Although the basic definitions of 'franchise' and 'franchise agreement' are set out in Chapter 1, it is considered appropriate to repeat them here for ease of reference. The Regulation contains the following definitions:

(a) 'franchise' means a package of industrial or intellectual property rights relating to trademarks, trade names, shop signs, utility models, designs, copyrights, know-how or patents, to be exploited for the resale of goods or the provision of services to end users;

(b) 'franchise agreement' means an agreement whereby one undertaking, the franchisor, grants the other, the franchisee, in exchange for direct or indirect financial consideration, the right to exploit a franchise for the purposes of marketing specified types of goods and/or services; it includes at least obligations relating to:

- the use of a common name or shop sign and a uniform presentation of contract premises and/or means of transport;
- the communication by the franchisor to the franchisee of know-how;
- the continuing provision by the franchisor to the franchisee of commercial or technical assistance during the life of the agreement;

(c) 'master franchise agreement' means an agreement whereby one party, the franchisor, grants the other, the master franchisee, in exchange for direct or indirect financial consideration, the right to exploit a franchise for the purposes of concluding franchising agreements with third parties, the franchisees;

(d) 'franchisor's goods' means goods produced by the franchisor or according to its instructions, and/or bearing the franchisor's name or trademark;

(e) 'contract premises' means the premises used for the exploitation of the franchise or, when the franchise is exploited outside those premises, the base from which the franchisee operates the means of transport used for the exploitation of the franchise ('contract means of transport');

(f) 'know-how' means a package of non-patented practical information, resulting from experience and testing by the franchisor, which is secret, substantial and identified;

(g) 'secret' means that the know-how, as a body or in the precise configuration and assembly of its components, is not generally known or easily accessible; it is not limited in the narrow sense that each individual component of the know-how should be totally unknown or unobtainable outside the franchisor's business;

(h) 'substantial' means that the know-how includes information which is of importance for the sale of goods or the provision of services to end users, and in particular for the presentation of goods for sale, the processing of goods in connection with the provision of services, methods of dealing with customers, and administration and financial management; the know-how must be useful for the franchisee by being capable, at the date of conclusion of the agreement, of improving the competitive position of the franchisee, in particular by improving the franchisee's performance or helping him to enter a new market;

(i) 'identified' means the know-how must be described in a sufficiently comprehensive manner so as to make it possible to verify that it fulfils the criteria of secrecy and substantiality; the description of the know-how can either be set out in the franchise agreement or in a separate document or recorded in any other appropriate form.

The Commission has identified in the Regulation those provisions regarded as restrictive of competition under Article 85(1) of the EC Treaty. Exemption is granted pursuant to Article 1.1 of the Regulation to franchise agreements entered into between two undertakings which include one or more of the following restrictions:

(i) The grant of exclusive territorial rights, which can include the franchisor agreeing not to supply its goods to third parties in the territory.

(ii) The imposition of a location clause restricting the franchisee to operating from premises specified in the contract.

(iii) A prohibition against a master franchisee concluding agreements with third parties outside the contact territory.

(iv) A prohibition against the franchisee seeking customers outside the contract territory. This prohibition is likely to affect mobile franchises more than those which are tied to premises.

(v) An obligation on the franchisee not to manufacture, sell or use in the course of the provision of services, goods competing with the franchise; where the subject of the franchise is to sell or use in the course of the provision of services both certain types of goods and spare parts or accessories thereof, this obligation may not be imposed in respect of these spare parts or accessories.

This list includes the provisions most frequently seen in franchise agreements which can be regarded as restrictive of competition.

Having identified the problem provisions the Regulation exempts them subject to compliance with the Regulation. There are a number of issues and these are considered by category.

TERRITORIAL RESTRICTIONS

1. The grant by the franchisor of exclusive territorial rights, coupled with undertakings by the franchisor not to appoint another franchisee or itself to carry on business within the territory, is permitted.

2. The franchisor may also undertake not to supply goods manufactured by him, to its specification or bearing its trademark to third parties within the territory allocated to the franchisee.

3. The franchisee may be restricted to trading only from the premises identified in the contract (i.e. a location clause).

4. The franchisee should also be permitted to move to alternative premises with the franchisor's consent. The franchisor cannot withhold its consent to such a move if the alternative premises match the franchisor's normal criteria for trading premises.

5. The franchisee can be prohibited from soliciting or touting for custom from those whose residence is or business premises are outside any allocated territory but the franchisee cannot be required to refuse to do business with a non-solicited customer from outside the territory.

6. A master franchisee can be prohibited from selling franchises outside his territory.

While the issue of exclusivity so far as Article 85(1) is concerned has been dealt with in the Regulation the commercial considerations, which have given rise to many difficulties in practice, remain.

The commercial considerations revolve round the difficulties, particularly in the early stages of the development of a franchise business, of fairly defining a territory. The tendency is to allocate an area which is too large. Many franchisors who have tried to establish exclusive territories have created problems for themselves by having unexploited areas and an inability to force the franchisee to expand his business to fill the demand which has been created for the goods or services offered by the franchised network. The impact of such a situation affects franchisees as well as franchisors since there is an open invitation to others to provide the facilities which the network is not supplying. The obvious solution of establishing performance targets, allowing for the effect of inflation on true growth, is also not so easy to achieve. It is not a separate issue since the performance capability of any territory which is allocated must be related to the correct assessment of its potential, giving the franchisee the necessary scope for establishing and developing his business without inhibiting the growth of the franchised network. If the franchisor cannot fairly define the territory he is unlikely to be able to establish fair and realistic performance criteria to apply throughout the term of the contract. The ability to grant exclusive territorial rights without adverse competition law consequences will not affect the commercial considerations and while location clauses will continue to be used widely there may not be an increase in the grant of exclusive territorial rights.

GOODS THE SUBJECT OF THE FRANCHISE

1. The franchisee can be prohibited from manufacturing, selling or using in the course of the provision of services, goods competing with the franchisor's goods (i.e. goods produced by the franchisor or according to his instructions and/or bearing the franchisor's name or trademark). The obvious course for franchisors to adopt would be to ensure that all goods involved in the franchised business should be manufactured by the franchisor or to his instructions or bearing the franchisor's branding. In some cases this is done but in many cases it will not be possible. A strongly branded product may just not be available for 'own brand' labelling or the range and volume of products involved may make it impracticable to arrange.
2. Without prejudice to the above the franchisor must not refuse, for reasons other than protecting the franchisor's industrial or intellectual property rights, or maintaining the common identity and reputation of the franchised network, to designate as authorized manufacturers third parties proposed by the franchisee.
3. The franchisee can be required so far as is necessary to protect the

franchisor's industrial or intellectual property rights or to maintain the common identity and reputation of the franchise network:

(a) to sell, or use in the course of the provision of services, exclusively goods which match minimum objective quality specifications laid down by the franchisor;

(b) to sell, or use in the course of the provision of services, goods manufactured only by the franchisor;

(c) to sell, or use in the course of the provision of services, goods manufactured by nominated third parties where it is impracticable owing to the nature of the goods which are the subject matter of the franchise to apply objective quality specifications;

(d) to sell the goods only to end users, other franchisees and others within the manufacturer's distribution network;

(e) to use his best endeavours to sell the goods;

(f) to offer for sale a minimum range of goods;

(g) to achieve minimum sales targets and plan orders in advance;

(h) to keep minimum stocks;

(i) to provide customer and warranty services;

(j) to honour guarantees whether the goods have been obtained from the franchisor, nominated suppliers, other franchisees or other distributors of the goods which carry similar guarantees in the common market.

4. The franchisee cannot be prevented from:

(a) buying goods from other franchisees or other distributors thereof;

(b) fixing his own prices, although the franchisor may recommend prices. It should be noted that the Commission can withdraw the benefit of the exemption given by the Regulation if 'franchisees engage in concerted practices relating to sale prices of the goods or services which are the subject matter of the franchise'. In view of this provision franchisors should prohibit such concerted practices in the franchise agreement so that action may be taken to require the practice to be discontinued or enable the agreement to be terminated;

(c) obtaining spare parts or accessories for the franchisor's goods other than from the franchisor;

(d) supplying goods or services to non-solicited end users because of their place of residence.

The provisions relating to products taken as a whole indicate that the position on tied supplies of goods may be summarized as follows:

1. The franchisee can be required to sell or use in the provision of services only franchisor's goods (as defined) and no others. This requirement cannot be imposed in respect of accessories or spare parts for these goods.

2. The franchisee must be permitted to obtain franchisor's goods from other franchisees or other distributors of such goods.
3. Insofar as it is necessary to protect the franchisor's industrial or intellectual property rights or to maintain the common identity and reputation of the franchised network the franchisor can require the franchisee only (a) to sell goods obtained from nominated suppliers where it is impracticable owing to the nature of the goods to formulate objective quality specifications; (b) to sell exclusively goods which match minimum objective quality specifications laid down by the franchisor.
4. The franchisee cannot be prevented from obtaining supplies of goods of a quality equivalent to those offered by the franchisor without prejudice to 1 and 3(a) above.

The combined effect of 3 and 4 is that the franchisee may be obliged to deal in goods supplied by a nominated supplier where it is impracticable to formulate objective quality criteria. In the Pronuptia case (2) the Court gave two examples to illustrate what this means. The first was the nature of the products, such as fashion goods (not a surprise since the case involved a fashion goods franchise), and the second was where the cost of monitoring compliance with the specification would be too expensive as could be the case if there were a large number of franchisees.

If one wished to take advantage of either or both examples it is probably sensible to use the opposition procedure under the Regulation given that the agreement otherwise complies with its requirements. To resolve these issues (apart from any others which may be relevant) the following questions will have to be addressed.

(a) Is what is proposed necessary to protect the franchisor's industrial or intellectual property rights or to maintain the common identity and reputation of the franchised network?
(b) Is it impracticable to formulate objective quality criteria by reason of:
— the nature of the goods; or
— the cost of monitoring compliance in the light of the numbers of suppliers involved?

There has been much commentary over the 'nature of the goods' provision which it is said *inter alia* prevents a fast food operation from nominating which particular brand of beverage should be served by franchisees. A case can be made that a franchisor should be able to nominate brands of product as it is necessary to maintain the common identity of the network. It is also suggested that a case can be made, as it was for fashion goods, that it can be impracticable to formulate objective quality criteria where subtle variations of flavour and consumer taste are involved.

COMPETITION

The franchisor can require the franchisee to comply with the following.

1. Not to manufacture, sell or use in the course of the provision of services goods which compete with the franchisor's goods. This requirement cannot be extended to spare parts and accessories for such goods.
2. Insofar as it is necessary to protect the franchisor's industrial or intellectual property rights or to maintain the common identity and reputation of the franchised network not to engage directly or indirectly in any similar business in a territory where the franchisee would compete with:
   — a member of the franchised network; or
   — the franchisor
   at all during the agreement and for a reasonable period not exceeding one year after the agreement ends in the territory where the franchisee has exploited the franchise. This prohibition can extend to non-solicited customers who reside or have their place of business outside the franchisee's allocated territory.
3. Insofar as it is necessary to protect the franchisor's industrial or intellectual property rights or to maintain the common identity and reputation of the franchised network not to acquire financial interests in the capital of competitors which would give the franchisee power to influence the economic conduct of the competitor.

It is understood that the Commission takes the view that 'power to influence' means power to compel by agreement or weight of voting. There is unlikely to be a problem in practice if the business in which the investment is made is a listed company. However, if it is a small proprietorial company there is great temptation for the investing franchisee to influence the economic conduct of the business by the power of his knowledge derived from the franchisor's know-how, if the business encounters difficulties. The franchisee may be prohibited from being personally involved in the conduct of a competing business in which he has invested.

KNOW-HOW

The franchisor is entitled to protect his know-how and can impose an obligation on franchisees:

1. not to use the know-how other than for the purpose of exploiting the franchise, during or after the end of the agreement but only until the

know-how becomes generally known or easily accessible other than by breach of an obligation by the franchisee;

2. not to disclose the know-how to third parties during or after the termination of the agreement; and

3. to require staff of the franchisee to keep confidential the know-how imparted to them to enable them to discharge their duties as employees of the franchisee.

GENERAL ASPECTS

1. The franchisor must oblige the franchisee to indicate his status as an independent undertaking. This is, in any event, quite a frequent requirement in franchise agreements. It will be appreciated that the Business Names Act 1985 contains provisions which are supportive of this approach.

2. Insofar as is necessary to protect the franchisor's industrial or intellectual property rights or to maintain the common identity and reputation of the franchised network the franchisee can be required to make advertising contributions and not to advertise unless the nature of such advertising shall have been approved by the franchisor.

3. The franchisor must not prohibit the franchisee from challenging the validity of the industrial or intellectual property rights which form part of the franchise. However, if a franchisee does mount such a challenge the franchisor can provide for the termination of the agreement.

4. The Regulation contains a list, which is not intended to be exhaustive, of typical franchise contract clauses which are not considered to be restrictive of competition and are thus permissible without any qualifications. They do not call for any special comment.

It should be understood that as EC competition law stands the conduct of the parties can be investigated to see whether, in practice, they are behaving in a manner which contravenes the requirements of the Regulation. This is recognized in the Regulation, which provides that the franchisor must not use his right:

- to inspect the location (or vehicle);
- to veto a move to new premises; or
- to withhold consent to an assignment of the franchisee's rights and obligations under the franchise agreement (i.e. sell the business)

for reasons other than:
- protecting the franchisor's industrial or intellectual property rights;

- maintaining the common identity and reputation of the franchise network; or
- verifying that the franchisee is performing his obligations under the agreement.

5. The franchisor can require franchisees to introduce modifications of the franchisor's commercial methods.

STRUCTURE OF FRANCHISE AGREEMENTS

It will be appreciated that not all the provisions referred to in this chapter will apply in every case, but some, indeed most, will feature in all franchise transactions.

The legal topics which have to be addressed in a franchise arrangement often involve a number of areas of law which are not usually dealt with by one practitioner. Indeed, some of the topics are quite specialized. Although in business terms the contractual obligations can be split into two stages, which are dealt with below, in framing advice to the franchisor or, even where the franchisor considers his own position, the transaction should be broken down into six phases:

1. The preparation of the franchise scheme for marketing. The development of the concept through the pilot operation during which are developed the industrial and intellectual property rights—the trademark, the service mark, the trade name, goodwill, trade secrets and know-how. This is the stage at which advice about how properly to protect these rights must be taken. The development of the system, apart from solving business problems, must not create legal difficulties which may later cause the system to be changed. This is also the time to consider the structure of the transaction: Will one be involved in property? What will be the policy in relation to territories or catchment areas? What will be the range of services to be provided to the franchisee and so on?

2. The marketing of the scheme. The promotion of the scheme; the preparation of the sales literature followed by the actual negotiations and discussions with prospective franchisees. When one considers the wide range of services to be provided by the franchisor, and the need to demonstrate to a franchisee the capacity of the business for success, the scope for the franchisor to make representations is very wide indeed. The larger the franchisor's organization, the more people there are involved in the selling effort, the greater the scope and the greater the risk of mistakes being made in the making of such representations.

The next four phases:

3. the period from the recruitment of a franchisee to the opening of the franchisee's business;
4. the continuing relationship;
5. termination; and
6. consequences of termination,

are now dealt with in detail.

Stages (3) and (4) have to be dealt with within the contractual framework and can be accommodated within one agreement although some franchise companies have two contracts, one for each stage. In such cases the first-stage contract is frequently called a purchase agreement and the second-stage contract the franchise or licence agreement. Although the invariable practice is to use one contract it is convenient to consider each of the two stages separately as they are dealing with different issues.

The first stage will deal with three aspects basic to taking the franchisee from the period of signing the agreement to the opening launch of his business.

1. The franchise package.
2. The price.
3. The initial services to be provided.

Before examining each of these aspects it should be noted that it is not essential that the premises from which the franchisee is to trade should be finally agreed upon before the contracts are signed. As long as it is possible to pinpoint an area within which the premises are to be located, the agreements may be entered into conditionally upon a mutually acceptable site being found. This may appear at first sight to be potentially dangerous, but a successful franchise will usually attract more prospective franchisees than can be placed at any given time. A waiting list will develop. In such a case a prospective franchisee will wish to join the queue and reserve an area; indeed it is possible in some cases to obtain an option from a franchisor for an area.

If a site is being sought the agreement will specify the area within which the premises are to be located and provide for the approval of the premises by the franchisor. If a decision has been made by the franchisor that he wishes to be involved in the ownership of the property the effect of that decision will need to be reflected in the contractual arrangements. The franchisor will usually provide assistance with the obtaining of any required planning permissions.

The franchise package

The extent and subject matter of the franchise package which is being sold will be listed. The list is sometimes called an inventory of equipment or perhaps just an equipment list. It must contain all items which are included; all items which the franchisee has been told to expect. Some franchise companies regard this list as being confidential and stipulate in the contract that it must be so treated by the franchisee. In such a case there will also be a provision requiring the return of the list if the transaction does not proceed.

The franchise package may involve a number of options about how the premises will be dealt with or if there is a mobile franchise how the vehicle will be provided and equipped. The options in relation to the premises include the following.

1. The provision by the franchisor of standard plans and specifications for the franchised outlets which will be adapted either by the franchisor or the franchisee's own surveyor or architect and subject to approval by the franchisor.
2. The provision by the franchisor of a manual, with property specifications from which the franchisee's surveyor, architect or shopfitter will prepare detailed plans and specifications for the franchised outlet.
3. The complete service by the franchisor of the preparation of plans and specifications followed by the necessary works to convert the premises into the franchised outlet (a turnkey operation).
4. The hiring by the franchisee of a shopfitter, either from a list approved by the franchisor or freely chosen by the franchisee, who will be employed to convert the premises into the franchised outlet in accordance with the franchisor's plans and specifications.

In cases where the franchisor is not actually doing the work the quality and standards will be monitored by the franchisor for compliance with his standards while the franchisee will have the responsibility for ensuring the correct quality of day-to-day supervision.

Where there is a vehicle to be acquired as part of the package the manner of fitting out and equipping the vehicle will have to be detailed with the franchisor either arranging for the works to be carried out or providing sufficiently detailed plans and specifications to enable the franchisee to organize it for himself. The specifications will include the colour scheme and a suitable livery for the vehicle.

The price

The price will be specified, as will the manner of payment. This may be cash in full on signature, although this is rare. More often a deposit is required on signature with payment of the balance to follow on delivery of the equipment or at other identified stages, e.g. commencement of training.

There may be allowance for the fact that finance has to be arranged. In this case the contract may be conditional upon satisfactory finance being obtained. What is to be regarded as 'satisfactory finance' should be defined carefully. If hire purchase finance is to be obtained for vehicles, fixtures, fittings, etc., the contract must accommodate the necessary arrangements for the finance house to acquire title.

The price may not include delivery charges, installation charges, shopfitting works and VAT. If this is the case it should be made clear, particularly in respect of the shopfitting work, as the equipment list will often include equipment and fittings which will be incorporated in the shopfitting.

If a deposit is paid at this stage, or indeed at any other, it should be made clear whether and in what circumstances it, or a part of it, is returnable to the franchisee. The franchisor will wish at this stage to retain the right to withdraw from the transaction. It may be that training will show the franchisee to be unsuitable for the particular type of franchise. In a case where the franchisor withdraws from the transaction the deposit should be returnable to the franchisee in full unless the reason is that the franchisee fails the training course when the franchisor should be entitled to recover his costs to date.

However, a different situation obtains if the franchisee wishes to withdraw. The franchisor may be prepared to take a risk on his own withdrawal, but if the franchisee can withdraw without cost after having caused the franchisor a lot of trouble and expense, then the payment of the deposit will not amount to much evidence of good faith. Provision is therefore usually made for the franchisor to be able to retain the whole or part of the deposit to reimburse him for the expenses in which he has been involved. The Code permits this practice. The franchisee should insist, if a deposit is to be paid, that the circumstances in which he gets it back or in which the franchisor may keep some of it, are very clearly and unambiguously set out in writing. Some franchisees have lost money by failing to read or understand what they were given or told. It is essential to take proper professional advice before parting with any money.

The initial services to be provided

The services which are to be provided to the franchisee are discussed in some detail in Chapter 8. The franchise agreement should reflect the obligation to provide these services and the franchisor should be prepared to undertake the commitment to provide what he has promised.

If there are two agreements the first agreement will contain the provisions relating to the initial training of the franchisee. This will mean that the franchisor will impose upon the franchisee a requirement to keep the franchisor's know-how, trade secrets and system private and confidential to ensure that if the transaction does not proceed the trained prospective franchisee cannot make use of, or disclose, the know-how acquired in training. These are the main features to be expected in an agreement dealing with stage one of the transaction whether or not there is a separate contract.

The stage two provisions can conveniently be divided into eight sections.

Section 1.   The rights granted to the franchisee.
Section 2.   The obligations undertaken by the franchisor.
Section 3.   The obligations imposed upon the franchisee.
Section 4.   The trading restrictions and requirements imposed upon the franchisee.
Section 5.   Sale of business/death of franchisee.
Section 6.   Dispute resolution.
Section 7.   The termination provisions.
Section 8.   The consequences of termination.

SECTION 1

The franchisee will be given the following rights so far as may be relevant in the particular circumstances.

(a) To use the trademarks, service marks and trade names of the franchisor and to benefit from the goodwill associated with them.
(b) To use the brand image and the design and decor of the premises (including layouts, fixtures, fittings and equipment) developed by the franchisor in projecting that image.
(c) To use the franchisor's trade secrets, know-how, system and methods.
(d) To use the franchisor's copyright material.
(e) In appropriate cases to use the recipes, formulae, specifications, processes and methods of manufacture developed by the franchisor.
(f) To conduct the franchised business upon or from premises approved by the franchisor (usually premises are specified in the agreement) identified under the franchisor's name, branding, etc. and in accordance with the franchisor's system and methods.

Many franchise schemes carry with them the promise of exclusive rights. These exclusive rights will vary according to whether the franchised business is physically immobile (e.g. a retail shop) or physically mobile (e.g. a Service-Master or Hometune franchisee). In the case of a retail shop the exclusivity would be based upon a radius within which the franchisor will not franchise another similar unit. In the case of a mobile franchise an area within which the franchisee may carry on his business may be exclusive or non-exclusive and the franchisee will be forbidden to solicit or tout for business outside such area. The grant of exclusive rights involves issues of competition law which are dealt with above. It is difficult to lay down any set radius, for what is reasonable will vary considerably from case to case. It is important to realize that the franchisor cannot hope for successful growth in his own business if his units are placed so close together that none can effectively operate on a profitable basis.

    (g) The right (as well as the obligation) to obtain supplies of products from the franchisor and/or nominated suppliers at special prices. The franchisor can often obtain quite good reductions for franchisees using the weight of the bulk-purchasing power of the whole of the franchised chain. The issue of product supply has been dealt with in detail above in the discussion on competition law.

SECTION 2
The obligations of the franchisor in the continuing relationship which exists after the business has opened are dealt with in Chapter 8. As is the case with the initial obligations, the franchisor's ongoing commitments to the franchisee should be detailed and the franchisor should be prepared to accept a legal obligation to provide them.

SECTION 3
The franchisee may have the following obligations imposed upon him:

    (a) To carry on the business franchised and no other upon approved premises and strictly in accordance with the franchisor's methods and standards. This provision may detail the range of products, their sources and/or services which the franchisee is permitted to sell or provide.

    (b) To observe certain minimum opening hours. These will usually be the hours which enable the business to be operated most profitably within the scope of the 'blueprint' and without incurring disproportionate overheads. For example, the franchisor may well through practical experience be able to demonstrate to the franchisee that the cost of staff and other overheads in remaining open for, say, a further two hours a day may not be covered by the additional trading which is likely to be done.

    (c) To pay a franchise fee. The various methods by which a franchisor receives payment of such a fee are dealt with in Chapter 7.

    (d) To follow the accounting and reporting systems laid down by the franchisor. The purpose is twofold. Firstly, the franchisor has a means of checking and calculating any fees to which he may be entitled. Secondly, these systems will be prepared in such a way that they will rapidly reveal vital management information and whether or not the projected gross and net profit margins are being achieved.

(e) Not to advertise without prior approval of the advertisements by the franchisor. As previously explained (Chapter 8), the franchisor will invariably handle all national advertising but this will not mean that there is no local or other advertising which cannot benefit the business. The franchisor will wish to have control of the contents of advertisements which make use of his trademark, service mark or trade name to ensure that the standards associated therewith are maintained.

(f) To use and display such point-of-sale or advertising material as the franchisor stipulates. Also to use bags, boxes, wrappers, and, in a food franchise, even such items as straws, cups, and serviettes bearing the franchisor's name and trademark. Point-of-sale and advertising material may be supplied free of charge, within the framework of the advertising arrangements, but the other items would, of course, have to be paid for.

(g) To maintain the premises in a good, clean, sanitary condition and to redecorate when required to do so by the franchisor. This is a provision which often causes difficulty in practice. The franchisor will always be striving to ensure that the premises have the best possible appearance while the franchisee will be reluctant to spend his money.

(h) To maintain the business insurance cover. The purpose of this provision is to protect the franchisee from the consequences of fire or public or employees' liability third party, product liability and other claims. It protects the franchisee's business and his livelihood. In some cases franchisors are able to arrange for insurance schemes to be established for the benefit of the network. Indeed some insurance brokers have offered specialist services in this respect to franchisors.

(i) To permit the franchisor's staff to enter the premises to inspect and see whether the franchisor's standards are being maintained and whether the terms of the agreement are being observed.

(j) To purchase goods or products from the franchisor or his nominated suppliers (see competition law above).

(k) To train his staff in the franchisor's methods and to ensure that they maintain the standards of service associated with the franchisor's branding and system.

(l) Not to assign the franchise contract without the franchisor's consent. All franchise contracts should be capable of assignment. If the contract is not assignable there is no incentive to the franchisee to invest and to build. The franchisor, however, will need to approve the purchaser. There is rarely difficulty in practice in arranging a transfer of the franchise provided the purchaser of the franchisee's business matches the franchisor's selection standards and successfully passes through any necessary training. Many contracts provide for a fixed or percentage fee based upon the sale price to be paid to the franchisor to cover his costs of processing the transaction and of training and establishing the new franchisee. Some franchisors are able to introduce purchasers from their waiting list of franchisees and make a charge for the introduction on a percentage fee basis as would a Business Transfer Agent. Some franchise agreements contain a grant of an option for the franchisor to purchase the franchisee's business when the franchisee wishes to sell. Any such option should secure at least as good a deal for the franchisee as he would get if he were to do a bona fide arm's length sale in the open market. Any provision which requires the franchisee to sell to the franchisor at a value (e.g. net asset value) which is less than the real market value should be unacceptable.

SECTION 4

The restrictions imposed upon the franchisee are affected substantially by the European Commission's block exemption regulation and are detailed above. The restrictions fall under four headings the last of which is not dealt with in the Regulation.

1. Product sourcing, supply and control of range of products to be dealt with by the franchisee.
2. Restrictions on other competing activities both during the term of the agreement and after its termination.
3. Protection of the franchisor's know-how during the term of the agreement and after its termination.
4. A restriction on the franchisee to prevent him taking staff away from other franchisees.

It will be recalled that the franchisor's control of products is considerable if they are 'franchisor's goods' as defined in the Regulation and controls on other goods are more difficult to impose except on quality criteria or where it is impracticable owing to the nature of the goods to establish quality criteria.

The franchisor can require franchisees to devote the whole of their efforts to the franchised business and can prevent franchisees from soliciting or touting for business outside their allocated territory.

SECTION 5

The question of assignability has been discussed in item 8 in the preliminary considerations. The problem of what should be done in the event of the death of the franchisee, or the principal shareholder of the franchisee if it is a company, should be dealt with in the contract. The franchisee or principal shareholder should ensure that in the event of death:

(a) his personal representative(s) and/or dependant(s) will be able to keep the business going until one of them can qualify as a franchisee and take an assignment of the franchise agreement or undertake the obligations formerly assumed by the principal shareholder; and/or

(b) that, if they cannot or do not wish to so qualify, arrangements can be made to keep the business going until a suitable assignee can be found at a proper price. In this respect the franchisor may agree to offer to provide management (for a fee) during the critical few weeks following the death. All reputable and ethical franchisors will be sympathetic and helpful whatever the contract provides, but it is best if the contract clearly specifies what will happen.

SECTION 6

There is an increasing tendency to introduce into franchise agreements a provision for the arbitration of disputes. The BFA introduced an Arbitration Scheme administered by the Chartered Institute of Arbitrators (see Appendix D). Arbitration is a useful procedure and is particularly apt for franchise transactions although it is not considered desirable by all franchisors and their advisers as a method of resolving disputes. However, there is a very definite role for arbitration as a method of resolving disputes or differences which can arise in a franchise transaction. A franchise agreement is the basis for a long-term arrangement which should be able to survive genuine differences of opinion. The alternative is confrontation, termination and litigation. Not that arbitration is not a form of confrontation but it gives the opportunity to deal with a difference speedily in confidence and largely at the convenience of the parties. Also, it is usually less expensive, and arbitrators can be selected from a specialist panel who will realistically understand and cope with the problems.

There are some aspects of the franchise agreement which are particularly appropriate for the arbitration procedure. Examples include:

(a) whether a franchisee has performed his contract sufficiently well to justify any renewal rights which the franchisee may have; and

(b) differences arising in respect of royalty or franchise fee calculations.

However, most franchisees would not wish to arbitrate about whether or not their standards had been observed. Also, care must be taken to ensure that when a franchisor needs to be able quickly to enforce his rights, for example on termination, that he can go to court for immediate action in appropriate cases.

It is likely that the recent trend towards the introduction of mediation and conciliation procedures will be introduced in franchising transactions. The BFA intends to introduce these techniques into the range of services which it offers.

SECTION 7

The agreement may be determined after the expiration of the fixed period or there may be express provision for the termination upon the service of a notice. Inevitably, the agreement will provide for termination by the franchisor in the event of any default by the franchisee of his obligations under the franchise agreement. Most agreements provide a machinery for the franchisee to be given an opportunity to remedy any defaults which can be remedied within a specific period before the franchisor can exercise the right of termination subject to safeguards against the habitual offender. Indeed, as is mentioned above, the Code requires such a provision to be inserted in agreements.

Many franchisors treat breaches with varying degrees of seriousness, but many take a very strong view of breaches which raise questions of whether the franchisee can be trusted. Therefore, some regard cheating over disclosure of gross income, and thus the amount of the fee to be paid, as fundamental and will wish to be able to terminate in such a case without giving the franchisee an opportunity to put matters right. Where the franchisee has provided misleading or false information in his franchise application a franchisor may wish to be able to terminate the agreement. A franchisor is also bound to take a very serious view of a franchisee who is found to be making confidential information available to competitors or potential competitors.

Even if a franchisee is in default under the terms of his agreement every effort should be made to investigate whether it is possible to find a solution which will not result in the termination of the contract. There are many steps which can and should be taken.

(a) Attempts should be made to persuade the franchisee to return to the performance of his obligations.

(b) Additional support should be offered to assist in a case where the franchisee is genuinely finding it difficult to cope. It may be necessary to provide the franchisee with additional training to try to improve his performance. If such a franchisee clearly has no long-term future it is best if both parties recognize the fact sooner rather than later so that a strategy can be developed to build up the business in order for it to be sold and the franchisee to receive the best possible recovery of his investment.

(c) If the franchisee is not responsive to the franchisor's attempts to help (and not all are) it may be worth suggesting that the franchisee sell his business.

(d) If all these approaches fail and the franchisee continues to be in default the franchisor should serve a default notice requiring the franchisee to remedy the breaches. A further attempt should be made to find a solution along one of the lines suggested above but if that fails the franchisor will be left with no alternative but to terminate the agreement.

SECTION 8

The termination of the agreement of a defaulting franchisee is always a sad time for the franchisor, but a bad franchisee will invariably cause disquiet among other franchisees, who could be adversely affected by his poor performance. Fairness and firmness should characterize the franchisor's dealing with all his franchisees but particularly with those with whom he experiences difficulties.

In whatever circumstances the franchise agreement is terminated the franchisee should be left with the assets of the business for which he has paid. He will be stripped of his right to carry on business under the trade name, and to use the franchisor's system and know-how, and he will lose all the other advantages made available to a franchisee. He may also have to move trading premises or substantially change his business in view of restrictive covenants in the agreement.

In some cases the franchisor will own the freehold or lease of the premises and will grant a lease or an underlease to the franchisee. In such a case the franchisee may find that upon the termination of the franchise agreement he has lost his lease also. In such a case the franchisee should at the time of the signature of the contract see that there are safeguards for the cash investment he is making. On termination in these circumstances the franchisee would be no worse off than he would be in the event of a termination where there is a third party landlord. It may be that he would be slightly better placed since if there is a third party landlord and the franchisee cannot trade from these premises he will have commitments under the lease until he can dispose of it. He would have no such commitments if the franchisor is his landlord and retakes possession.

The franchisee must appreciate that the basic cause for him finding himself with problems on termination will invariably be his own default.

The objective in framing these provisions is to ensure that the franchisor recovers total control of his industrial and intellectual property rights, his system and his goodwill.

   (a) The use of the brand name and goodwill associated with it must be discontinued.

   (b) The use of the system and know-how must be discontinued.

   (c) All outward signs, appearance of premises and vans must be changed to avoid confusion and to prevent the franchisee from cashing in on the franchisor's goodwill.

   (d) Customer contact must stop. Their custom is part of the franchisor's goodwill.

   (e) The franchisee must be prevented from competing with the franchisor and the network from the premises on which he conducted the franchised business.

In view of the close working relationship that will exist between a franchisor and a franchisee all requirements must be clearly stated in the contract. This is a transaction in which no small print should exist.

Chapter 13

Techniques of multiple franchising

One of the ways in which a significant number of franchise companies in the USA develop their networks is by the use of the technique of area development. This technique, by whatever name it is called, has as its purpose the more rapid growth of the network. There are many similarities between this technique and that which is employed in international master franchise arrangements, which are dealt with in Chapter 14. There can be a number of approaches to area development arrangements, such as:

- an arrangement in which the developer is given the right to open a multiple number of outlets to a predetermined schedule and within a given area; and
- an arrangement in which the developer is given the right to establish to a predetermined schedule and within a given area, a combination of his own outlets and those of subfranchisees.

In the USA, by the use of this sort of system some networks achieve a phenomenal growth rate of many hundreds of outlets each year. The technique has not been used much in the UK owing to several considerations. One of the major factors is that the UK is much smaller in area and the concentrations of population are far greater. This means that a franchisor can cope more easily with growth in the UK in compact and sensible marketing areas than can a franchisor in the USA.

What are the advantages for the franchisor of expanding through area development agreements?

1. As is the case with the franchising of individual units, the franchisor will be making use of the financial and manpower resources of the franchisee. However, with the area developer these resources will need to be that much greater. If the cost of opening an individual unit is, say, £100,000 and the developer has undertaken to open 25 outlets he will need to find, in total, £2.5 million to open all of them, and within a given period of time. One should also not lose sight of the fact that further working capital will be required to develop and invest in the creation of the right infrastructure for the area developer's business. This will require a franchisee of a different type with much more substantial financial resources than is the case with the individual unit operator. Furthermore, the amount of capital required will necessitate a different approach to financing and a very professional attitude to the marketing of the resulting business.

2. The financial strength of the area developer will have to be geared up to permit the rapid growth of the required number of outlets so as to obtain the maximum benefit from the rapid saturation of his marketing area and the organizational infrastructure which he will be creating.

3. The area developer, with the sort of resources which will be required and with the commitment which he will undertake, will probably need to be far more experienced in business than an individual outlet operator and he will have to build an effective team to work with him. The procedure which the franchisor will adopt when selecting an area developer will be very different, and the franchisor will apply criteria which are radically different, from those which apply to the selection of unit operators.

4. The usual fee arrangement for such a transaction would fall into the following four categories.
   (a) A lump sum payment to secure the right to open an agreed number of outlets. This payment, in some cases, may be treated as a payment on account of the initial franchise fees to be paid in respect of each outlet as it opens. (The receipt of such a front-end payment can provide a franchisor with a welcome cash injection.)
   (b) Initial franchise fees to be paid on the opening of each outlet. These may be discounted (see above) by an agreed amount to reflect the fact that a lump sum payment has been made for the rights, or they may be at the same rate as applies to individual outlet operations.
   (c) Continuing franchise fees.
   (d) Advertising contributions.

These latter fees would be the same as those which apply to the rest of the network, although sometimes a developer will claim to be entitled to some special deal.

One can expect the claim to be supported by the argument that since there are so many outlets to be in operation and the area developer will have his own management structure, the franchisor will have less to do in return for the fees. Indeed, there may be some saving in this respect, but it will more often than not be less of a saving than might be suggested.

A franchisor should not accept that there will be less to provide in the way of services to an area developer than to an individual outlet operator. All the normal range of services will have to be provided, as will the periodic visits from field support staff to ensure the maintenance of standards of operation, as well as providing assistances with problems, either on site or at the area developer's central office. Indeed it may be more necessary for the franchisor closely to supervise an area developer's activities since given his larger size and resources as compared with the 'one-off' franchisee he is more likely to feel competent to challenge the franchisor's wisdom and to seek to cut corners and introduce his own ideas. Furthermore, if an area developer encounters problems they will be much greater than will be the case with an individual unit operator. The franchisor will find disproportionately heavy demands upon his resources with which he will find it difficult to cope economically.

In the case of advertising contributions, an area developer may argue that as in aggregate his contribution is disproportionately high he should have some concession. This is of course a fallacy since on an outlet-by-outlet basis there would be no disproportionate contributions. Any such concession would inevitably mean that those who did not benefit from the concession would be making a proportionately higher contribution which they would resent. Also, it is sometimes argued that part (if not the whole) of the area developer's contributions should be concentrated in his marketing area. This, of course, is what every franchisee would like and, if followed, would result in a loss of the benefits of co-operative network advertising and promotion. The fundamental principle that franchisees should be dealt with on an equal and consistent basis must be observed even where there are area developers involved in the network. Special cases make for discontent and resentment.

In theory, it should be easier for the franchisor to control the network operated by an area developer, but the reality may well be different. The area developer will have his own management infrastructure and he will want to ensure that all outlets operate the system properly and that full advantage is taken of the opportunities to develop the business. But, while the area developer and some of his senior staff may well be extremely well motivated through capital investment and share option schemes each outlet will be, in fact, under management, and that management has to be provided with the right degree of motivation and supervision.

The franchisor still has a responsibility to ensure that everything which should be done is being done at both levels. Care must be taken to ensure that the franchisor is not caught between an area developer, who refers him to an outlet which is in need of assistance, and the manager of the outlet, who blames the area developer for all his problems, or who will not accept direction from the franchisor unless the area developer agrees and so directs him.

The area developer should have, or will acquire, a broader-based local knowledge, extending throughout the whole of his marketing area, which should enable him to capitalize upon the opportunities. There will be greater scope than exists for individual outlet operations, given the larger area, for a comprehensive saturation of the market-place and the benefits from the greater concentration of exposure which will be obtained in the market area. In the case of the individual outlet the franchisee would have to want the establishment of other franchisees to achieve the same comprehensive saturation of the market-place. This would not be without trauma for the individual franchisee, who would be concerned that the development of saturation would introduce a competitive element which he would wish to avoid.

The area developer's own business organization should provide substantial back-up to the franchisor's efforts. Since the area developer's presence at each outlet will be by staff and not an owner, the need for supervision will be greater and so will the need for constant training and retraining, as well as the recruitment of personnel. The area developer will have to provide these facilities in some respects as an addition to the services provided by the franchisor. The area developer will not be replacing the franchisor in the areas of training and supervision, but will be able to provide these services more economically, given his scale of operation, than can each individual outlet operator.

CONTRACTUAL DOCUMENTS

The franchisor who seeks to benefit from the advantages of offering area development agreements will have to face the burden of complex contractual and structural arrangements. There will invariably be two, and possibly three, contractual documents.

Development agreement

This will contain detailed provisions in relation to the development programme and the procedure for selecting and approving locations, as well as the detailed infrastructure to be established by the area developer. The area developer will have to undertake certain central obligations in terms of business organization and functions. His senior staff will have to undergo specific training, and it is likely that the franchisor will require the person who is appointed managing director (general manager) to have passed the training course. In addition it is not uncommon to find a requirement that the managing director (general manager) should have a minimum equity stake in the business.

Operational unit agreement

This will usually be on the same basis as that used for individual unit operators and will be signed when each location is approved, at which time any initial fee will also be payable.

Funding agreement

Unless the area developer has considerable resources it is possible that, in addition to the above agreements, there will also be a funding arrangement. This will be governed by a complex contract and if the sums involved are significant there could be a syndicate providing the funds. Further, it is likely that there will be a shareholders' agreement to protect the interests of the area developer's shareholders. This agreement will have to reflect the safeguards which the franchisor will require to prevent any change in the control of the area developer's organization with which he might not agree.

STRUCTURING THE AREA DEVELOPMENT AGREEMENT

There are a number of problems to be considered in structuring the arrangements.

1. What is to be the number and density of the outlets?
2. Are exclusive or non-exclusive rights to be granted?
3. Will the area developer be limited to opening the number of outlets agreed upon in the contract, or will he be permitted to open more? If so, on what basis?
4. What degree of transferability will there be? Will the area developer be permitted to dispose of his right to develop the area? That would be unusual, as most franchisors would expect an area developer to complete the development schedule before seeking to sell the business. The franchisor is essentially seeking a relationship with those who will develop the area and who will have been selected for that purpose. The franchisor would not expect the area developer to enter into an area development agreement in order to profit from its sale and thus not be involved in the crucial development stage of the system for which purpose he was expressly recruited. Such a course of action would be fraught with problems, which might extend beyond the relationship between the franchisor and his developer;

they will undoubtedly involve also those who have put up the funds for the area developer's business.

Does the franchisor really want to permit a change in the person who has undertaken the development schedule and who is, in reality, the franchisee before the network is fully in position? The break in continuity may prove a stumbling-block and the individual may be difficult to replace. A change may also result in the development schedule being difficult to sustain and the area developer's team of senior executives may well lose interest if the person who recruited and motivated them is to depart before the development phase is complete. On the other hand, those who have provided the financial back-up will not want to be prevented from changing the person who has been selected if they have lost confidence in his ability to take the business forward effectively. These are all difficult matters which will have to be considered and common ground found in the course of negotiations.

Again, it is necessary to emphasize that in structuring these arrangements, the fundamental features and requirements of a franchise transaction must be maintained no matter what pressure the funding sources try to impose. They will try to impose pressure since many funding sources do not possess the requisite levels of knowledge of franchising, and they would find many features puzzling and possibly contrary to some of their normal thinking. This should not prevent them from investing since given care their involvement could be very worthwhile. The franchisor must not compromise on franchising principles since once the integrity of the franchise concept and system is undermined, the future development of the franchise is put at risk. As is the case with individual outlet operations where uniformity of treatment is essential, so it is with area developers: once the format for dealing with area developers is established it must remain the same for them all.

5. To what extent will the area developer be permitted to dispose of individual units without affecting the development right and on what conditions? Bear in mind that each unit operated by the area developer should be on the same contractual basis as those operated by individuals. The issue is not whether the area developer can sell individual units, but whether he can do so before he has fully developed (as required by the contract) or if he does so thereafter, must he replace the outlet sold with another; if so, on what terms?

6. When one considers the problem of termination of these arrangements, the position becomes even more difficult. There are three possible arrangements to terminate: (a) the development right; (b) the overall development agreement; and (c) individual outlet agreements. Let us consider each in turn.

The development right

This would normally be capable of termination in the event of a failure to perform the development schedule. If the area developer has exclusive rights, does he not merely lose his exclusivity? Whether or not he has exclusive rights, does he lose the right to continue to exploit the development schedule in the future? If so, are there ways in which he may be able to protect himself against a slower rate of progress than he had planned? These are issues to be considered. One should remember that the franchisor will attach great importance to the maintenance of the development schedule and may feel that failure to do so would be to the detriment of the development of the network in the target territory. Whichever way the franchisor decides to approach the problem there is no clear answer. At the worst the franchisor would have parallel systems being operated by the original area developer and one subsequently appointed. The practical problems which can arise in such circumstances where there are in essence two developers within a given territory may lead some franchisors to require that the defaulting developer's agreement should be capable of being terminated in its entirety for a failure to sustain the development schedule.

The overall development agreement

This would apply to failure by the developer to observe and perform the 'non-development right' provisions in the development agreement, i.e. the detailed infrastructure referred to earlier. One would normally expect that such failure would not lead to termination unless the developer had been given an opportunity to put matters right. However, given that despite warnings and in the face of a failure to remedy the default, the franchisor terminates the agreement, one would expect such termination to bring the development agreement to an end, including any development right. This would have to be the case, since if the general provision relating to the area developer's business structure is ignored it would be futile to permit him to continue to develop by opening further outlets. Similarly, such a breach would also be expected to lead to a position where the individual outlet agreements would also be capable of being terminated since the business structure, designed to provide the basis for the supervision and control of those outlets, would not be in existence.

Individual outlet agreements

One might expect that there could be problems with individual outlets which could lead to termination of the agreement relating to such an unit. Whether or not that termination should affect the main agreement must depend upon:

- why the agreement is terminated; and
- how many such agreements are terminated within any given period of time; and
- whether or not the breach of the individual unit agreement involved a sufficiently serious breach of the main agreement.

One then has to consider what should be the consequences of termination of each of these three agreements.

1. Does the loss of the development right affect the continued operation of the individual outlets, and if not, can the developer still apply to open new outlets, but independently of the developer arrangement? What would be the consequences if he did?
2. If the overall development agreement is terminated should the individual unit agreement also be in jeopardy?
3. One would also expect that all the normal consequences of termination of a franchise agreement would be equally applicable. In cases where the franchisor has an option to purchase on termination, the scale of the business to be purchased could cause problems for him because the amount of money involved could be considerable.

FURTHER CONSIDERATIONS

Besides the complexity of the contractual and structural arrangements, there are also other important considerations for the franchisor in deciding whether or not to grant area development agreements.

1. Entry into development agreements has to be handled with great care so that a proper balance of power is maintained between the franchisor and his franchisees. A franchisor with, say, four area developers covering the whole of the UK and with no other franchisees is clearly vulnerable to challenge. Each of the area developers will represent a substantial part of the franchise, and if two or more 'gang up' on the franchisor, unless he has considerable resources he could be in great difficulties. A franchisor should, therefore, never structure his arrangements so that he is creating a franchisee network where the franchisees or a small group of franchisees could have such power that he is at a serious disadvantage. A balance must be maintained between single unit operators (or company-owned units) and developers so that the franchisor has a powerful business base from which he can operate without threat.
2. Having chosen to appoint an area developer, a franchisor is committing himself to that one person to exploit an area and open a

number of outlets, consistent with the size of the area. If the area developer does not proceed at the agreed rate of openings, then the growth of the franchisor's network will be inhibited. It may be difficult later on to regain the impetus and put the network back on course.

3. If a area developer proves unable to cope, the problems for the franchisor will be that much greater, depending upon the size of the area developer's operation at the time when the problems arise. Dealing with individual unit operations which experience difficulties will always be part of life for the franchisor, but normally those operators will only represent a small percentage of his network. Dealing with the area developer whose operation has gone sour will probably involve all the area developer's outlets, which in aggregate will be a larger percentage of the whole network, and these problems will have to be coped with in addition to the normal volume of problem cases from individual unit operators.

4. The above factors emphasize the need for the franchisor to ensure that the developer's management team is of the right quality (see below).

5. The existence of a large organization as franchisee, with the likely transient nature of its employees, makes it more difficult for the franchisor to protect the spread of his know-how and confidential information. Great care will have to be taken by the franchisor to ensure that the correct steps are introduced to provide the necessary protection for his system.

6. The elements of motivation and incentive at operational outlet level, which are such important fundamental features of franchising, are considerably diminished because the outlets are operated not by franchisees but by managers. The supervisory ability of the area developer's management team, and the existence of incentive schemes are, of course, valuable aids to the solution of this problem. It is, therefore, vital that a way is found to provide incentives and motivation at outlet level, and to encourage the stability and long-term loyalty of the management staff.

7. The introduction by the development agreement system of a layer of management between the franchisor and the operational outlet staff can create difficulties. The franchisor must be in the position of being allowed to intervene at the unit level if standards are not maintained.

Area development arrangements are not, as yet, a significant feature of UK franchise systems. As we have seen, they present challenges as well as benefits. However, the issues which they raise have relevance also in other 'multiple franchisee' arrangements, such as situations in which the franchisee through his ambition and ability becomes the owner and operator of a significant number of operational outlets. Area development arrangements also provide lessons which are relevant to international agreements, where, in many cases, the master franchisee in the target territory is analogous to the area developer.

Another technique which is being used in the USA is that described as 'combination' franchising. This is where the same franchisee operates a number of complementary franchises from the same premises. An example which illustrates the technique would be a franchisee with, say, three different fast food franchises each with a service counter and a common area for sitting and eating, similar to a mini-food hall in a shopping mall. With increasing cost and scarcity of accommodation the technique may have some appeal. However, there are pitfalls in such an arrangement which all franchisors must consider. There are two ways in which the arrangement can be structured. In the first the physical facility would be occupied by different franchisees who would each occupy part of the premises under franchise from different franchisors. This type of arrangement presents the least of the difficulties so long as each franchisor ensures:

- that each franchisee operates the franchise properly from his portion of the premises;
- that the areas used in common are compatible with the franchisor's branding and image;
- that there are adequate contractual obligations to ensure that this common area is properly maintained;
- that the facilities available are consistent with the franchisor's requirements; and
- that the franchisor is able to enforce his standards.

There is clearly room for conflict between the franchisors or the operators over the way in which the common areas are fitted out and maintained. There is also the problem of who will be the tenant of the total facility as well as of the common area.

1. Will one franchisor or franchisee lease the area and sublet to the others?
2. Will the other franchisors and/or franchisees be able to exercise the level of control which they require over the common area?
3. Will the other franchisees operate to a standard which will not detract from the standard imposed by one of the other franchisors?
4. Will the association with the franchise operation in one section of the property harm the others?
5. What should happen if one of the franchisee's operations fails?

6. With whom would it be replaced and who would have the responsibility for ensuring this?
7. What would be the position if one of the franchisors or his franchisee decides that the location is wrong for them or that they are not doing as well as they should?
8. Should they be able to 'opt out'? If so, on what basis?
9. By whom should they be replaced, on what terms and whose responsibility should it be to deal with the problem?
10. If the franchisor and franchisee whose operation is not doing well decide that the location and/or conceptual approach is wrong, who will find the replacement and should the other franchisors and/or franchisees have any say in who replaces them and what their operation should be?
11. If one of the franchisees runs his operation within the facility on a substandard basis so that the other franchisees suffer, what redresss should there be and who will enforce it?
12. Similarly, if one franchisee does not meet his obligations for the maintenance of the common area who will enforce these obligations against him and secure his compliance?

Should there be an overall agreement between all the franchisors to regulate the operations? If there is such an agreement should the franchisees also be a party to it so that they can enforce its provisions?

The second arrangement is where there is one franchisee for all the operations to be conducted from the common facility. In this case there are further difficulties to consider. The most striking disadvantage appears to be a risk of the loss of control with a consequent lowering of standards. It is not difficult to see how this happens since the arrangement has built into it some fundamentals which are likely to give rise to these difficulties.

1. The franchisee is not under the control of any one franchisor.
2. The franchisee is entering into the arrangement to maximize the utilization of space and staff and minimize expense.
3. The common area is not strictly under the control of any of the franchisors to the point where one of them can impose standards of uniformity, supervision and cleanliness which match those found in a unit wholly dedicated to that particular franchise.
4. The franchisee is in a position to play one franchisor off against another and to display a degree of independence to each (because he has other franchises in the same location) which undermines control and standards.
5. The franchisee has no incentive to promote all operations if he can

achieve the financial result he seeks by concentrating his efforts on the one which he considers will produce the best results for him.

6. Each franchisor's position in relation to the franchisee is weaker since the existence of the others may be a viable fall-back situation for the franchisee.

7. The franchisors are placed in a situation in which conflicts of interest can develop between them; even businesses which appear to be complementary can be competing and can have overlapping product, service or menu items.

8. Where such overlapping exists, the temptation for the franchisee to standardize the product, service or menu item—despite the normal differences imposed by the franchisors in terms of quality of product supply and methods of preparation—is considerable and difficult for each franchisor effectively to monitor on a regular ongoing basis.

9. It is difficult, if not impossible, to contemplate the sale by the franchisee of each franchise individually. The criteria for franchisee selection by each franchisor may differ and a prospective purchaser from the franchisee may not satisfy the approval requirements of all the franchisors involved.

10. Each franchisor runs the risk of being associated with another franchisor whose business may:
    - fail;
    - suffer a loss of credibility;
    - fall into disrepute; or
    - become heavily involved in litigation with franchisees.

    It is likely that the impact of any of these events could adversely affect the innocent franchisors not only in terms of the consumer's association with them but also because they may become involved in any litigation arising from these factors, particularly where bankruptcy or liquidation may be involved.

11. The participation by the franchisee in any of the franchised networks, marketing, promotional and advertising campaigns, particularly those involving point-of-sale material, may be in question since the others may resent the promotion of one franchise without the other. Liaison between all within the framework of their own marketing, promotional and advertising strategy may well be impossible bearing in mind the size and spread of their own networks. To try to establish contractual commitments in this area would not make sense or be practicable.

12. The franchisors will probably have put themselves under the pressure of seeking to use this technique as a method of achieving quicker growth than would otherwise be available to them, thus putting themselves under what might be the wrong pressures. In addition it would probably be difficult for them to resist further growth by this

method by their common franchisee within the area of this operation or the surrounding area.

Anyone considering this particular method of growth must take considerable care in structuring the arrangements and should seriously question whether the likely benefits in terms of any 'improvement' over their normal method of expansion are worth the undoubted risks.

Chapter 14

Franchising internationally

Franchising has grown considerably throughout the world in the past three decades, but the rate of growth which has occurred during the last 3–4 years, and that which is projected, indicates that its development is continuing to accelerate.

Many franchisors are recognizing that a franchise scheme possesses many of the elements which are required to take a business from one territory to another. The existence of a system which is well recorded in a manual, together with the in-built training programmes, enables a franchisor to transform a new foreign 'partner' into a person capable of running his system successfully.

In this chapter the international master franchise agreement will be called the master franchise agreement; the parties to the agreement will be called the franchisor and the sub-franchisor, respectively; and the operator of a franchised unit will be called the sub-franchisee. This terminology is recommended by the International Franchising Committee of the Business Law Section of the International Bar Association, which has prepared a lexicon of terms in an effort to promote the uniformity of use of terminology in international transactions. The text of the lexicon appears in the *Journal of International Franchising and Distribution Law* (1987/2, p. 58) and is available from the International Bar Association at 2 Harewood Place, London W1R 9HB, UK.

There are many issues which have to be considered when taking the business from one territory to another and these are dealt with in some detail. Suffice to say that those franchisors who treat a target territory with the most respect and who understand the differences which exist are those who at the end of the day do the best. Thorough preparation is essential in taking one's franchise overseas, in dealing with not only the business, but also the legal issues. The legal issues to be considered when conducting the essential legal audit of the target territory include the following.

LEGAL STATUS OF THE PARTIES AND THE NATURE OF LEGAL RELATIONSHIPS

Quite apart from an investigation and assessment of the capacity in which parties can contract, particularly if one of the parties is an overseas company, consideration must be given to whether or not there are special local laws which might result in the franchisee being regarded as an agent or employee of the franchisor. In most franchise arrangements, the parties go to great lengths to ensure the establishment of the franchisee as an independent contractor, and to ensure that the franchisee has no power to bind the franchisor and that the franchisee is not the agent or partner or employee of the franchisor.

There can be special laws which might override the contractual arrangement between the parties and impose upon the franchisor obligations, both to third parties and of a financial character in the form of social welfare contributions, which are not part of the normal calculations made, or considerations taken into account, when establishing a franchise scheme.

GOVERNMENT ATTITUDES

It is important to ascertain whether the government has an attitude towards franchising and to the import of know-how and trade secrets. By investigating government attitudes and existing policies, it may be possible to take advantage of special incentive schemes and grants that can be available for certain types of business or industry, which would make the franchise venture more certain of success and more profitable from the point of view of the franchisor and franchisee.

COMPETITION LAWS

The competition laws of the territory must always be considered. Many countries are now adopting competition laws, the stated objective of which is to make anti-competitive practices unlawful and thus stimulate competition. These laws are not directed at franchise transactions, but often affect franchising because of the generality of their application.

Many of the practices inherent in a franchise transaction, such as tied sales, price fixing and other controls, are capable of being affected by anti-trust legislation whose effect must be taken into account.

UNFAIR COMPETITION

No franchisor will want to train franchisees so that they are equipped to trade competitively with the franchisor. The franchisor has two basic defensive weapons available:

- restraints against in-term and post-term competition; and
- protection of the franchisor's know-how.

Both weapons have to be contractually based and the nature and extent of the protection available in any given territory must be investigated. In-term restraints are usually easier to enforce than those which become effective post-term. The latter are increasingly affected by competition law and in some cases constitutional rules and are based upon the reasonableness of the restraints in regard to the area within which they are to be enforced and the length of the period of the enforcement.

Protection of know-how may not be affected by the latter considerations but there will often be disputes as to whether the know-how was really confidential or in the public domain. In franchising the individual elements of know-how may well lack confidentiality but the strength of the franchisor will come from the skill employed in the completion of the total know-how package and its application to the franchised business. This fundamental character of know-how in franchising is recognised by the European Commission's block exemption regulation for categories of franchise agreements.

INDUSTRIAL AND INTELLECTUAL PROPERTY LAWS
The franchisor's industrial and intellectual property form the backbone of the franchisor's business. It includes:

- trademarks and service marks
- trade names
- goodwill
- know-how, methods, trade secrets
- copyright material including designs
- sometimes also patents

The method of registering and protecting these rights must be investigated in each territory since although the law in many countries follows a similar pattern there can be significant differences. It is not unknown for franchisors to seek to set up business in a country only to find that someone else is already using their name and has established rights to it which have priority over the franchisor's no matter how long he has used his name in his own country.

In franchise transactions the use of these rights is permitted by licence in some form or other and it is essential to use the correct method of licensing each different right to avoid adverse claims and to enable control to be maintained by the franchisor over these valuable rights.

TAXATION

The taxation effects on the franchise scheme have to be considered. There may be local sales taxes to be taken into account and certainly, in operating the pilot scheme, care has to be taken to ensure that the effect of local tax laws on the scheme is fully taken into account. Variations in accounting and reporting systems and procedures which may be necessary also have to be considered and incorporated into the locally developed concept.

From the point of view of international tax considerations, one should commence by investigating whether double-taxation agreements exist between the franchisor's own country and the target territory. If there are no direct double-taxation agreements, or if the terms are not thought sufficiently beneficial, then investigation should be made of the best route for the franchisor's income to enable the effects of multiple taxation to be minimized. It may be necessary for the franchisor to establish a licensing entity in a foreign territory to achieve his objectives.

Very often careful selection of the route through which the monies flow by taking advantage of double-taxation agreements can achieve a great deal in ensuring that the maximum amount of money reaches its ultimate intended destination. There are, of course, cash-flow considerations, and if withholding taxes are imposed to any substantial extent it can have a considerable adverse effect on the cash-flow of the franchisor and on his ability to finance his obligations from the income which is generated in the initial stages of the foreign operation.

CORPORATE LAW

In deciding whether to set up a branch or operational subsidiary, apart from the taxation implications of operating in this way, local corporate laws have to be considered to see whether some form of incorporation is necessary or desirable, or whether there are, as is often the case, requirements for registration of foreign companies which establish a place of business. Some territories have prohibitions against foreign nationals owning the majority of shares in companies which are incorporated although there is a trend away from that sort of restriction.

Corporate laws should also be studied as franchises may choose to incorporate the business which is to be licensed. The franchisor will have to develop some method for ensuring that shareholders and directors cannot acquire the know-how and trade secrets, and subsequently use them in competition with the franchisor. There must be a clear understanding of the corporate laws, and the roles, duties and responsibilities of shareholders and directors. Appropriate steps must be taken to ensure their compliance with the terms of contracts, particularly in limiting the scope of the use to which they can put the franchisor's know-how and trade secrets and to retain control over the transfer of shares in the corporation.

SPECIAL FRANCHISE LAWS

The USA, with its federal and state system, abounds in a multiplicity of franchise laws. There are disclosure requirements, registration requirements, and some statutes affecting franchisors' rights to terminate or to refuse renewal to franchisees. So far as the USA is concerned, one can be offending against some legal requirement even in discussing the grant of a franchise. Legal advice at the earliest point, even before negotiations, is essential.

There are franchise laws in only one European Community member state since France introduced pre-contract disclosure requirements early in 1990. These requirements affect all licensing transactions in France and not merely franchising. There are no franchise specific laws in any other European Community member state. The European Commission has legislated for franchising by exempting certain franchise agreements from the application of EC competition law. This law is explained in some detail in Chapter 12. In the UK there are laws which have general application to commercial transactions including the Pyramid Selling Schemes Law contained in the Fair Trading Act 1973 which affect franchising. There are some franchise laws in Canada and South America (Andean Pact countries), and Japan has issued guidelines on the application of anti-trust laws to franchising. In Brazil there is a proposal for a franchise law which is being considered. The OECD is known to be preparing a report on franchising from the viewpoint of competition law and UNIDROIT is studying franchising with a view to preparing guidelines for international franchising.

At present—apart from the above and the effect which competition laws have on franchising—there are few countries throughout the world which have special laws that directly affect franchising. Indeed, Australia, after a detailed study, rejected the need for franchise laws as existing remedies to law were regarded as adequate, although the Minister with responsibility for small business has advocated self-registration of franchising and in December 1990 appointed a task force to look into the issues and to make recommendations.

SPECIAL INDUSTRY LAWS

The franchisor should investigate whether his target territory has any laws which concern or affect the type of operation in which he is engaged. For example, fast food or restaurant businesses will invariably be affected by legislation which regulates standards of cleanliness in the interests of public health. These requirements must be carefully checked out by the franchisor because it is only in recognizing the existence and extent of these laws that the franchisor can properly adapt his concepts to the target territory's requirements.

VICARIOUS LIABILITY

One of the fundamental features of franchising is that the franchisee is an independent business person responsible for running his own business, albeit in accordance with the franchisor's format and using the franchisor's branding. The franchisee will have total control of the day-to-day conduct of the business operation, will own all the assets and will hire and fire staff. The franchisor does not expect to be considered liable to those with whom the franchisee deals for any acts or defaults by the franchisee. The possibility that third parties dealing as customers or suppliers with the franchisee will not recognize his status as being independent of the franchisor can be dealt with by various methods. In the UK the issue of a trader using a name other than his own is dealt with in the Business Names Act 1985 which requires notice to be given in a particular way. The European Commission has made it a condition of the application of the block exemption regulation for categories of franchise agreements that the independent status of the franchisee is made clear. At the time of writing the European Commission is considering a proposal for a directive requiring European Community member states to introduce legislation dealing with liability for the supply of defective services. As the proposal stands it is intended to make franchisors and franchisees jointly and severally liable so that a franchisor would be equally liable with the franchisee to those to whom the franchisee provides defective services. It is not known yet whether this proposal will be adopted.

PROPERTY LAWS

Laws affecting real estate and leasehold property vary from territory to territory and what may be permissible in one country may not be in another. In some cases, there may be protection for business tenants and in others there may not be. Careful evaluation has to be made of property laws to see whether the manner in which the franchisor's scheme is structured in his home territory is capable of being repeated in the target territory. If it is not, adjustments may have to be made to take into account the differences and some fundamental rethinking may have to be engaged in. This is particularly the case where franchisors wish to retain the ownership or control of premises.

CONTROLS ON EXPORT OF CURRENCY/LIMITS ON ROYALTY PAYMENTS

Some countries have restrictions on the import and export of currency. It is necessary to ascertain whether such restrictions exist and, if so, what they are. There may be a requirement that consent is obtained from inward investment, and that it is given only subject to certain conditions. These conditions may affect the right of the investor to remit profits in whole or in part. Careful evaluation will have to be made to see how these laws will affect the franchisor's investment.

There is little point in selling know-how and granting rights to others to exercise the right to carry on business under a franchise agreement if it is a profitless exercise for the franchisor, in the sense that he is unable to turn his entitlement to income into cash in his hand except in the target territory where he may have little use for it.

In some territories, usually coupled with the exchange control requirements, there can be limitations imposed on the rate at which royalties are permitted to be paid and whether or not royalties can be paid at all. Certain countries take the view that low-level know-how and trade secrets should not entitle the owner to any royalty income. Some take the view that the royalty income should be limited for a period of time, after which no further charge can be made.

CONTRACT LAWS
The law of contract will differ from country to country. There are different legal systems—the common law system and the civil law system—and even in dealings between countries where the same systems apply, different legislative approaches lead to differences in the legal requirements which have to be considered and taken into account. One cannot assume that contracts can necessarily be entered into on the same basis from one country to another. Great care must be taken before entering into any commitments to ensure that the correct form and procedures are followed.

ZONING/PLANNING LAWS
Careful investigation has to be made into the extent to which there are any restrictions on the use to which premises can be put. Are there any building requirements or building regulations affecting the proposed schemes? This difference can have a marked effect on the operation, the layout of facilities, the availability of suitable premises in the right location and thus the rate at which the franchise network can grow.

It often transpires that when the calculations of growth rate are taken into account, coupled with the difficulty in obtaining situation locations for particular types of business, a completely different financial projection emerges from that which the franchisor originally anticipated. The local regulations in relation to building may require a higher standard of construction than is normally built into the capital requirement projections, and unless a thorough investigation is made of these factors, the franchisor is not in a position to give the right guidance to franchisees or, indeed, to know the extent to which his operation is viable.

EMPLOYMENT LAWS
There are wide variations in employment laws, and a wide range of add-on

costs to the employer, depending upon the degree of social security available in the jurisdiction. There can also be legislation which inhibits the ability of the franchisor or the employer to dismiss staff without being liable for compensation payments. These laws must be assessed and realistic decisions made about how to cope with the differences which exist between territories while keeping the basic business viable.

EXCISE AND DUTIES

The cost (including shipping costs) of importing any materials, equipment and plant and machinery which cannot be obtained locally must be taken into account as well as any excise or other customs duties (including VAT) which may be levied on them in the target territory. This, coupled with the need to make technical changes in equipment to which reference has already been made, may require the franchisor to use locally manufactured products, or products manufactured in a company whose imports to the target territory do not bear excise taxes and custom duties at such a high rate. It is clearly important to include the cost of import and excise taxes and duties, which can be significant in the cost calculations and profit projections.

IMPORT/EXPORT CONTROLS

Some territories have restrictions on what may or may not be imported or exported, and also certain standards may be set which must be achieved before imports are allowed. There may also be quotas limiting how much can be imported from certain countries. The franchisor must be sure that it is possible to import into a target territory whatever he requires. His product requirements in this respect must be capable of meeting the criteria established by the target territory in order to qualify for import, or alternative arrangements must be made.

DECIDING WHETHER OR NOT TO FRANCHISE INTERNATIONALLY

International franchising is not easy, but if done properly for the right reasons and with the availability of the right resources it can, in time, produce positive results. However, many franchisors have made fatal mistakes in overseas operations. These mistakes have not been limited to smaller companies which might be regarded as lacking in experience. Some well-known and successful names in franchising have found, to their cost, just how difficult it can be to transplant their formula with success to another country. There are a number of business and practical issues which have to be considered in coming to the decision to begin franchising internationally.

Firstly, there must be a sound business reason for overseas development. A mere ego trip in order to try to satisfy a craving to be in a position to boast that one is an international franchisor is simply not good enough. There have to be better reasons. For example, is the home market saturated or approaching saturation? Is the franchise so well established in its own country that the time is now propitious to broaden its horizons? Are there market opportunities abroad which present themselves and which are too good to miss?

In the same way as some domestic operations start up as a result of the pressure of interest from those who would like to take up a franchise, many successful franchisors find that they receive approaches from abroad from those who would like to introduce the franchise into their own countries. Such approaches are fine and very flattering, but whether or not one is in a position to accede to them will involve a proper and very thorough evaluation of all the many basic issues. There are, of course, franchises which particularly lend themselves to being operated on an international scale, such as product distribution franchises at retail or wholesale levels, and hotel and car rental firms catering for international business travellers and tourists.

Is the reason or desire to become international in scope merely there in order to be able to claim one is ahead of competitors in the race for growth? Again, as with the ego trip, this can be a dangerous approach, particularly if the other relevant factors are ignored in a wave of blind optimism and an arrogant belief that it would be an easy task to achieve. If the international expansion is not done at the right time or well enough, it can significantly harm the franchisor's domestic operation and also the franchisor's reputation by failure in one or more overseas countries. Considerable harm can be caused to the domestic operation if the international activities create a heavy drain on the franchisor's financial and manpower resources.

In order to franchise successfully overseas, the franchisor must have a sound and successful home base which is sufficiently profitable. The financial position of the franchisor must be secure and he must have resources which are surplus to, or which can exclusively be diverted from, his domestic requirements. He must also have manpower resources available which can be devoted solely to the international operations, and, above all, he must be patient. On the whole, the development of international markets will always take longer and make greater demands on both the financial and manpower resources of the franchisor than is first anticipated, and probably by a surprising margin.

The buildup of the international operation will take time because just as it is strongly advisable to operate pilot outlets in one's own domestic market, it is equally prudent to do so in the target country. This is necessary not only to ascertain whether the business is viable in the new country, but also to fine-tune the operational side to conform to local customs, culture, habits, business practices and laws, and not least to cope with the problems which may arise through the need to use a different language, necessitating the translation and revision of operational manuals and other written material. The issue of pilot operation is dealt with in more detail below. There are other factors which can have an impact and to which consideration must be given.

1. Is the target country one which has a history of political stability? The less stable the political climate, the more difficulties are likely to arise, particularly where there may be controls over the movement of funds, or over the activities of foreign companies in that country.
2. What degree of government control over, or interference with, the normal arm's length negotiating process between the parties can be expected? Will these requirements impose fresh negotiations and a dilution of the franchisor's bargaining power?
3. Are there exchange controls which might limit the amounts of franchise fees or prevent the repatriation of profits, or the remittance of funds? If so, can consents be obtained and will they be honoured over the long term? How long will it take for funds to be remitted? Can one only rely on a steady flow of cash or will it be intermittent? In some countries, funds can even be delayed for which permission to remit does exist. These delays can sometimes be for long periods because the country's central bank does not have adequate foreign currency resources to enable the payments to be made. There are sophisticated methods of barter and counter-trade which can sometimes be used to overcome this problem, but there has to be a reasonable scale of business to justify these types of complex arrangement.
4. Are communications good? As with domestic operations, the speed and effectiveness of communications are an important factor.
5. Many franchise operations rely on what is described as the discretionary spending power of their customers. The product or service supplied is not essential, and customers do not necessarily need to buy it. Here the question of how much money is available in consumers' pockets after they have met their essential living requirements is an important issue.

The franchisor will also have to cope with the provision of training programmes. If he is geared up to provide a high level of training in his own domestic market-place, he will find that he is well placed to extend the programme to cope with the overseas operation. Many consider it invaluable, certainly in the early days, to provide training at the domestic training facility so that an in-depth understanding of the operation can be achieved. It is essential to be sensitive to the requirements and conditions in the target territory.

Finally, and by no means the least important factor, is that the right person or company with whom it would be fitting to be associated has to be found for the target territory. What is surprising is how many companies with significant experience in franchising fail to recognize that this is such a vital matter. In the same way that many franchisors find it difficult to recruit the right people as franchisees and to display the patience which is necessary, so franchisors venturing abroad are confronted with a similar problem, but in a foreign country it is compounded by the fact that they are operating in an unfamiliar environment. There have been many who have made bad choices which could have been avoided had they been patient and exercised the same degree of care in selection as they would have taken in choosing franchisees in their own country.

If the prospect of expanding internationally continues to appeal after considering and evaluating these factors then the various alternative methods available for franchising overseas must be evaluated.

METHODS OF INTERNATIONAL EXPANSION

Having taken the decision to operate in a foreign market, the franchisor then has to consider the method by which such an operation will be established. There are a number of different approaches which are commonly in use. These include:

- a company-owned only operation
- direct franchising
- a branch operation
- a subsidiary company
- a master franchise arrangement
- a joint venture

Each of these options will be examined in turn.

Company-owned operation

In the case of a company-owned operation, the franchisor decides not to franchise in the target territory and instead establishes his own operation. In order to do this, the company would need to have the manpower and financial resources to set up and sustain such an operation. A successful company-owned network would in the future provide the basis for the introduction of franchising should a change of course ultimately be considered more desirable.

Direct franchising

Direct franchising means that the franchisor enters into direct franchise agreement with each individual franchisee, and provides the basic back-up and continuing support. As a technique it is normally limited in scope because the further away the franchisor is from the target territory, the more difficult it becomes to service the franchisees. Very often direct franchising, combined with the establishment of branches or subsidiaries, can provide tax advantages. The use of the direct franchising route also makes the franchisor vulnerable to the possibility that he will fail to recognize the differences which exist between the territory in which the business originated and the target territory. Pilot operations are advisable in order to achieve the transition.

For those intending to do business with or within the European Community it is relevant to consider the effect on such arrangements of the Single European Act, which is aimed at eliminating fully the internal barriers within the European Community by the end of 1992. Although there will be considerable uniformity achieved by the removal of barriers which are physical (e.g. the movement of people and goods), technical (e.g. product specifications, professional qualifications) and fiscal (e.g. harmonization of tax rates), there will remain some vital differences throughout the European Community. These will include:

- language barriers;
- local laws which could impact upon franchising, franchise operations, and agreements, although special industry laws should be standardized;
- cultural and life-style differences;
- the tastes and habits of the nationals of each of the member states will continue to be different;
- national characteristics will not change at all.

The need to adapt the franchise system to local conditions will continue to be essential.

The territorial scale of the European Community may make it more feasible for franchisors to consider the use of area development agreements, which are discussed in Chapter 13.

Branch operation

A branch operation may be established in any of the following circumstances:

- the franchisor may be operating his own outlets;
- the franchisor franchises direct into the target territory and has established a branch operation to service franchisees; or
- the branch has been established as a regional base to provide services to franchisees within the region.

The business decision as to whether or not a branch should be established may well be more affected by fiscal or legal considerations than the business need to have a presence in the territory. These considerations may as an alternative lead the franchisor to follow the next course available to him, the establishment of a subsidiary.

Subsidiary company

The establishment of a subsidiary company may fulfil any of the following four functions:

1. The franchisor who is franchising directly from his domestic territory into the target territory will use the subsidiary to service franchisees.
2. The franchisor may grant master franchise rights to the subsidiary and the subsidiary will either open its own operations or sub-franchise, or both.
3. The subsidiary may be involved with a joint venture partner.
4. The subsidiary may be used as a regional base, either to provide services to sub-franchisees, or sub-franchisors in the region.

The service which the branch or subsidiary would provide would be similar in nature to those provided by the franchisor and would cover the whole range of franchisor services, including, as the network develops, a training facility.

Master franchise arrangement

The sub-franchisor will usually have the exclusive right for a whole country either to open his own outlets or to sub-franchise, or do both. The sub-franchisor in essence stands in the shoes of the franchisor in the territory and is to all intents and purposes the franchisor of the system in the territory. As is always the case, there are advantages and pitfalls. The franchisor has to consider the following basic pitfalls to which reference has already been made.

1. The difficulties in identifying and selecting the right person or company as a sub-franchisor.
2. The need to have a strong home base to sustain the demands which will be made upon the franchisor.
3. The diversion of manpower and financial resources from domestic operations. It should be emphasized that it will always take more people and cost more money than anticipated.
4. The time factor: it will also always take much longer than one anticipates.

The other advantages and pitfalls to be considered include the following.

1. The franchisor has only one entity with which to deal with in the target territory. All his dealings will be with the sub-franchisor and he will not be concerned in day-to-day direct dealings with the sub-franchisees who operate the outlet. The similarity with domestic operations where the franchisor is not concerned with the day-to-day problems of the franchisee's operations is not coincidental. However, the franchisor must not ignore the sub-franchisees—they are the life-blood of the network and the quality of their operations will either bring credit to the business or harm its reputation.

2. The quality of the sub-franchisor's services in the selection and training of sub-franchisees, site selection, and all the other services he provides to his sub-franchisees is vital. The franchisor needs to be satisfied that these services are of the requisite standard, and he must have an interest in ensuring the quality of the ongoing controls and the supervision of standards. The neglect of these areas will mean that the franchisor will find himself with a sub-franchisor whose agreement will probably have to be terminated and a troublesome substandard network of sub-franchisees to be coped with. The maintenance of standards and the control of the quality of the network's operations is crucial and at the same time difficult to maintain.

3. The franchisor should make some effort to attend sub-franchisee gatherings and encourage foreign sub-franchisees to attend the franchisee gatherings in his domestic market. This form of contact, together with the regular 'quality control' visits, which he should undertake, will demonstrate to the sub-franchisees that the franchisor is indeed interested in them and that they are part of the global network and family of franchisees. The franchisor, however, should never permit himself to usurp the functions of the sub-franchisor so long as the sub-franchisor is running the operation correctly. There is a balance which has to be maintained.

4. In the same way as the franchisor operating in the domestic market expands his network using the resources of the franchisees so does the franchisor under the master franchise agreement. Indeed, the franchisor does so at two levels instead of one. In the first place, the sub-franchisor will be required to provide the financial resources to establish and exploit the system in the target territory. Whatever financial resources are needed to establish the system and operate it, they will have to be found by the sub-franchisor. The franchisor will require the sub-franchisor to demonstrate his financial capabilities before entering into the master franchise. Additionally there will be the second tier of financial and manpower resources, which are

contributed by the sub-franchisees who are operating the trading outlets.

5. The sub-franchisor should be making his own financial calculations to see whether he considers the proposition to be financially worthwhile. There is some discussion below about pilot operations which are necessary, but suffice it to say that decisions will have to be taken during the course of the negotiations as to the nature and extent of pilot operations, as well as what contribution will be made to their establishment by each of the parties. The sub-franchisor will be responsible for the recruitment of staff for the pilot operations, as well as for the establishment of the sub-franchisor's own business organization.

6. The arrangement encourages the blending of the franchisor's developed system with local conditions by the application of the sub-franchisor's local knowledge. This sort of knowledge cannot be acquired sufficiently quickly by a 'visitor' to the target territory. The local businessman will have the basic knowledge of local business practices, legal issues, banking and financial sources, and will know, or be able more quickly to identify, companies in the territory which would be suitable as suppliers to the network.

7. In the same way as a franchisor in a domestic operation will earn less in cash terms from a franchised outlet than he will from an operational outlet, so is the case with master franchising when the fee income available from the sub-franchisees is divided between franchisor and sub-franchisor. The sub-franchisor will be charging franchise fees to his sub-franchisees and from these fees he will not only have to finance his own operations, but also to make a payment to the franchisor. What that fee will be, and how it is calculated, will be a matter for negotiation. It is unlikely that the fee charged to sub-franchisees in the target territory will differ much from that charged to franchisees in the franchisor's domestic territory so the amount available to be shared will be limited. There is a discussion of this issue below.

8. Mention has already been made of the vulnerability of the franchisor to any fall in standards of the network run by the sub-franchisor. The franchisor must, therefore, develop a strategy for the establishment and maintenance of the correct quality standards. This will be achieved by the quality of the sub-franchisee selection criteria, initial and continuing training, and through a contractual framework supported by inspection visits, sanctions and general alertness.

9. The problems which arise when the franchisor reaches the point where he has no alternative but to terminate a master franchise agreement are many and varied. It is likely in such circumstances that the franchisor will inherit problems because termination will either

result from the sub-franchisor having done his job badly, or because he is not doing very well financially, and in either case he will have neglected the network. Franchisees always find a change of ownership troubling, but often in a master franchise arrangement there are mixed feelings. On the one hand, the sub-franchisees are pleased that the franchisor (the 'fountain' of all knowledge and innovation so far as the system is concerned) has taken over the reins, but, on the other hand, there will inevitably be a feeling that perhaps it should have been done sooner and that the franchisees have in some way been let down. The franchisees may also have developed feelings of hostility and resentment which will take a lot of careful handling and an outstanding performance by the franchisor before they are overcome.

Joint venture

It is not the purpose of this chapter to consider the advantages and disadvantages of joint venture arrangements, but only the issues which are particularly relevant to franchising. The franchisor who enters into a joint venture will still find that many of the problems we have discussed will exist. The need to identify and do a deal with the right person is just as much of a problem. But there is more to it than that. The franchisor will have to negotiate what share he wishes to take up and decide how he will finance his contribution. The joint venture company will become the sub-franchisor of the franchisor's system. In some instances, the franchisor's contribution to the share of the joint venture will take the place of the front-end fee normally payable, and on occasions the front-end fee is paid, but returned in whole or part by the franchisor to the joint venture as his contribution. Sometimes a value is placed on the services and/or know-how provided by the franchisor and this value is taken as the measure of the franchisor's contributions to the capital of the joint venture.

The joint venture company will help the franchisor establish the system in the target territory on a shared basis, with the local partner operating under a master franchise agreement. The franchisor will find that he has become involved in the risk of operational losses which he would otherwise have avoided. He will also find that there is much scope for disagreement on operational matters with joint venture partners who will resent the fact that the master franchise agreement will give the franchisor (a joint venture partner) the last word on many issues. This highlights the two roles which the franchisor has in this type of arrangement and which create scope for friction in the relationship.

Finally, the franchisor who is confronted with a buy-out situation, or the need to terminate the joint venture, or the master franchise agreement, will find himself in a potentially difficult position. The joint venture partner will be established in the territory and in operational control, and unless the franchisor has a presence in the territory, or the ability rapidly to put the right person in position (which will be rare), he will be at a considerable disadvantage in trying to take over the operation. It is infinitely more difficult to divest oneself of an unsatisfactory joint venture partner than it is to terminate a sub-franchisor (not that the latter is an easy option). To have to face the prospect of coping with both at the same time is something to contemplate long and hard.

MASTER FRANCHISE AGREEMENTS

Before considering the provisions which one can expect to find in an international master franchise agreement, it is necessary to delineate the functions of the parties and purposes of the transaction as well as the consequential requirements. The master franchise agreement reflects the commercial bargain which has been struck by the franchisor with the sub-franchisor to:

- introduce the franchisor's system to the target territory;
- evaluate the viability of the system in the target territory;
- equip the sub-franchisor to become the franchisor in the target territory;
- develop the growth of the system in the target territory at an agreed pace and within an agreed time schedule; and
- result in the sub-franchisor providing the full range of the franchisor's on-going services to sub-franchisees in the target territory.

In these transactions the aspirations of the parties and balance of negotiating power will vary from case to case as will the skill, financial resources, knowledge and experience of the prospective sub-franchisor.

Negotiations of these agreements are prone to failure for the following reasons.

1. The franchisor overvalues the initial fee by requiring the payment of a sum which bears no resemblance to the reality of the prospects for the business or the value of the services and know-how which are being provided.
2. The franchisor requires payment of too high a proportion of the continuing franchise fees which the operation of the system will generate in the target territory.
3. The prospective sub-franchisor (and this is particularly the case where a large company is involved) cannot come to terms with the conceptual issues involved in franchising and the controls to which he

will inevitably be subjected. Whatever the nature of the agreement, the fundamentals of franchising do not change and cannot be compromised however much of a culture shock it may be for the prospective sub-franchisor.

4. The prospective sub-franchisor has underestimated the capital cost and the time frame involved before the operation will generate profits.

5. The franchisor will not accept the need to consider if, how, and to what extent the system and operational manuals require adjustment to the business, legal and other relevant factors (including the market realities) which are to be found in the target territory.

Structure of the master franchise agreement

The master franchise agreement will have to accommodate the issues which the commercial discussion will have confronted. In many of these issues, there is no such thing as the right answer since these agreements, unlike unit agreements, are all negotiated on a case-by-case basis. However, the fundamental principles must remain, as is the case throughout all franchise transactions. It is necessary to emphasize, yet again, that in structuring these arrangements the fundamental features, characteristics and requirements of a franchise transaction must be maintained. Once the integrity of the franchised concept and the system is undermined the future development of the franchise is put at risk.

The main issues to be dealt with in negotiating and preparing master franchise agreements are:

(a) The rights to be granted.
(b) The term of the agreement.
(c) Territory.
(d) Initiating the sub-franchisor.
(e) Exclusivity.
(f) Performance schedule.
(g) Franchise fees (including exchange controls).
(h) Withholding taxes, and gross-up provisions.
(i) Advertising.
(j) Training.
(k) Trademarks and other industrial and intellectual property rights.
(l) Sale of the business.
(m) Protection against misuse of know-how and unfair competition.
(n) Default issues.
(o) Choice of law and venue selection.

Each of these subjects is examined in turn.

THE RIGHTS TO BE GRANTED
These will always include the use of the franchisor's trademarks, service marks, trade names, know-how, confidential information, copyright material and all the usual elements which one finds in franchise transactions. The nature, extent of the rights, and the obligations attached to them are dealt with separately below.

THE TERM OF THE AGREEMENT
The term of the agreement does not usually present too many problems, although there have been draft agreements with what is clearly an unrealistic 5-year term proposed. Since the nature of the transaction involves establishing the sub-franchisor as the franchisor in the target territory with a corresponding investment, the longer the term, the greater the opportunity to develop the territory properly. With a 5-year term, in many cases a sub-franchisor would have a shorter term available to him than the sub-franchisees would expect. This is clearly unworkable.

The clauses in the contract which will deal with these issues will have to recognize and cope with the problems involved in the grant by the sub-franchisor of a longer term to sub-franchisees than the sub-franchisor has left under his agreement. If the problem is not considered and dealt with, the sub-franchisees may find that their agreement is terminated by operation of law because the sub-franchisor's agreement has come to an end. This can happen sooner rather than later if the sub-franchise agreements are for a 10-year term since any sub-franchise agreement granted after 15 years where the master franchise agreement is for 25 years will create a problem unless the issue is dealt with properly in the master franchise agreement. The more realistic terms are from 25 to 50 years with rights of renewal.

Assuming that it is agreed that the sub-franchisor should have a right of renewal there will be the normal issues to consider. In what circumstances should the right of renewal be denied? On what terms should it be granted? Will there be scope for the franchisor to introduce changes, particularly bearing in mind the likely time-scale since the original document was entered into? If so, on what basis can that be done? Will any charge be made for the extended rights which are to be granted and if so how will the charge be calculated? Leaving negotiation to the time the right is exercised could effectively leave the sub-franchisor with no rights at all since if the charge cannot be agreed there could be no contract. What will be provided for as the ongoing development schedule? How will one cope with changes in the method of exploitation of the franchised business?, e.g. one could find larger regional franchise units with satellite operations instead of smaller stand-alone units. This would have an effect on the number of outlets which are required to be opened and kept in operation, even though turnover may be enhanced.

TERRITORY

As is the case with operators of individual units who seek the comfort of territorial rights, most sub-franchisors also seek the widest possible territorial rights. In fixing the extent of the territory to be exploited by the sub-franchisor, regard clearly has to be paid to the franchisor's overall inter-national marketing strategy and how each of the individual sub-franchisors will fit into the pattern of that strategy.

Ideally, the territory should be one in which the sub-franchisor has the knowledge, experience and capacity to cope. One of the reasons for master franchise agreements is to have the sub-franchisor stand in the shoes of the franchisor in relation to the market-place. It somewhat defeats the objective of the exercise if territories are granted of such a nature and/or extent that the sub-franchisor is not capable of achieving proper exploitation. The question of exploitation and the degree of exploitation will be dealt with later in this chapter.

Care should be taken not to add on a nearby territory merely because the sub-franchisor wants it. The exploitation by one sub-franchisor of more than one territory may not be a sensible arrangement and should be avoided. This has been the case in Australasia where the Australian sub-franchisors com-monly ask for the rights to New Zealand to be included and often succeed in obtaining them. However, New Zealand tends to be treated as the poor relation. The country is a long way from Australia. It is a different market and it is likely to be neglected.

INITIATING THE SUB-FRANCHISOR

The sub-franchisor is being trained to be the 'franchisor' in the territory. This will mean that the franchisor will have to provide a range of services to enable the sub-franchisor to undertake that role. There are probably two categories of services in addition to training.

1. Evaluation of the piloting and the adaption of the system to the territory.
2. The services which enable the sub-franchisor to become established and to operate the system.

Each will be considered in turn.

Evaluating the piloting and adapting the system

The franchisor must be sufficiently receptive to other ideas and face up to the need to recognize that there are differences. They may be slight; they may be subtle; they may not affect the actual operational procedures within the unit, but they will be real. They are likely to be people-related: attitudes will be different; social and cultural attitudes may have an effect. The ultimate outcome may not result in the franchisor compromising the way in which the basic business is operated. Changes may have to be made in marketing methods, staff recruitment, training, management and accounting, procedures and methods.

There may be different business flows during the course of the opening hours. This could result in the outlet being busy in the target territory at different times of the day from those which are most popular in the original territory. This may mean that not enough business flow is generated overall to make the business in its current form a viable proposition. Experimentation will be needed in order to resolve the problems and gear up the business to be successful in the target territory.

All franchisors will use the existing operating manual as their starting point. How much change will be necessary will depend upon the nature, range and scope which the manual covers. If, for example, it deals in detail with the hiring and firing of staff with an explanation of the legal issues and procedure, this section will need to be changed for use in the target territory. Terminology will have to be changed as well as other features where the pilot operation has shown the need to do so.

After the initial shock to the franchisor and his system has been overcome, it will be necessary for both franchisor and sub-franchisor to liaise in regard to the future development of the system in the target territory. The franchisor's development of his system in the territory will have to be shared with the sub-franchisor; the sub-franchisor's response and input must all be considered and appropriate changes introduced. The franchisor will always wish to retain control over whatever changes are made to the manuals and system in the target territory. The franchisor will also require that the ownership of the manuals and the system are retained by him. The manuals may have to be translated into the language of the target territory. The responsibility for doing this and bearing the cost must be agreed upon; the franchisor must also secure ownership of the copyright in the translation.

The provisions in the contract have to be drafted to allow sufficient flexibility to:

- leave the franchisor with control, but
- provide for the co-operation to allow the business to develop as the years pass.

Part of this aspect of the matter will include developing the operational franchise agreement into which the sub-franchisor will enter with sub-franchisees. Normally, the franchisor will start with the form he uses in his domestic operations and try to keep to it as far as possible. This is often not possible since legal systems differ, as do the terminology and the approach adopted to certain issues, e.g. corporate law, real estate law.

The important issue for many franchisors is to ensure that contractual requirements can, in substance, be enforced in the target territory. The franchisor will always want to have ultimate control over the form and text of the operational agreements which are so crucial in protecting his name, trademarks, service marks, know-how and systems. The franchisor will also wish to have confidence in the operational agreements he may inherit on termination.

The services which enable the sub-franchisor to become established and to operate the system

These services are important to the arrangement for without them the sub-franchisor would not be able to maximize the benefits to be obtained from the franchisor's experience. The areas in which the sub-franchisor will need assistance will include the following:

1. Site assessment, evaluation and choice. The franchisor will not have the detailed knowledge in the target territory of premises and the market which is possessed by the sub-franchisor, but he will know the type and size of premises required for the concept's equipment and furnishings. There will also be some common criteria for the evaluation of sites.
2. Providing the sub-franchisor with operational assistance:
    *   in developing the pilot operation for the commencement of the business; and
    *   on an on-going basis to help monitor performance and offer advice.
3. The preparation of criteria for the selection of sub-franchisees. The franchisor cannot expect to be involved in the recruitment and selection of sub-franchisees, but he may have some valuable guidance to offer to the sub-franchisor.
4. The selection and approval of the right suppliers may be an important feature of the franchise. Indeed, if the franchisor has products for which a proprietary specification exists or there are secret formulae the franchisor will have to grant rights to manufacturers to produce the products to the franchisor's specifications and to enable the franchisor's trademark to be affixed.
5. The provision of marketing, promotional and advertising materials used in the territory of origin which may be useful in the target territory.
6. Access to the ongoing research and development which the franchisor may be conducting.

7. The ability to participate in franchise seminars and get-togethers organized by the franchisor.
8. Training in how to be the franchisor in the territory.

Not only would these services be provided but frequently there is a requirement that there should be a managing director or general manager who must have a minimum equity stake in the business of the sub-franchisor. The franchisor will not only want to be satisfied with the quality of the sub-franchisor's management but also its commitment through equity participation. The managing director or general manager and their successors would also have to be approved by the franchisor and would be required successfully to complete the franchisor's training programme. The sub-franchisor will also be required to establish a proper business structure to ensure that he is in a position to provide the right degree of supervision and control as well as the secure proper reporting and the payment of sums due to the franchisor.

EXCLUSIVITY

Most sub-franchisors would wish to have exclusive rights to the territory which is allocated to them. This enables them to invest with the comfort of knowing that they are investing in a market in which they will be the sole exploiters of the opportunity. Exclusivity is normally tied to performance criteria and can be lost if these criteria are not met. This can lead to practical problems if one has a network which is being developed by a sub-franchisor who fails after a period of time to meet the performance schedules.

The consequences of such failure need to be carefully thought through. Many sub-franchisors would consider the franchisor to be behaving extremely unfairly if the whole contract were to be terminated. Many might say that loss of exclusive rights merely because there is perhaps a temporary hiccup, which can be attributed to economic circumstances or unavailability of suitable premises, is a harsh and unjust outcome.

Terms can sometimes be negotiated to provide for a sub-franchisor who expresses these concerns to make payments to the franchisor to compensate him for the loss of the revenues by the non-achievement of the performance schedule in cases where the sub-franchisor wishes to preserve his position. This method is only a temporary expedient and does not necessarily compensate the franchisor for the fact that there has been a loss of impetus, unless, of course, it can be recovered later.

In practical terms, the mere loss of exclusivity without the loss of the continuing right to grant further sub-franchises could result in parallel networks being operated—one by the sub-franchisor, and the other by the franchisor or by another sub-franchisor (recruited by the franchisor to replace the one in default). The loss of exclusivity would also create additional problem areas.

1. The sub-franchisor so affected would be significantly demotivated. There will no longer be the incentives to continue to develop the network since for all practical purposes it will have reached its peak with no prospect of further expansion.
2. There will be problems when a sub-franchisee has need to relocate because his lease has come to an end or because trading conditions require a move. Relocation may bring conflict with a sub-franchisee of the successor sub-franchisor.
3. How will the issue of the renewal of a sub-franchisee's agreement be dealt with?
4. If the sub-franchisor has become involved in the property chain he could be in a position to harm the sub-franchisees' interests and their future development.
5. The sub-franchisor will inevitably reduce the level of 'franchisor' services to his sub-franchisees which will harm the franchisor's name and goodwill and any subsequently appointed sub-franchisor and his sub-franchisees.

In short there will be a mess which should be avoided by addressing the issue and not limiting termination to a mere loss of exclusivity. The totality of the arrangements and the possible implications must be reviewed and the franchisor's branding, goodwill and system put first so that sub-franchisees will emerge with a proper structure and support.

PERFORMANCE SCHEDULE

The agreement of a performance schedule which sets out the projected annual and cumulative rates of growth of the network in the targeted territory is a common feature of these agreements. Indeed, without it, the franchisor would not have the confidence that the commitment exists which can result in the proper exploitation of the territory. Unless a sub-franchisor is prepared to accept a realistic performance schedule for the establishment of operational units, the master franchise route can lose some of its attractions for a franchisor. The performance schedule is obviously of great importance where exclusive rights are granted because this is the franchisor's insurance policy against under-exploitation.

There are practical difficulties in establishing performance schedules. It may not be possible at the time the contract is being negotiated to have an accurate idea, or sufficiently accurate knowledge, to enable the parties to judge what would be an achievable rate of expansion. What is certain is that the franchisor's expectations are likely to be on the high side, while those of the sub-franchisor will be on the low side. However, most sub-franchisors will prepare business plans in the process of deciding whether or not to take the opportunity on board and these must include some assessment of the growth rate which the business is capable of achieving. Otherwise, the sub-franchisor would not be able to make a balanced business judgement about whether or not to go into the proposition, and the level of resources which would need to be committed to it.

The experience of the market-place obtained from the pilot operations can determine whether the development schedule which has been established will be effective, or whether it is in need of change by mutual agreement to reflect the reality which has become apparent. Indeed, the sub-franchisor may conclude that he does not wish to continue in the light of the results obtained in the market-place from the pilot operations. The master franchise agreement has to be sufficiently flexible to accommodate the practical realization of the parties' understanding and agreement of what is achievable based upon experience.

How the parties initially come into contact with each other will also have a bearing on the negotiations as there are many instances in which the prospective sub-franchisor, having seen a business in another country, makes a judgement that the concept will undoubtedly succeed in his own country and subsequently approaches the franchisor for the master franchise rights. Such enthusiasm by the prospective sub-franchisor should not lead to the franchisor accepting him without question. There are many who are prepared to take this sort of initiative but who following careful patient evaluation will prove unsuitable. There cannot be any relaxation in selection standards which must be set and maintained at a high level.

It is important that the terms of the contract should fairly reflect the reality of the market-place, and that the terms which are agreed are those with which the parties are comfortable and which will make them feel that the arrangement is equitable.

FRANCHISE FEES

Front-end fees
One of the most difficult questions to come to terms with in the negotiation of a master franchise agreement is how much should the franchisor receive for:

- the grant of the rights;
- the transfer of know-how; and
- setting up the sub-franchisor in the territory.

If this was an easy question to answer, it would not cause the problems with which one is so often confronted. Indeed, there are many franchisors whose expectations are such that any would-be sub-franchisors are frightened off. The author is aware of a significant number of such cases. There are also instances in which unrealistic figures have been agreed only to be resented by the sub-franchisor when he realizes that he cannot make money at all, or at least sufficiently quickly to justify the high level of the initial cost. This leads inevitably to conflict and harm to, if not a breakdown of, the relationship.

It seems that there are a number of factors which could be taken into account when trying to calculate what would be a proper level of front-end charge by a franchisor. The degree of importance to be attached to each will differ from country to country, depending upon the practices to be found in each. The factors are given below.

1. The actual cost to the franchisor of dealing with the sub-franchisor; setting him up; and proving or assisting in proving that the concept works within the target territory.
2. How much it would cost, and how long it would take the sub-franchisor to acquire the requisite know-how and skills to operate a similar business in his territory.
3. The value of the territory as estimated by the franchisor based upon the projected number of units which could be established.
4. The estimated aggregate amount of the initial franchise fees which could be charged by the sub-franchisor to his sub-franchisees in the development of the network.

Franchisors who are based in those countries where high initial fees are charged to franchisees tend to have much higher expectations under the latter two factors, and therefore demand far more than may be considered realistic in the targeted territory. As the medium- to long-term interests of the franchisor probably are best served by having well-motivated and successful sub-franchisors this type of attitude has to be reconsidered.

The first two factors are probably the more sensible avenues of approach. The timing of payments may differ, and in some cases an agreement of a sensible up-front figure may enable the parties to agree some sort of split of the initial franchise fees which are received from the sub-franchisees as they are established.

Continuing fees (royalties)

These are normally calculated on the aggregate amount of the gross network sales to the ultimate consumer. The level at which they are fixed obviously has to provide the franchisor with a good economic reason to be involved, but it must be appreciated that these payments represent a straight deduction from the gross income of the sub-franchisor, and that if they are too high, the sub-franchisor will not be able to run his business profitably. In such circumstances, the network will not be given the proper support and cannot succeed and the franchisor will be presented with problems and conflict rather than an income flow.

One often sees an initial presentation by franchisors (who operate their domestic operation on, say, a 5 or 6% fee to their own unit operators) in which they ask for a 3 or 4% fee from the sub-franchisor. That sub-franchisor in market terms may not be able to charge more than 5 or 6% to his sub-franchisees. Indeed, if he were to be receiving an income based on that sort of percentage, and there was no involvement by the franchisor, he would be able to run a very viable and profitable business. However, if he loses 60–80% of his gross income to the franchisor, he is doomed to failure.

The financial effect on the network of establishing fees has to be very carefully thought through. Proper financial projections must be prepared to demonstrate the effect which the level of fees payable by the sub-franchisor would have on the viability of his business and the benefits to the franchisor. Sometimes one sees arrangements where there is a variation in the level of fees as the amount of the total gross network sales rises.

The method of making payments also has to be carefully related to the way in which the sub-franchisor will be dealing with sub-franchisees. For example, if sub-franchisees pay their fees monthly by the tenth day of the month, an obligation on the sub-franchisor to make payments to the franchisor monthly on the tenth day of the month would not be possible. Yet one frequently encounters provisions of that nature in contracts. The payment periods and accounting periods at both levels must tie in with each other.

Another question to be considered is whether the sub-franchisor is to be responsible for paying franchisee fees to the franchisor whether or not the sub-franchisor has been paid by his sub-franchisees. This will be a subject for negotiation but the franchisor's view will be that he should not share the sub-franchisor's credit risks with his sub-franchisees. There should always be a provision requiring the sub-franchisor to ensure that sub-franchisees observe and perform the terms of sub-franchise agreements which would mean that a failure by the sub-franchisor to collect fees and financial reports would be a breach of contract. In practical terms, a defaulting and non-paying sub-franchisee will not only not be paying fees, but will also probably not be submitting returns of gross sales, which, of course, will mean that no-one will know what should be remitted. A formula can be written into the contract to cope with such a situation.

Exchange controls
There may be exchange control requirements to be complied with in some countries. The mere fact that exchange control permission has been obtained does not necessarily mean that payments can be made with any degree of regularity because payments can be delayed administratively by the country's central bank when it assesses the total outflow of funds from the country during any particular month.

The franchisor considering the establishment of a bank account in the territory into which the sub-franchisor should make payments must ensure the quick flow and availability of funds as the international banking system does not always move funds as rapidly as one might wish. It is not unknown for payments to take an inordinate time to travel from bank A in country X to bank B in country Y.

The franchisor will invariably stipulate the currency in which he wishes payment to be made. In most cases franchisors prefer payment to be in their own currency. This requires the establishment in the agreement of a conversion date, and it is also sensible to identify which bank's quoted rate will be used for conversion on that date, so that there is a proper method for the franchisor to check that the right amount of currency has been remitted. Provision will usually be made for the cost of remittance and conversion to be borne by the sub-franchisor. If by reason of exchange controls, currency conversion cannot take place, provision should be made in the agreement to establish the alternative action to be taken.

Bearing in mind the long-term nature of these contracts, provisions are often inserted to allow for the possible introduction of exchange controls, as the mere fact that a country has no controls at the time when the contract is negotiated does not mean that at some time during the ensuing period of the contract such controls will not be introduced.

WITHHOLDING TAXES, AND GROSS-UP PROVISIONS

In dealing with the payment provisions in the contract, the way in which the payments will be treated and characterized for tax purposes in both the franchisor's country and the target territory should be considered. Any double-taxation agreement which exists should also be examined to ensure that if the franchisor wishes to receive payments which are free of withheld tax, this can be achieved. Provision should be made in the contract to enable the franchisor to obtain the benefit of any double-taxation agreement by the provision of evidence of payment in the target country in such form as may be necessary to enable the relief to be claimed.

Some franchisors insert gross-up provisions in their contracts which provide that if tax is deductible, effectively it has to be borne by the sub-franchisor by increasing his payment to the franchisor so that the franchisor receives the amount net, which he would have received had there been no deduction. The effect of such a provision is to increase the level of fees payable by the sub-franchisor as he is effectively paying the franchisor's tax liability on the payments which are remitted to him. This would be a cost which would not be recoverable from the franchise network, and if a sub-franchisor is forced into accepting such a provision, then the sub-franchisor should check his projections and cash-flow forecasts to ensure that this additional burden does not make the proposition unacceptable.

ADVERTISING

It is likely that the operational agreements will deal with advertising and promotion in the usual fashion. The sub-franchisor will obviously have to be in a position to meet his obligations under such a provision.

The international dimension with the ultimate control resting with the franchisor will mean that the sub-franchisor cannot do or permit to be done any advertising by sub-franchisees unless it has been approved by the franchisor. The arrangements do not need to be cumbersome, but they need to be carefully considered so that they are practical and capable of being operated effectively in practice without causing any unnecessary delays and inconvenience to the sub-franchisor or sub-franchisees. In some cases, where international advertising can have a value for the network (e.g. car hire, hotels), the allocation of part of the advertising contributions for international promotional marketing and advertising activities can be beneficial to the network.

TRAINING

The degree of training support will vary from case to case. However, many franchisors find it sensible, particularly in the early stages, to ensure that both the sub-franchisor's staff, and the sub-franchisees and their staff, are trained at the franchisor's domestic training facility. There are many who find that the quality of training and the absorption of the franchisor's philosophy and style at the domestic base just cannot be reproduced and, even though there have to be changes made to accommodate local requirements, this quality of training and exposure to the original concept is essential.

One would expect that the contract would contain the details of how, and how many of, the sub-franchisor's team will be trained and for them to be identified by their job description. In appropriate cases, it may be that the franchisor will provide an opening crew for the first few outlets and will provide on-site training for the sub-franchisor's staff. The sub-franchisor and his sub-franchisees would be expected to pay all their expenses relating to getting to and from the training site, and their subsistence and other expenses during the course of the training.

The sort of training resources which the franchisor considers have to be made available for a successful launch of the business in the target territory will have a bearing on the level of the initial fee to be charged to the sub-franchisor. The intensity of training and support which is given during the piloting stage in the target territory can, in some cases, be quite high. The agreement would also provide for the sub-franchisor to establish his own training facilities in the course of time, and for the franchisor to provide the necessary back-up and training aids to enable this to be done.

TRADEMARKS AND OTHER INDUSTRIAL AND INTELLECTUAL PROPERTY RIGHTS

These issues are discussed above.

SALE OF THE BUSINESS

The master franchise agreement will have to contain provisions dealing with the basis upon which the agreement may be assigned and the sub-franchisor's business sold. The basic principles are the same as those which apply to the sale of a franchised business by a sub-franchisee. However, there are some differences in detail because the level of investment will inevitably be much greater, and the skills which the purchaser will require will not be the same as those which are required for the day-to-day operation of a franchised unit.

A purchaser of a sub-franchisor's business will not only have to demonstrate his financial capacity, but also his ability to understand the franchise system and to manage the business of a sub-franchisor. The criteria to be applied should be specified as should any conditions which are considered appropriate. One should bear in mind the possibility that an interested purchaser could be a competitor. The purchaser might also be a large company which is wishing to expand and diversify its business. In these circumstances, special considerations may have to be given as to how the franchisor's know-how and confidential information can be confirmed to the franchised business, and not made available elsewhere within the purchaser's organization, or group of companies.

On the takeover of the business, it may be necessary to impose training and approval requirements on the purchaser as well as for the appointment of a managing director or a general manager for which provision should be made in the agreement.

PROTECTION AGAINST MISUSE OF KNOW-HOW AND UNFAIR COMPETITION
These issues are discussed above.

DEFAULT ISSUES
Of prime concern to the franchisor will be the degree to which the sub-franchisor monitors and controls the quality and standards which are achieved by his sub-franchisees. One must not lose sight of the fact that the sub-franchisees are trading, using the franchisor's know-how and systems, and are benefiting from the goodwill associated with his trademark/service mark/trade name. It is the franchisor who is running the risk of events occurring which are adverse to his interests. The sub-franchisor is the custodian of those interests in his territory. Provision should be made in the agreement for the policing of those standards, but if all else fails, the franchisor must have remedies. These would obviously be built around default provisions in the contract.

One often finds attempts are made to introduce into contracts working formulae using expressions such as 'material or substantial defaults', but these are often difficult to interpret. What a franchisor regards as 'material or substantial' a sub-franchisor may regard as not being so 'material or substantial', and how a court would determine the dispute could be open to question. It seems far better, therefore, if one is to use an expression, such as 'material default', to have a precise definition which may, for example, describe it as any default under the agreement of which the franchisor has given notice to the sub-franchisor requiring it to be remedied to cure and which remains unremedied after a fixed period of time, which may be as much as 30 or 60 days. Money defaults may be treated more seriously with a shorter period of notice. Quality control default may need a longer period in order for the default to be put right because it may involve enforcing rights against another.

The failure by the sub-franchisor to ensure that his sub-franchisees comply with the terms of their contracts is a serious issue, but one which may, depending on its nature, require reasonable time and careful handling to secure compliance. The problems may also not best be solved by requiring the sub-franchisee to undertake legal proceedings. The solution of operational problems leading to a lowering of standards can often be dealt with by direct discussion and persuasion, rather than by resorting to law. The parties must acknowledge that there are a wide range of methods available to cope with these problems. Ultimately, of course, the franchisor must be able to bring matters to a head to protect his interests and the integrity of his industrial and intellectual property rights.

There will, as in most commercial agreements, be provision for termination in the event of insolvency, bankruptcy or liquidation. The consequences of termination are usually drastic. In brief terms, one would expect that the sub-franchisor will lose the right to continue; will have to de-identify his business premises; and be bound by effective post-term restraints on competition and the use of the franchisor's know-how. There are other considerations, of which one of the most important is, what is to happen to the network of sub-franchisees?

1. Will their contracts survive the termination of the sub-franchisor's contract?
2. If so, will the franchisor be entitled to take them over?
3. Will the franchisor be obliged to take them over?
4. Will the sub-franchisor be able to make a virtue out of termination and claim payment of a sum of money by way of compensation for 'the takeover of his business'?
5. Will the franchisor, now that he has terminated the sub-franchisor for good cause, want to take over what could be a badly run network of disgruntled sub-franchisees, who are intent on making difficulties, and be faced with considerable expense to put the business right? Rather than the sub-franchisor expecting to be paid something (as mentioned above), should he, on the contrary, be liable to pay the franchisor for the costs the latter will have to face in coping with the problems which he will inherit?
6. What is to happen to any property (including leases), which the sub-

franchisor has acquired for leasing or sub-leasing to the sub-franchisees, and which may have a capital value which the franchisor cannot afford to pay? This can create difficulties which arise from the integrated structure of the sub-franchise arrangements.

Another issue is whether the master franchise agreement should terminate as a whole if the development schedule is not maintained. This issue has been discussed above.

Should the sub-franchisor be entitled to terminate the franchise agreement if the franchisor is in material default of his obligations, or becomes bankrupt or is put into liquidation? If so, what should be the consequences for the sub-franchisor and his network? Should the sub-franchisor be entitled to continue as before, using to the full the franchisor's industrial and intellectual property rights, including the name and know-how, and, if so, on what basis? Is it right that the sub-franchisor may have to run the risk of losing his business when the franchisor is at fault, whether the fault arises voluntarily or involuntarily?

The issues are many and varied, and the list which is given is far from complete, but will serve to indicate the complexity of this particular subject.

CHOICE OF LAW AND VENUE SELECTION

All contracts should specify the law which is to be applied to the contract, and the venue for the resolution of disputes. Consideration should also be given to whether the parties wish to have disputes referred, or capable of being referred, to arbitration or the growing practice of mediation. So far as choice of law is concerned, there are some jurisdictions in the world where one might not feel comfortable with the local laws or legal systems, but, invariably, the ultimate sanctions which would have to be brought under any contract against the sub-franchisee would have to be taken in the country in which the business was being conducted. Although there are contrary views, on the whole one should tend to select the law of the country where the sub-franchisor will be conducting his business.

There are other considerations in making this choice. Most courts will not enforce 'public policy issues' provisions in accordance with foreign laws. Restrictive covenants, competition law and exchange controls are the type of provisions which fall into this category. The treatment of the intellectual and industrial property rights, which the sub-franchisee is licensed to use, will fall to be dealt with under the law of the country in which the business operates. The laws of state A relating to trademarks would not affect the treatment of trademarks in state B where the sub-franchisor is carrying on business. Another factor is that the sub-franchise agreements would undoubtedly be subject to the law of the country in which the sub-franchisor is operating. It does not seem to make sense to have the master franchise agreement (out of which all rights are granted to the sub-franchisees) governed by a different legal system from that which governs the contracts for the operational units.

It should be emphasized that this chapter has not attempted to deal with every single provision to be found in an international master franchise agreement. Obviously, the final terms will vary from case to case, and will reflect the outcome of the give and take of the commercial negotiations. International franchising is growing fast. Given the right care in choice of 'partner', the correct structuring of the arrangements, infinite patience, and the right level of financial and manpower resources, it can be a very successful way of expanding one's business.

Chapter 15

Case studies: UK franchises

In this chapter we examine six franchise operations which have been developed in the UK:

1. Apollo Window Blinds
2. Autela Components
3. Colour Counsellors
4. Fastframe
5. Hometune
6. Prontaprint

They represent a wide geographic spread, from the Home Counties to Glasgow. All of these companies are well established and are members of the British Franchise Association (BFA). Three of them have provided chairmen of the BFA (Apollo, Hometune and Prontaprint), one of them has provided a vice-chairman (Fastframe) and another (Autela) a council member.

One of the companies (Fastframe) has been voted 'Franchise of the Year' and another (Prontaprint) has been runner-up. At least four of these companies came from a small beginning and none of them is what one might describe as big business, although one (Autela) had its origins as a division of a very large company, one (Prontaprint) was taken to the unlisted securities market (USM) and is still there although it was taken over by another USM company and two (Apollo and Hometune) have been taken over by larger groups.

Many of these companies display how a business developing from a humble start and moderate size can achieve considerable success using the business format franchise method of marketing. Even though most remain moderate in size by big business standards they have made a significant contribution to small business activity and employment.

One of these businesses, Colour Counsellors, is unique. It was started by a woman, Virginia Stourton, has particular appeal to women and has only women as franchisees. The Autela business is interesting because it involved the successful change of format to achieve franchising. Hometune has undergone three changes of ownership yet emerged strong and effective.

All these franchise systems are organized along traditional business format principles. They represent the hard core of franchising activity and have experienced growing pains along their path as do all businesses. Not all dealings with franchises go smoothly, as will be apparent on reading about their experiences. Despite the inevitable problems and setbacks all have managed to develop and grow with basically sound and successful formats. They would all agree from their experiences with many, if not all, the principles set out in this book but they have undoubtedly each found their way to the achievement of their objectives by different routes within the established framework of franchising's basic principles.

There are three factors which call for some comment. Of all these franchises only Apollo points to franchise exhibitions as a source of new franchisees. Given that there are three major exhibitions each year in the UK this must raise a question about the effectiveness of exhibitions as vehicles for recruitment. Secondly, considering the size of operation all six franchisors manage to sustain operations with remarkably low 'head office' staffing levels. All of them involve most of their 'head office staff' in contact with franchisees, which helps the 'belonging to a family' feeling which exists in many franchise networks. Thirdly, without exception all six have concluded that considerable effort has to be put into franchisor–franchisee relations. This is a lesson which must be taken seriously (see Chapters 10 and 11). There is a similarity in approach to handling such relations with a heavy emphasis on communication and regular meetings. The case in practice for and against franchise associations appears to be supportive of the views expressed in Chapter 11 of this book.

Apollo Window Blinds (Apollo; case study 1) commenced business in 1973 when the McNeill brothers set out to fill a gap in the market-place. The gap was the lack of availability of high-quality, made-to-measure, fashion window dressing outlets in the high street shopping areas. Until Apollo was established the only way to obtain window blinds was by mail order or from non-specialist retailers. Inevitably choice was limited and consumers were usually left with the inconvenience and uncertainty of DIY measuring and installation. Apollo provided a specialist product and service which removed the inconvenience and uncertainty while broadening the choice for the consumer.

Case study 1

Name of company	Year established business
Apollo Window Blinds	**1973**

Year commenced franchising	Type of business
1975	**Retailer of blinds and curtains, manufacturer of blinds**

Countries in which company operates	Outlets outside UK
2	**1**

Number of outlets open before franchising	UK company-owned outlets	UK franchised outlets
5	**1**	**96**

	Employees:	
In franchising activities	In company-owned outlets	In franchised outlets
40	**4**	**180**

The brothers saw the potential but recognized their shortcomings so far as operating a network of outlets was concerned. They were basically in the business of supplying materials and facilities, and franchising enabled them to continue to do that while at the same time providing a network of outlets run by well-motivated owners rather than managers. The formula worked, thus justifying their confidence in the franchise method of marketing when it was not so well established and understood as it is now. The two-way flow of ideas between franchisor and entrepreneurially minded franchisees has proved beneficial in improving and expanding the system, product and range.

Apollo acquired its franchising know-how from experience building upon its knowledge of a home-grown agency concept reinforced by specialist legal advice. Apollo considers that there are three categories of benefit which have emerged from its use of franchising:

1. Motivation: the higher level of motivation throughout the network resulting in higher expectations of support services from the franchisor than an employee would demand tended to raise standards of achievement through proactive and reactive contributions by both parties.
2. Expansion throughout the UK enabling swift growth of corporate

image and identity. Experience thus obtained enabled the development of swift assessment of and response to local product requirements.

3. Improvement of the effectiveness and scope of the system and business by the constant two-way flow of information, ideas and suggestions.

Apollo was quick to recognize the importance and value of good communications. As the network grows in size and geographical spread so the problems of maintaining good communications become more acute. Apollo has established systems to overcome these problems. These systems include the following techniques and services.

1. Operations team: field based to offer regular commercial advice and practical help.
2. Bulletins: monthly, to update on news and events.
3. Fact sheets: whenever relevant, produced to fit into manual, and providing product and marketing information.
4. Business development: a forum for presentation of new products/ ideas/training.
5. Association meetings: twice yearly; managed by franchisees and attended in part by franchise director; for presentation, or to answer questions. Association chairmen meet at Head Office prior to meetings to update and be updated (see below).
6. Focus Groups: groups meeting at Head Office to give feedback on support service/systems. Meetings whenever relevant.

Apollo recruits franchisees by a combination of sources:

- advertising
- exhibitions and trade shows
- referral from franchisees
- approaches from customers
- through BFA membership
- seminars

An applicant for an Apollo franchise has an initial informal interview preferably in his home. If that is satisfactory it is followed by a full-day meeting which takes place at Apollo's offices to enable both parties to get to know each other better. Apollo also uses the techniques of psychometric testing.

Once the applicant is accepted an agreed territory is allocated to him pending acquisition of premises. During this period Apollo's Franchise Development Manager keeps in contact on a regular basis and bulletins, information packs and newsletters are sent to the franchisee. The candidate is trained for 2 weeks at Apollo's Head Office so that he can operate the system and cope with the practical and administrative tasks which are necessary for its operations. Operations and property teams seek suitable premises, organize shopfitting and assist the candidate with preparation for trading including an opening advertising campaign. The operation manager works alongside the franchisee when he opens for business to assist in building confidence and improving working knowledge.

Support is given to the franchisee on an ongoing basis with:

- field support staff visiting every 4–5 weeks offering commercial advice and practical help;
- ongoing training for franchisee and staff including:
  - product knowledge
  - commercial selling
  - time management
- marketing: ranging from Yellow Pages adverts and major exhibitions to point-of-sale advertising and other material;
- monitoring legal and contractual aspects of the property with advice and support.

Apollo did establish a franchisee association which was abandoned owing to franchisee disinterest. Since Apollo is concerned to emphasize good franchisor–franchisee relations it has revived interest in holding meetings between the franchisor and the franchisee. Regular meetings are now held with franchisee representatives which in time are expected to become valuable tools in maintaining good relations. In addition, as mentioned above, Apollo has Focus/Advisory Groups which are used to monitor the feedback on product and systems and to provide a focus for reaction to new ideas. Apollo also recognizes that it is important to speak to all franchisees on a 'one-to-one' basis to reduce opportunities for dissatisfaction.

Autela Components Ltd (Autela; case study 2), the automotive parts distributor, is the successor in business to AP Autela, which was originally a trading division of Automotive Products plc. Autela was the subject of a management buy-out by the team which ran the business as a division of Automotive Products plc. Automotive Products originally operated a sub-depot/distribution system alongside its wholly owned branch operation and was accustomed to dealing with 'branch' owners within the network. However, it found that the system of dealing with sub-depot/distributors was not satisfactory in terms of contractual arrangements, financial arrangements and operational standards. The company recognized the limitations of its existing arrangements and wished to increase the rate and improve the quality of network development as well as to promote an effective vehicle for expansion into continental Europe. These reasons are still regarded as valid. In addition,

Case study 2

Name of company **Autela Components Ltd**	Year established business **1971**
Year commenced franchising **1982**	Type of business **Automotive parts distributor**
Countries in which company operates **2**	Outlets outside UK **1**
UK company-owned outlets **37**	UK franchised outlets **26**

Employees:

In franchising activities **7**	In company-owned outlets **265**	In franchised outlets **127**

Autela has found that it is able to offer the ultimate career opportunities for the better-quality branch managers to become their own boss by taking up a franchise. There are now five former managers who are franchisees.

Autela acquired its franchising know-how by an evolutionary process. During the 1970s a sub-depot/distributor system was operated alongside company-owned branches. Dealing with depot operations and distributors enabled the company to acquire some expertise in handling a relationship which had some features in common with franchising. The depot/distributor system was not as effective in practice as Autela would have wished. It decided to develop a business format franchise and to offer the opportunity to existing depot operators and distributors to convert to the new format.

Autela embarked on the detailed preparation of the system, system manuals, corporate identity, training capacity and acquiring franchising knowledge by attending seminars, contact with the British Franchise Association (BFA) and by taking specialist advice. Autela discovered, as it had hoped, that there were significant benefits:

- higher-quality entrepreneurially minded individuals joined the network;
- the rate of expansion was increased;

- the quality of operations was improved;
- the network's buying power was improved.

The principal problems with which Autela was confronted relate to franchisor–franchisee relationships and include:

- communications;
- problem solving;
- franchisees with difficulties;
- breakdown of partnerships between franchisees.

Autela has found that a positive attitude with a combination of services has improved or eliminated problems. The services include the following.

1. Quarterly Newsletter: information regarding the network, development, market trends, seminar/conference information, Government policy, budgets, etc.
2. Franchisee visit reports: concentration on individual franchisee comments and questions, trading experiences and personal details, site quality, general state of repair, quality of operation.
3. Franchisee seminars: area meetings arranged to encourage two-way discussions franchisee–franchisee and franchisee–franchisor, and to exchange experiences and problem solving techniques.
4. Franchisee Conference: particularly designed to include and involve the franchisees' spouses in the environment of the franchise network and colleagues; engenders family and team atmosphere away from working surroundings and pressures.

Autela recruits prospective franchisees by advertising, word of mouth referrals and from the publicity about members which the BFA distributes. Upon receipt of an initial enquiry, Autela responds by sending an initial information pack including an application form. This is followed up a week or so later to confirm or otherwise whether or not there is continued interest. Upon receipt of a completed application form Autela can judge whether the applicant appears to be a viable prospect, both financially and from the point of view of his trade knowledge which is essential. An initial interview is held between the applicant and Autela's Franchise Manager either at Autela's Head Office or at some other convenient place. A second interview is held if both parties are still interested in each other. The applicant is advised to visit operating franchisees to observe and question existing franchisees. After this a decision will be made by both Autela and the applicant about whether or not to proceed. If it is decided to proceed the applicant will be provided with the franchise contract for advice from his solicitor. The applicant will pay a deposit and sign the contract.

Autela assists the applicant with the preparation of a business plan, including the first year's cash flow and projections, and a bank presentation to assist the applicant in obtaining finance. During this time Autela helps the applicant with his property search, the conversion of these premises and training. The applicant is trained and assisted in setting up and opening for business. In providing these services Autela also prepares a sales plan for the franchisee including the first year's monthly sales budget in line with the bank presentation and a sales plan covering the first 3 years of trading. The Autela system provides computer installation and set-up, price file software set-up and back-up tapes and computer system training. Finally, Autela provide an opening launch which includes initial local newspaper editorial and advertising articles, as well as a special marketing launch with special offers and mailshots.

Autela provides a number of continuing services for its franchisees which it divides into six categories:

1. System: ongoing computer training; monthly supply of computer price update tapes including standardized selling discount structure; system manuals, training and updates.
2. Property: property inspections by Property and Assets Manager; rent review negotiations including if necessary advice in connection with insurance and assistance with any claims.
3. Marketing: monthly sales offers, bulk purchasing arrangements and supplier co-ordination and support.
4. Accounts: litigation and accreditation support with back-up from Autela's Accounts Department.
5. Field support: six-weekly visits cycle to franchisees by field support staff to discuss business problems, sales success, staffing and control of overheads and general matters.
6. Conferences and seminars: Autela holds annual conferences at which there is an appraisal of annual business and general trade trends. Supplier input and support is also provided at the conference. In addition, Autela provides 6-monthly seminars for two-way discussion with franchisees on a regional basis.

As mentioned above, Autela has concentrated upon franchisor–franchisee relations in view of the nature of some of the problems with which it has been confronted in the past. As a consequence it has in position a developed range of techniques, which have already been referred to, for maintaining good relations. The Franchise Department includes a Franchise Administrator whose job is to provide a link between franchisees and the Head Office administration.

Case study 3

Name of company **Colour Counsellors Ltd**	Year established business **1970**	
Year commenced franchising **1978**	Type of business **Interior design**	
Countries in which company operates 2	Outlets outside UK 1	
UK company-owned outlets 0	UK franchised outlets **58**	
	Employees:	
In franchising activities 3	In company-owned outlets **N/A**	In franchised outlets 0

Colour Counsellors Ltd (CC; case study 3) was established in 1970 by Virginia Stourton to provide an interior design service. Arising from the difficulties inherent in choosing soft furnishings including fabrics, carpets and wall coverings in shop surroundings, Ms Stourton developed a mobile service which enables customers to choose such products in their own homes. Samples of fabrics, carpets and wall coverings are catalogued into eight transportable boxes. Each box relates to a main colour and is organized so that suitable harmonies immediately become apparent.

Having demonstrated the success of her ideas Ms Stourton had to make a decision about how to expand the business. CC did not have surplus capital and decided that franchising would provide a suitable method for its expansion programme. As this franchise was developed by a lady it is perhaps not surprising to find that CC's expansion plans showed great sensitivity to the working aspiration of home-bound women who had placed their family commitments at the top of their priorities. The CC business is ideal for women in such a situation and although they can work full time if they wish their financial arrangements are structured to allow for part-time operations but nonetheless provide the necessary incentive to secure a minimum commitment to developing the franchised business. CC manages a network of 58 franchises with only three staff, all of whom deal with franchisees.

None of the franchisees has any employees since the business is not designed in that way and employees would not be appropriate. The fact that the franchisees lead a full life probably results in less discontent and fewer franchisor–franchisee relations problems, which permits CC to keep its staffing to a very low level.

In 1978 when CC started its franchising programme there was not so much guidance available as there now is. Consequently CC learned its lessons the hard way, by trial and error resulting in steady rather than spectacular growth but set on sound foundations.

After its years of experience CC is satisfied that its reasons for introducing franchising were correct and that they still hold good. Furthermore the concept has stood the test of time and has required remarkably little change. This is not surprising since the basic format is very simple. The key to success will be the selection of the right franchisees, establishing the right areas of operation, keeping the catalogue boxes up to date with modern patterns, and establishing good lines of supply with manufacturers.

The benefits of franchising to the company have been that expansion has been achieved with minimum capital. The role of a franchisee in contributing to the development of a good name and the franchisees' dedication to success developed from an understanding of their motivation in becoming involved in the network. The biggest problems which CC has encountered have been in franchisee selection. The characteristics which CC seeks in franchisees are honesty, determination and an outgoing personality. As is the case with so many franchisors CC's choice of early franchisees did not always produce those who matched these characteristics. CC thought that it could train them into the right mould but found that this was not possible. CC cautions franchisors against believing that it is possible fundamentally to change the character and make-up of an applicant who does not meet established criteria.

CC recruits franchisees largely by recommendation and word of mouth although some advertising is used, particularly in recessionary times. Once identified, prospective franchisees are invited to attend a presentation course when CC explains what the franchise is and what it involves. This is followed by a buffet lunch and further discussions. If interest is aroused the prospective franchisee completes an application form. CC then evaluates each applicant and arranges a second interview with those considered suitable. After further discussions if both parties wish to proceed the contract is signed and the franchisee undergoes a 2-week training course at CC's Head Office where there is a small in-house exhibition.

CC's franchisor–franchisee relations are handled by Virginia Stourton, who does not regard it as a burden to set and maintain the highest standards. On the contrary she regards it as an essential feature of her business activity in which she enjoys the success she assists the franchisees achieve. CC regularly meets with a committee of six franchisees to discuss and resolve issues and problems which have arisen in the field.

Case study 4

Name of company **Fastframe Franchises Ltd**	Year established business **1983**
Year commenced franchising **1984**	Type of business **Retail picture framing**
Countries in which company operates **5**	Outlets outside UK **120**
UK company-owned outlets **7**	UK franchised outlets **83**

Employees:

In franchising activities	In company-owned outlets	In franchised outlets
21	**26**	**315**

Fastframe (case study 4) was founded in June 1983 when Ian Johnson realized that custom picture framing was not being adequately serviced. At the time the market was very fragmented so it was difficult to find a picture framer, and typical delivery times were 3 weeks or more. Mr Johnson, who owns a substantial commercial printing company, realized that the framing market was ripe for its establishment on the high street in a similar way to which the successful high street printing operations had positioned themselves. The objective was to provide a genuine while-you-wait service from a retail environment using traditional materials and modern marketing methods coupled with on-the-spot manufacture. Fastframe was one of the few companies whose system was designed from its conception with franchising in mind rather than franchising an already successful concept.

Fastframe decided to use the franchise method of marketing because it felt that it would enable it to saturate the market rapidly. It considers that its decision is justified by events and still holds good. In addition, Fastframe has discovered that the techniques of franchising lend themselves to international development and has been able in the relatively short time it has been operating to establish master franchise arrangements in the USA, Japan, Australia and France.

Fastframe acquired its knowledge of franchising by relating its business opportunity to the Speedy Print Shop franchises, with which it considered there were similarities. The principal benefits which Fastframe considers have flowed from its franchising can be summed up as:

- a reduction in the amount of capital required by Fastframe for the development of its network;
- a more rapid rate of expansion was achieved;
- Fastframe required fewer employees, thus avoiding the problems associated with recruitment and control of large numbers of staff, particularly where branch operations would have been involved;
- the rapid rate of growth of the operation has attracted the interest of foreign companies requiring master franchise opportunities.

Fastframe has discovered, as do all franchisors, that franchising presents its challenges as well as its advantages. The challenges which it has identified include:

- the difference in approach which is necessary between dealings with franchisees and staff in company-owned operations;
- that it is difficult to please all the people all the time;
- that management decisions involve a great degree of consensus and sensible compromise.

To meet these challenges, Fastframe concentrated its efforts on the recruitment of suitably qualified managerial staff who are trained to appreciate the need to behave diplomatically.

Franchisees are recruited mainly by national advertising. After completing an application form which is evaluated to see whether the applicant is suitable interviews are conducted with Fastframe's Franchise Director. There are at least two interviews followed by liaison with the Property Manager in the search for a suitable location. The prospective franchisees' reactions to the difficulties involved in such a search are also evaluated.

The upfront services include:

- complete training for the franchisee and staff;
- assistance with property location and lease negotiation;
- assistance with the preparation of cash-flow forecasts;
- assistance with the preparation of business plans for bank presentations;
- complete installation and stocking of the outlet, i.e. Fastframe provides a turnkey operation;
- organization of initial advertising and public relations for the opening of the outlet;

- support with 'hands-on' assistance in the early days following the opening of the outlet.

Fastframe also provides a wide range of continuing services:

- monitoring of corporate presentation;
- help with rent reviews;
- assistance with any necessary refinancing arrangements;
- assistance, in some cases, with rental payments;
- marketing, advertising and public relations support;
- continuous training and retraining.

In the 1990/91 regime of high interest rates Fastframe issued new franchisees with an agreement to pay all interest charges in excess of 14% on agreed borrowings for a Fastframe franchise.

Franchisee relations are recognized as complicated and warranting a concentration of effort. Fastframe, apart from the normal day-to-day contact, holds regional meetings, twice each year and in three different locations to permit brainstorming sessions between Fastframe and its franchisees. There is an annual conference at which the following year's marketing campaign is presented. Fastframe also regularly publishes a 'newsy' magazine which features network news as well as technical information.

Fastframe is in the process of formulating a franchise advisory council and has an open mind on what its objectives should be. Experience tends to show that such councils are manipulated by those with extreme views and questionable motivations. Fastframe prefers to have a one-to-one dialogue with franchisees, which it considers to be the best method of communication. Fastframe takes the subject very seriously and has had discussions with other franchisors to understand the problems with which they have been confronted to assist Fastframe in the development of its strategy.

The **Hometune** mobile engine servicing business (case study 5) was founded in 1968 by Duncan Whitfield and was franchised right from the outset. The network grew to some 180 franchisees and in 1986 Mr Whitfield sold the business to MCL Ltd so that he could retire. The transfer of the business was followed by changes in policy introduced by the new owners which led to widespread defections by approximately one-half of the network. In 1990 the management team of Hometune bought out the business and established the present company, Hometune Ltd (Hometune).

The original rationale for franchising was to minimize the capital required for expansion by the Hometune business and to utilize the energy and commitment of self-employed operators. These reasons are still considered valid and Hometune finds that the 1990/91 recessionary economic climate reinforces the case for franchising.

Case study 5

Name of company **Hometune Ltd**	Year established business **1968**
Year commenced franchising **1968**	Type of business **Mobile engine servicing and tuning**
Countries in which company operates **1**	Outlets outside UK **None**
UK company-owned outlets **None**	UK franchised outlets **120**

	Employees:	
In franchising activities **10**	In company-owned outlets **None**	In franchised outlets **200**

The knowledge of franchising which was acquired by Mr Whitfield sustained the operation until he sold the business. After the sale the business was taken over by professional managers (Mr Whitfield was retained as a consultant for a period of time) and a level of expertise developed which has resulted in a very professional operation.

Franchising enabled the Hometune business to expand rapidly. The concerned personal involvement of 'owners' as individual operators has enabled a high-level quality of service to be provided for customers. In addition the franchisees are prepared to work longer hours and on more days in each week than would be the case with employees. Hometune is able to run all its operations with only 10 staff, all of whom have contact with franchisees.

Franchisee recruitment is carried out by a team of two who organize all advertising and conduct interviews with prospective franchisees normally at their home. Following the initial interviews, financial projections are provided to the prospective franchisee with such follow-up interviews as Hometune consider necessary. Once the decision is made by both Hometune and the prospective franchisee to proceed, Hometune provides a range of services:

- assistance with the preparation of a presentation to the bank for finance;

- assistance in the preparation of cash-flow forecasts, profit projections and analyses;
- assistance with the identification and determination of a suitable location and territory;
- offers of special van leasing schemes with a special fleet rate;
- fitting out and equipping the Hometune van;
- discussions with Hometune management to assist with the organization of the franchisee's business;
- provision of initial stock of parts;
- franchisee insurance scheme;
- extensive training for 3 weeks at the Hometune Training Centre followed by experience in the field with an experienced Hometune operator;
- operational manuals are provided.

The ongoing services are an extension of the comprehensive initial services and include:

- updating of operational manuals, particularly with technical information in relation to the vehicles on the market;
- regular field support and contact;
- regional meetings;
- conferences;
- marketing materials;
- advertising and public relations support;
- technical support;
- ongoing field support;
- equipment evaluation and reconsideration.

Hometune has given a great deal of thought to the handling of franchisor–franchisee relations. Regular contact with franchisees is maintained through personal visits, regional meetings and conferences. Hometune insists that franchisees accept that two-way communication is essential and must be a feature of the relationship. Hometune finds that its efforts are rewarded by a high level of motivation in its network. Hometune has decided not to establish a franchisee advisory council since its own experience suggests that it is better to have regular communication with each franchisee direct rather than through a representative body.

Prontaprint's rapid printing business (case study 6) was established in 1971 by Edwin Thirlwell with the intention of franchising if the pilot operation proved successful. Franchising commenced in 1973 and the company is the largest wholly UK developed franchise. Mr Thirlwell took the company to the Unlisted Securities Market in 1985 and in 1988 the company was taken

Case study 6

Name of company **Prontaprint plc**	Year established business 1971
Year commenced franchising **1973**	Type of business **Print and business services**
Countries in which company operates 14	Outlets outside UK 121
UK company-owned outlets 4	UK franchised outlets 282

Employees:

In franchising activities 82	In company-owned outlets 16	In franchised outlets 1300

over by Continuous Stationery plc. Mr Thirlwell's intention had always been to franchise. He had had previous experience as a franchisee and having sold out that business went to the USA to review the franchised businesses on offer there so that he could make a decision about what would be a suitable business to develop in the UK. He decided on the speedy print business for a number of reasons, not least of which was that it involved quick turnover of work and payment on delivery of the finished product. He also recognized that franchising offered an ideal vehicle for rapid expansion with a lower capital requirement than would be required for a wholly owned retail operation. These reasons remain valid, but the company points out that many franchisors make the mistake of underestimating the capital requirement in setting up since the revenue flow takes some years to establish.

The benefits of franchising have been demonstrated to Prontaprint in a number of ways. The involvement of franchisees in a business in which they have made significant personal investment is, in Prontaprint's view, the greatest incentive to improve performance. Other benefits include:

- the mix of local personality and attention with a strong national brand is a powerful combination;
- the franchisor's capital needs are reduced;

- once the business is established (this will take time, see above) there is a positive cash flow;
- there is a proven formula which can be taken across national borders.

There are practical problems with which Prontaprint, like all franchisors, is confronted. Prontaprint's major problem area has at its root franchisor–franchisee relations, the indiscipline of franchisees and their challenges to the system designed and developed by the franchisor. This is not unfamiliar territory as earlier chapters in this book have revealed. This sort of resistance and challenge if taken to a logical conclusion is a classic case of franchisees shooting themselves in the foot. Again this has happened before in other cases. This issue is discussed in some detail in Chapter 10. Franchisees have to accept the disciplines involved in joining a network. Each attempt by a franchisee to impose his own ideas, to ignore the franchisor's developing strategies and to challenge innovation adds considerably to the franchisor's cost of providing services, diverts manpower resources from productive effort and weakens the national perception of the brand. This sort of problem becomes more difficult to handle the larger the network and is perhaps a reflection of Prontaprint's success. The selection of entrepreneurially minded franchisees is always considered desirable but methods have to be found to keep their entrepreneurial interests focused upon making a success of the operation of the franchisor's system and not unilaterally seeking to develop their own.

Franchisees are recruited by advertisements in Sunday newspapers, selected franchise journals and occasionally advertising in the regional press. Applications are required to complete an application form which provides initial screening to see whether Prontaprint's basic requirements are met. If they are, the selection procedure which follows involves a number of inter-views at which in the initial stages some effort is put into providing the applicant with sufficient information to enable him to judge whether the franchise is right for him. Once the applicant is satisfied Prontaprint makes a detailed assessment of his suitability, evaluates his financial status and conducts psychometric tests.

Prontaprint's initial services to the franchisee commence with a 4-week induction programme consisting of 2 weeks' theoretical and 2 weeks' practical training. During that period the franchisee has access to the Estates Department to assist with site selection and lease negotiation if required. Shopfitting is arranged by Prontaprint, who have approved suppliers offering beneficial rates. Similarly, equipment ordering is arranged through central purchasing. Prontaprint also has legal facilities in-house from which franchisees can benefit. After training and shopfitting, a schedule of 5 weeks is arranged with the franchisee during which period he is heavily supported in-store by field trainers. The schedule is designed in such a way that the attendance of the field trainers progressively reduces, and during the fifth week an assessment is made by the respective trainees as to whether the franchisee is ready to be incorporated into the general field support schedule or whether the 'hand-holding' support should be extended further. Once Prontaprint is happy that the franchisee is comfortable with the running of the business an official opening and publicity campaign is organized.

On a continuing basis Prontaprint provides support under seven categories:

1. Sales Operations: the Sales Operations team consists of field trainers and sales promotion executives. They provide a regular 6-weekly visit of one day in length to each franchisee during which they assist in the planning and implementation of promotional activities. The field trainers provide continuing in-shop training for staff, together with regional training courses around the country throughout the year.
2. Marketing: the Marketing Department provides all promotional advertising material for use at local level by franchisees. It also organizes all national advertising promotion and public relations activities in conjunction with the sales operations development.
3. Technical support: the Technical Department provides a development role, assessing new equipment or services prior to introduction to their system. It also provides training and support teams to advise on optimum use of print equipment.
4. Central Purchasing: Central Purchasing negotiates with all suppliers to establish the best rates for both capital equipment and consumables. This includes not only items relating to the operation of the business but also such things as shopfitting, fascias and insurance. The benefits resulting from these negotiations are passed directly to franchisees.
5. Commercial Department: the Commercial Department provides commercial assistance to any franchisee who find himself in difficulties. It works on an *ad hoc* basis, spending as much time as required with the franchisee, assessing difficulties and seeking solutions to problems.
6. Estates: the Estates Department negotiates on behalf of franchisees in lease renewals, rent reviews, and business rate assessments.
7. Legal Department: the Legal Department provides ongoing information to franchisees relating to changes in legislation, i.e. copyright law, and where necessary assists franchisees in the event of litigation against them.

As will be appreciated from the practical problems outlined above, Prontaprint has had to concentrate heavily on franchisor–franchisee relations. To this end it has, during the last 4 years, developed a more open management structure in respect of communications with franchisees. Prontaprint recognizes that good communications are inevitably the key to good franchisor–franchisee relationships.

Prontaprint's communications strategy is broadly based and includes a number of components.

1. Regular bi-weekly mailouts to franchisees (Postbag) containing general information of interest to the franchisees. These are accompanied by a regular league table of performance, which engenders healthy competition between franchisees.
2. Technical news: despatched every 2 weeks with Postbag. This provides updated information on approved suppliers, equipment, and supplier prices.
3. Promotional news: despatched with Postbag. This provides an update on all marketing activities and includes additions to the range of promotional material.
4. *Prontaprinting*: produced every quarter. This magazine provides general hints and tips on the business and highlights any major successes by individual franchisees.
5. Regional meetings: regular regional meetings are arranged around the country when small groups of seven or eight franchisees meet, usually during the evenings, with Prontaprint staff to discuss their problems or successes.
6. Prontaprint National Conference: held each April over a period of 3 days. It provides the major forum for discussing strategy for the forthcoming year. An exhibition of all approved suppliers runs concurrently.
7. Regional Roadshow: held during October/November each year, usually in six venues around the country and is attended by Directors and key management staff. This forum is intended to provide an update to franchisees at the half-year stage.
8. Directors' visits: each Director schedules 10 shop visits every quarter to ensure that there is a continued direct contact between the board of Prontaprint and the franchisee base as well as to ensure that directors do not become too detached from the 'sharp end'.

The Prontaprint Franchisee Association (PFA) was established in 1988. This is a body of 12 representative members of the network elected by franchisees annually. The PFA meets with Prontaprint for 2 days every 2 months to discuss policy and new initiatives. One of the two days is spent in working parties covering areas such as marketing, technical and training, and it is in these that policies agreed at the PFA are put into practice.

The PFA was established following an invitation to the network by Prontaprint to vote for elected members. After the initial and inevitable early stage where some mistrust was apparent, the PFA has proved to be a very effective body; not only in the discipline it imposes on the franchisor to justify activities, but also in the exposure it provides to franchisees of the very real difficulties in running a franchised business. During recent years it has helped implement many new initiatives, including the move to a Business Service Centre and the expansion into more commercial services.

In addition to the PFA, Prontaprint has a Business Development Group which meets quarterly for 2 days. Its members are franchisees, invited by Prontaprint, who are showing the highest rate of performance in terms of growth, market penetration, etc. The forum is used to discuss activities being undertaken by the individuals and offers the opportunity to discuss new ideas which ultimately can be evaluated and passed on to the remainder of the network.

Chapter 16

Case studies: international franchises

In this chapter four case studies are examined:

1. Budget Rent-a-Car
2. Burger King Corporation
3. Dunkin' Donuts
4. Service Master

All four companies are excellent examples of the way in which franchising can assist in the development of a global network. Each of these companies began operations either in the late 1940s (Service Master) or the mid-1950s. None pretends that international franchising is without its problems and difficulties. What they have all managed to do is to overcome these difficulties and to establish effective worldwide networks. In the case of Burger King Corporation and Dunkin' Donuts they have both become ultimately owned by UK companies as a result of acquisitions, which may increase the interest of UK readers.

In the case of Burger King, which has acquired the UK Wimpy network, there will be problems which arise when seeking to absorb another network and convert its members to different branding. These sorts of problems have been experienced on many occasions in the USA and have in some cases resulted in litigation. There is already litigation in one case where a franchisee with 11 Wimpy outlets does not wish to convert to the Burger King branding. If Burger King is to avoid further difficulties it will have to handle disputes with skill and a level of sensitivity to the franchisee's inevitable problems. Franchisees who change branding will probably find competing

Burger King outlets near by, changes in corporate style and the way in which services are provided and a cost of conversion. It will be inevitable that businesses will suffer. Burger King's skill will be evidenced by the way in which it is able to assist franchisees to overcome the short-term difficulties and succeed in the medium- to long-term.

The interest in Burger King and Dunkin' Donuts by large multinational groups has demonstrated that franchising systems can indeed become big business. There are, of course, many other examples of big business in franchising, where there are a significant number of franchise companies each with outlets in excess of 500. The four companies featured in this chapter all have a well-established presence in the UK. Dunkin' Donuts has shown resilience in coming back to the UK after an earlier premature and unsuccessful attempt to enter the market in the early 1960s. The growth in the UK of the other companies featured in this chapter has been steady rather than spectacular but the UK market-place is probably a more difficult one with which to come to terms than many others, particularly for American companies, who can be lulled into believing the differences between the USA and the UK are less than they really are.

The worldwide development of the networks in widely differing cultural arenas demonstrates that not only does franchising have universal appeal but that the services and products of these companies also have universal acceptance. That level of acceptance is sufficient to sustain the basic operational outlets or units on a profitable basis which is essential to make franchising possible. All companies recognize the value of their system and the need to be sensitive to local markets, the language, the culture, different business practices and the many variables to be found when entering a foreign territory. The important factor for those who would follow these companies into the international arena is to learn from their experience. Much of what emerges from the case studies includes the principles which are explained in Chapter 14 and which ideally should be read before reviewing the case studies.

If the lessons to be learned from the experience of others are taken into account an entrant to international franchising will find it possible to reduce risks and to use his resources in a far more cost-effective way. It may be that the lessons produce an intimidating and inhibiting effect; in some cases that may be a good thing. The importance of these lessons and having them available is that the informed decision which can now be taken adds to the likely effectiveness of the franchisor new to international activity. It is appreciated that rules are made to be ignored or circumvented. There will always be exceptions: there will be those who follow the lessons and who will fail; there will be those who reject the lessons and who will succeed. These will be isolated exceptions; for the vast majority, ignoring the experience of others will be an expensive and damaging exercise which can not only adversely affect further international growth but which can also cause difficulties in the domestic operations that can significantly set back progress.

Case study 1

Name of company	Year established business	
Budget Rent-a-Car	**1958**	

Country of origin
USA

Year commenced franchising	Type of business	
In USA 1960	**Vehicle rental**	
Internationally 1964	**services**	

Outlets worldwide	Outlets in USA	Number of countries in which company operates
3600 (see note)	**1225**	**140**

International outlets	International outlets company-owned	International outlets franchised
2375	**150**	**2225**

Note: This includes locations at 710 national and international airports

The **Budget Rent-a-Car** business (Budget; case study 1) was founded in 1958 by Morris Mirkin in California. Mirkin's philosophy was to offer real value for money with high-quality services. He undercut the competition by charging approximately one-half the standard industry rates. This proved to be a ready formula for success and the company was incorporated in 1960 in Chicago, when it immediately commenced franchise operations. Its first international operation was established in 1964 in Zurich. Budget was established as a franchise operation to benefit from the strength which a franchise network can offer while also developing a strong corporate operational base. In recent years this combination of franchised and corporate development has enabled the company to continue to expand its operations on a world-wide basis, with countries such as Poland, Czechoslovakia and Hungary added to the network as Eastern Europe opened up to Western business.

The Budget network has grown from the original branch in Los Angeles with 30 cars to one which has branches in 140 countries, offering over 225,000 vehicles for rent from over 3600 branches, including 710 national and international airports. Budget has Reservation Centres in 23 international 'key' countries which are connected to its computer centre in Dallas, USA and it continues to develop and expand this vital aspect of its worldwide service.

Budget now offers its customers a wide range of business facilities such as the Rapid Action Card, the Budget Credit Card and the Identification Card, enabling both private and corporate customers to tailor their vehicle rental services to their own needs. The worldwide Budget network also offers a variety of retail products such as Holiday Drive and Business Traveller, designed to meet the needs of the business and leisure travellers. All these products can be booked through travel agents.

Recognizing the fast-paced development needs of the international car rental industry, as Budget developed into a worldwide company, Budget established an international division in England and moved into its current headquarters in Hemel Hempstead in 1987. From these headquarters the company provides operational, reservations, accounting, training, sales and marketing support.

While Budget was primarily created as a franchise organization, the structure of the company today reflects the company policy of providing continued development with prudent management. To achieve this, Budget has taken responsibility for operating a number of key locations. For Budget this strategy particularly calls for corporate investment in key travel centres such as airports, where the worldwide strengths of the organization are best exploited by the single, corporate operating body. In recent years, the success of this mixed strategy has been recognized by all the larger operators in the field, who now have a growing number of franchised locations to support their corporate base.

In the major European market-places Budget enjoys a significant share of the total vehicle rental market, a share which it has consistently maintained in recent years, achieving market leadership in several countries. Budget is committed to continuing its aggressive growth plans by the combination of both franchised and corporate operations. Budget's basic philosophy of 'focusing on value, i.e. delivering "more" car for the customer's money', is forefront in developing its network. Development of the Latin American and Asia Pacific areas has meant that Budget is now well placed to respond to the needs of both the international business traveller and the holiday-maker.

Budget has been active in the UK since 1966 when it set up operations in Romford, Ilford and Croydon. There are now 144 branches in the UK of which 110 are franchised and 34 company-owned. Budget employs some 200 people in the UK for its franchising activities, which include overseeing company-owned outlets, and head office staff including those engaged in international activities. Of these, 80% employed in franchising have direct regular contact with franchisees. In addition, there are approximately 275 employees at company branches and approximately 700 employees in franchised branches. Budget (UK) is a founder member of the British Franchise Association (BFA), which it has supported actively throughout its existence and has in the past provided the chairman of the BFA.

It was natural for Budget to move into the international arena. Its business is providing people with means of transport and as the customer travels the world it is natural for a transport provider to think in global terms. The air travel explosion probably made a considerable contribution to this development, as shown by the 710 airport locations from which the Budget service is available. The reasons for moving into the international arena not only still hold good but are reinforced by experience.

Budget finds the master franchise arrangement the most satisfactory for its international development because the master franchisee has local contacts and knowledge, e.g. legal obligations, business contacts, local customs, etc. While master franchising is considered the best method for them, Budget is sufficiently flexible to be able to consider each country on its own merits and select the most suitable method of entry bearing in mind the circumstances. The use of the master franchise method has brought many advantages to Budget; in addition to those mentioned above there is a local commitment to profit and efficiency. Furthermore, franchisees are often linked with other service industry interests and both parties benefit from reciprocal business opportunities.

Budget has had its fair measure of problems over the nearly 30 years of its international activity, but which franchise company has not? The problem areas include the following.

1. The grant to a master franchise of more than one territory which involves either the neglect of one territory while another is developed or the sub-master franchising of one or more of the territories which creates even more problems. The control mechanisms become very difficult as the loss of direct relationship between franchisor and master franchisee makes the parties too remote. The amount of money reasonably available from operations to be allocated to franchise fees is unlikely to be sufficient to sustain the extra level in the chain of command. This thin spread of fee income results in fewer resources being made available for the provision of services and tends to make the arrangement counter-productive.
2. Different attitudes between various countries are evident and have to be taken into account.
3. Budget tries to do the same things and use the same system in each country because there is a need for uniformity. In the early stages of its development it allowed franchisees to blur the system's identity and did not exercise the degree of control which it should have done. This has been remedied.
4. There are difficulties in getting master franchisees to operate as an international team. Promotional efforts have to break down barriers and overcome market segmentation.
5. Many master franchisees and their sub-franchisees do not attach the degree of importance to holiday trade which Budget considers they

should, resulting in the loss of business opportunities. Today's holiday-maker customer may be tomorrow's business customer and vice versa.

6. Budget has experienced the difficulties which arise on termination of master franchise arrangements and the takeover of the sub-franchised networks to which reference is made in Chapter 14.

Budget makes contact with master franchisees in a number of ways. In many instances it receives approaches from those who are interested in becoming a Budget master franchisee. Other contacts are made through commercial sections of embassies, a local tourist board, Budget bankers and trade sources. The qualities for which Budget is looking in franchisees include:

- ambition;
- ability to raise substantial capital and loans to acquire a suitably sized fleet;
- business experience supported by a track record in a related industry, usually tourism, hospitality, leisure, transport and services.

Budget focuses on the proposed master franchisee's General Manager, who should preferably have an equity interest and whom Budget must train and approve. The master franchisee will have a dedicated contact with Budget's Regional Manager and will be trained at the Budget training school in the UK. Assistance will be given in fleet acquisition (range and number of vehicles to be acquired), negotiations with factories and in the preparation of business plans. Budget organizes advertising and promotion both nationally and internationally, and organizes a series of meetings and seminars for franchisees and staff, the subjects of which include:

- reservation procedures   1   seminar per year
- sales/marketing   3   seminars per year
- operations   2   seminars per year
- accounting   1   seminar per year

Budget also holds an annual convention which all franchisees are expected to attend. The level of franchisor support for the network is therefore quite high.

Future developments, for the benefit of franchisees, include the introduction of a state-of-the-art car and hotel reservations system to bolt on to existing systems, which will enable franchisees to access a wide range of choices of services for customers including choice of beneficial packages and prices available from hotels and rental centres.

Budget's progress over the 33 years of its existence has been impressive. It has overcome many of the traditional problems and is determined to upgrade franchisee services to keep the network competitive. Its success in using reservation systems has been of great benefit to franchisees, with over 9 million international reservations through its central system in 1990 and a rate of growth of 75% between 1989 and 1990 in intra-European bookings. The change in emphasis in the source of bookings is demonstrated by the fact that 80% of all European bookings up to 1985 were from within the USA while now only 45% come from that source with 55% from within Europe.

Case study 2

Name of company	Year established business	
Burger King Corporation	**1954**	
Country of origin **USA**		
Year commenced franchising **In USA 1962 Internationally 1975**	Type of business **Fast food hamburger restaurant**	
Outlets worldwide	Outlets in USA	Number of countries in which company operates
6330	5500	37
International outlets **830**	International outlets company-owned **189**	International outlets franchisor **641**

Burger King Corporation (BKC; case study 2) was founded as Burger King of Miami Inc. in 1954 by James W. McLamore and Daniel Edgerton. The first restaurant was located in Miami and sold broiled hamburgers and milk-shakes, each for 18¢. BKC grew steadily through its first 10 years, commencing franchising in the early 1960s in order to accelerate the expansion of the business and to be able to develop markets at a faster pace than would have otherwise have been possible with its own capital and other resources. BKC considers that these reasons are still valid. In addition, it has found it possible to extend to areas which would not meet criteria for company-owned outlets but in which franchisees are interested and can (and do) thrive.

Its first international activity was the establishment of two restaurants in Puerto Rico in 1964. BKC's development enabled it to reach a total of 275 restaurants with 8000 employees by 1967, when it was acquired by the Pillsbury Company for $18 million. In 1975 BKC opened its first European outlet in Madrid. By 1977 the 2000th Burger King restaurant was opened in Hawaii, which completed Burger King's coverage of all the 50 states of the USA. In 1978 BKC established the Burger King University in Florida as the company's international training centre. By 1986 BKC had 4743 Burger King restaurants in operation with $4.5 billion of system-wide sales. There were 402 Burger King restaurants established in 25 foreign countries. In 1986 a record number of 546 new Burger King restaurants were opened worldwide. Since 1986 the number of international Burger King restaurants has more than doubled to 830 and a further 12 countries have joined the Burger King worldwide family to bring the total to 37.

The Pillsbury Company was acquired by Grand Metropolitan plc in 1988, following which in 1989 in the UK, UB Restaurants was acquired. UB Restaurants had owned the Wimpy franchised takeaway restaurants chain and some 200 former Wimpy restaurants are, have been or will be converted to Burger King restaurants.

BKC has been active in the UK since 1977, where it set up two company-owned restaurants before commencing franchising activities in 1980. There are now 105 franchised and 63 company-owned Burger King restaurants in the UK. BKC (UK) employs 25 staff for its franchising activities of whom 80% have regular direct contact with franchisees. There are also in the UK approximately 3000 employees in the company-owned restaurants and approximately 5000 employees in the franchised restaurants.

BKC was able to operate internationally for many years owing to the proximity of its centre of operations in Miami to the Caribbean, which was a logical international destination. In the early 1980s BKC made a positive decision to take international activity more seriously since it had reached the conclusion that the US market was nearing saturation level and new markets had to be found. BKC's experience reinforces this decision even allowing for the fact that the US market-place has proved larger than it was thought to be. The increase in travel, both business and leisure, has led to the world 'becoming smaller', and the travellers create a demand which has its origins in what they see and experience. This has resulted in a huge demand from prospective franchisees throughout the world—over 6000 enquiries each year from the international markets alone.

BKC basically uses direct franchising as its method of international franchising with subsidiary companies providing whatever local or regional presence is considered appropriate. There are some master franchise arrangements. BKC has found that it is best to maintain its US system as closely as possible with occasional minor local adjustments to menu to accommodate local tastes. The basic franchising approach is more flexible. In the USA,

BKC policy is to maintain owner operations in small groupings of restaurants. In international activities where investment is substantially higher, large corporations, small companies and partnerships are considered. If a franchise is developing an entire country through a master franchise arrangement the financial investment involvement is even higher with major expenses in start-up costs for storage facilities, production facilities and the expense of the usual pilot operations and development of the franchisee's business infrastructure.

BKC finds that the benefits of international operations may be summarized as:

- faster brand expansion;
- steady income with low investment;
- providing a training ground for management.

There are two particular problems with which BKC was confronted:

1. Handling the desire for expansion by US franchisees into international markets. It has been found that this is not successful owing to language barriers, cultural diversity and a lack of familiarity with foreign business practices.
2. The grant of territorial rights to individuals has resulted in slow growth by tying up the market and precluding the establishment of other franchisees to ensure an adequate presence and full market penetration.

Contact is made with prospective franchisees through the reputation and scale of BKC's operations, resulting in the 6000-plus enquiries received (as mentioned above). Above all, the Burger King franchise is a soft sell. In those areas where BKC wishes to expand but which do not produce sufficient leads by the direct approach, BKC uses many of the methods traditionally used by those less fortunate with unsolicited enquiries. These methods include:

- advertising in trade journals;
- attending franchise shows or exhibitions;
- meetings with various business groups;
- using the contacts which their bankers have in the business community.

Once the prospective franchisee is identified he is subjected to extensive interview procedures to evaluate entrepreneurial spirit, management/supervisory experience, commitment, drive and other relevant factors as well as financial strength. This is followed by an evaluation of a 50-hour in-store performance.

BKC also provides:

- procurement and quality assurance investigation;
- set-up of suppliers;
- real estate and construction support;
- training;
- marketing and restaurant opening assistance.

Ongoing support is provided throughout the life of the contact in all areas of operations, quality assurance, marketing plans, accounting, technological and product innovations.

Case study 3

Name of company **Dunkin' Donuts Incorporated**	Year established business 1950	
Country of origin **USA**		
Year commenced franchising **In USA 1955 Internationally 1964**	Type of business **Retail donut and related bakery and snack items**	
Outlets worldwide	Outlets in USA	Number of countries in which company operates
2895	2525	16
International outlets 386	International outlets company-owned 16	International outlets franchised 370

Dunkin' Donuts (case study 3) was established by William (Bill) Rosenberg in 1950. Bill is recognized as one of the pioneers of franchising and was the catalyst for the creation of the International Franchise Association which was formed to promote franchising and protect the interests of franchisors. Coming from a humble background Bill was determined to make his way in life and established an industrial catering business in which he sold food and drink to factory workers from mobile units. He noticed that 40% of his sales were coffee and donuts and decided that this would provide a business opportunity. He therefore established his first store, concentrating on selling coffee and a variety of donuts in 1950. By 1955 when he introduced the franchise method of marketing he had established five outlets. The reason for franchising was to attract capital and motivated management at the operational outlet level. This reason still holds good.

In 1964 the company tried its first international development by opening two units in London. This development was premature since the domestic US operation was not able to sustain the foreign activities; it was growing too quickly and could not spare the resources. The decision was taken to withdraw from the UK and to concentrate on the domestic US market. This decision was a difficult one for any company to make but was undoubtedly correct since the US operation developed rapidly and successfully. When the time came in 1971, following an approach by a Japanese company, for the company to re-enter the international market-place by establishing its presence in Japan, the company was well placed to do so, with the strength of its US operations enabling it to approach the international challenge from a strong base with realistic resources available.

The company's international activities now cover 16 countries (other than the USA) in which some 370 franchised outlets are operated. The success of the Japanese venture encouraged the company to expand further throughout SE Asia and the Americas as well as into Europe through the UK. The company considers that with a widespread consumer acceptance of the US style of retailing, e.g. self-service, convenience stores, etc., opportunities for its growth in world markets are considerable.

The company has found that from its experience other benefits from and justifications for its international expansion have emerged. These may be summarized as including:

- improved international identification and recognition of the Dunkin' Donuts brand due to the increase in international travel;
- cross-cultural media which make the introduction of the concept easier to achieve in countries where it has not previously been experienced;
- the product has a wide appeal in all countries whether developed or developing;
- eating patterns have changed and more snack food eating is now widely acceptable, which is positive so far as the company's range of products is concerned.

In its early international development the company concentrated on master franchise arrangements covering an entire country. The company intends to reduce its emphasis on master franchise arrangements in favour of a number of different approaches which it considers will enable it to grow more effectively. These other methods include:

- regional exclusive licences;
- alliances with existing retail distribution systems such as petrol companies, convenience stores, hotels and contract suppliers.

The company has found it possible to use the same concept as it uses in the USA with minor adaptations for local tastes and preferences. This is interesting when one bears in mind the wholly novel nature of the business for most countries other than the USA. Indeed the company has benefited from the introduction, in some franchised areas, of new retailing concepts, e.g. kiosks from the Philippines, and products, e.g. Boston Bun from Indonesia.

Some of the problems with which the company has been faced, apart from its premature international franchising attempt referred to above, include:

- difficulties in terminating agreements where a poor master franchisee is selected;
- the difficulty in establishing and maintaining proper controls over operations;
- an inability in some countries to enforce contract provisions;
- the need to recognize when the product has to be adapted to local ingredients and to cope with the problems which arise in this respect when importing is restricted.

The company comes into contact with prospective franchisees through:

- referrals from existing franchisees;
- direct enquiries from prospects;
- using contacts made through the commercial attaché at a local US Embassy;
- business contacts.

A prospective franchisee has to meet the company's criteria, which are:

- sufficient financial resources to ensure proper development of the territory;
- a demonstrated ability to develop and maintain a qualified organization;
- retailing experience;
- experience in real estate acquisition and leasing;
- he must be a national of and resident in the country in which the franchise will be operated;
- he must have the vision to take a long-range view of the business;

- the individual or company must have a high level of energy;
- the ability to recognize the importance of marketing.

Dunkin' Donuts provides assistance to franchisees in the following areas:

- guidance in establishing real estate selection criteria;
- the provision of standard building plans and specifications;
- the provision of equipment and raw material specifications;
- supplier development and quality control;
- formal operations training (6–8 weeks in the USA);
- initial store opening assistance;
- advertising, merchandising and sales promotional direction;
- ongoing communication and periodic visits to provide operational guidance.

The franchisee has significant responsibilities in developing his area of operation which include:

- identification and development of real estate locations;
- completing construction and/or remodelling of the location;
- securing necessary equipment and raw materials;
- establishing and maintaining an operations and management organization;
- funding all capital and ongoing financial requirements.

ServiceMaster (SM; case study 4) was founded by the late Marion Wade in 1946. Mr Wade was a truly remarkable man with a deeply held Christian faith which guided and influenced him in the establishment and development of SM and in his dealing with his family of franchisees. His story is told in a book entitled *The Lord Is My Counsel*, which was published by Prentice-Hall Press in a special edition in 1987. It is a book well worth reading and will serve to provide an understanding of how Mr Wade conducted his business life and the way in which he was able successfully to apply biblical teachings to the running of his business and his relation with those with whom he dealt. These principles are fundamental to SM and continue to this day to be the foundation of the business philosophy of the company.

The name ServiceMaster itself has significance. Mr Wade poses this question in his book: 'Does the businessman have to make a choice between God and man?' His reply is in Matthew 6:24. The Lord says: 'no man can serve two masters: for either he will hate the one and love the other, or else he will hold to the one, and despise the other. Ye cannot serve God and mammon.' Therefore the businessman must make a choice. If he has any spiritual consciousness at all he will choose God and he will service God by using the Bible as the handbook for his relations with men. The meaning of the two

Case study 4

Name of company	Year established business	
ServiceMaster LP	**1946**	

Country of origin		
USA		

Year commenced franchising	Type of business	
In USA 1958	**See note 1 below**	
Internationally 1959		

Outlets worldwide	Outlets in USA	Number of countries in which company operates
5428	**4473**	**25**

International outlets	International outlets company owned	International outlets franchised
955	**See note 2 below**	**955**

Notes:

1. The ServiceMaster business originated as a moth-proofing service, which was later expanded into the on-site cleaning of carpets and upholstery. However, the company has diversified considerably and made acquisitions. Its total range of businesses now include: on-site carpet and upholstery cleaning; cleaning services for businesses; cleaning services for the home; MerryMaids service; termite and pest control; lawn care services; home service contracts for the repair or replacement of heating, cooling, plumbing and electrical systems, water heaters, built-in appliances, etc. ServiceMaster has also developed a non-franchised Management Services Division which operates in the health care, educational and industrial markets.

2. ServiceMaster LP operates directly through subsidiaries in some European countries. These operations are included in the franchised outlets total.

words 'Service' and 'Master' in the name of the company assumes a majestic dimension in the light of this expression of belief and faith. Its use repeats message whenever the company name is used and in all communication. The objectives of SM are clearly and proudly stated in its literature:

To honour God in all we do
To help people develop
To pursue excellence
To grow profitably

The spirit of Marion Wade remains, and his philosophy and these objectives are daily practised by those who run and work in the SM businesses. That this approach can work successfully is amply borne out by the financial record of success which SM has established. In 1989 *Fortune* magazine extracted from its 'Service 500' list 'nine that light the sky' during the period 1979–88. SM was top with an average return on equity of 63.7%. Its best year was 1987, with a return of 142.2%, and its worst(!) year 1980 with a mere 30.9% return. It is worth noting that number 2 on the list of nine achieved an average return of 28.5% with a high of 43.2% and a low of 19.3%. This indicates the magnitude of the achievement.

It is necessary to understand this underlying nature of SM, since SM regards it as fundamental to its success. One cannot explain, describe or understand SM without this knowledge. Peter F. Drucker in an essay which appeared in the 1989 accounts of SM stated: 'ServiceMaster provides a purpose and network objective for the worker and his or her work and therefore contributes to that essential ingredient of dignity that has been lacking in the past.'

SM has been active in the UK since 1959. It was a founder member of the British Franchise Association (BFA) and has played a leading role in its activities. SM has provided two chairmen of the BFA including the chairman current at the time of writing. In the USA and Canada SM employs approximately 6000 plus at least 75,000 employed in the franchised outlets.

The company started to franchise because Mr Wade had a vision of travelling across the USA without needing to stay in a hotel because he would be able to stay 'with family' at each stop-off point. Franchising was the tool by which Mr Wade believed the concept of service could best be delivered. It provided family values in that the franchisees would find that they were part of a large family and so that they and their customers would feel better off for having been 'served' by ServiceMaster. Franchising also met the corporate objective both ethically and morally. SM considers that these reasons are still valid. The moral and ethical tone of the SM approach does not mean that the company is a soft touch and can be taken advantage of by franchisees or other businesses with whom it deals. Integrity of contractual relationships can be consistent with ethical and moral obligations if the right framework is established. SM would prefer to see the weight of the ethical and moral values govern its dealings with others and in practice invariably finds that its approach is effective. This must say a lot for the skill of its executives and managers and the people handling skills in which they are trained.

SM commenced international operations in 1959 since when it has achieved steady and significant growth travelling both east and west from the USA. The company decided to 'go international' for reasons which perhaps are unique to SM since it found that its culture, philosophy and system were broadly accepted and encouraged wider growth in other markets. Its experience justifies the decision.

SM prefers the master franchise partner (SM's word) route for international expansion. Every country is different and local knowledge is essential. SM prefers to work with existing companies rather than adopt a direct approach. It recognizes that it does not have all the answers and so remains open-minded, which enables it to retain the maximum flexibility. The master franchise route enables the operation to be established more rapidly in the target territory and also helps overcome the traditional problems which arise when setting up in a new country (Chapter 14). As will be seen below, SM is very thorough in its selection and has many procedures which have so far enabled it to avoid significant problems in its master franchise relationships. There are always worries about maintenance of standards and the effectiveness of control mechanisms but so far SM has not been confronted with a breakdown in the relationship with any master franchisee. SM recognizes the risk that the grant of exclusive rights to a territory could result in sterilization of that territory through inadequate growth.

SM contacts prospective master franchisees through:

- the national chamber of commerce;
- trade missions;
- introductions from business contacts;
- banks.

SM has developed a profile of the sort of company it is seeking and its size, and the selection process involves a number of interviews. A European prospect would be required to visit the UK and spend time with the vice president of international operations reviewing the franchise offering and meeting franchisees. This would be followed by a visit to the USA with time spent at Head Office in Chicago, then to Memphis where some of the operations are based, followed by some time in the field. The visit will finish with a meeting with the chairman of SM, who has the final word on the acceptability of the prospective master franchisee. Once approved the franchisee will have to send at least two staff members to the USA for training after which local support will be given, if needed, in the territory. The ongoing services are still provided from the SM US base, which is also the source of innovation for the total network. SM accepts that even after 32 years of international experience it is still learning how best to develop support services on an ongoing basis. In Europe specific assistance may be given through the SM subsidiaries if that is necessary and expedient. SM clearly still considers it has a long way to go in refining its already successful international operations.

Chapter 17

The British Franchise Association

The British Franchise Association Ltd (BFA), a company limited by guarantee, was incorporated in 1977. There were eight founder members.

1. Budget Rent-a-Car (UK) Ltd
2. Dyno-Rod plc
3. Holiday Inns (UK) Inc.
4. Kentucky Fried Chicken (GB) Ltd
5. Prontaprint Ltd
6. Service Master Ltd
7. Wimpy International Ltd
8. Ziebart Mobile Transport Services Ltd

Five of these companies, Budget Rent-a-Car, Holiday Inns, Kentucky Fried Chicken, Service Master and Ziebart, had clear origins in the USA. Wimpy originated in the USA, although the franchise development was devised and executed in the UK. Dyno-Rod, the idea of an American, was also developed in the UK, while Prontaprint was the only one devised and developed in the UK, by an Englishman.

The BFA has clearly defined membership criteria, and in joining all members, whether full or associate, commit themselves to comply with the terms of the following policies and procedures published by the BFA.

- The Code of Ethical Conduct
- The disciplinary procedure
- The complaints procedure

- The appeals procedure
- The terms of annual re-accreditation

(The current terms of these policies, procedures and the Code of Ethical Conduct are contained in Appendix B.) Members also agree to comply with the Code of Advertising Practice as published by the Advertising Standards Authority.

In addition, members also agree to provide to the BFA any non-confidential information relating to their franchise business, or relating to the standing and qualification of their Directors, as may be requested by an authorized official of the Association. Members also agree to grant a full-time official of the BFA, so authorized by Council, access (at reasonable times and on reasonable notice) to confidential information relating to the franchise and its standing (on the understanding that such information remains confidential to the authorized official).

The BFA offers a conciliation service, and an arbitration scheme under the auspices of the Chartered Institute of Arbitrators (see Appendix D for details) which is available to franchisors and franchisees who jointly agree to use the service. Members of the BFA also seek to comply with the spirit and intent of the *Guidelines to Best Practice* as published by the Association from time to time. While the BFA will use its best endeavours to establish the eligibility of an applicant, the onus for demonstrating that its criteria have been met on initial accreditation or re-accreditation lies finally with the applicant or member.

The BFA has two categories of membership, full membership and associate membership. Full members meet all the BFA criteria while associate members are on the whole more recent entrants to franchising who have yet to establish a proven trading and franchising record. The following four specific terms of membership apply to both associate and full members. Each term sets out a general condition which the applicant must fulfil. Each general condition is followed by examples of how applicants will ordinarily be expected to demonstrate that the condition has been met.

1. **Demonstrate that the business itself is viable**. The production of the most recent 24 months' audited accounts, including trading accounts, which show that the business is capable of being run at a profit which will support a franchised network.
2. **Demonstrate that the operating units in the business can be successfully replicated**. The production of the most recent 12 months' audited accounts for a managed arm's-length pilot operation, or a fully fledged pilot operation, which show a trading performance

at least in line with the business plan set for it and which is supported by a developed operating system.

3. **Demonstrate that the contractual terms to be offered to prospective franchisees comply with the BFA's Code of Ethical Conduct and such other terms as it may publish from time to time**. Lodge with the BFA for its accreditation, and make available for inspection by appointed franchisees, a copy of the then current agreement and any changes thereto.

4. **Demonstrate that the offer documents to be used with prospective franchisees present a full and realistic picture of the franchise proposition**. Lodge with the BFA for its accreditation, and make available for inspection by appointed franchisees, a copy of the then current offer documents and any changes thereto.

Applicants who comply with the foregoing general conditions of membership and the specific terms 1 to 4 set out above will be eligible for admission as associate members.

Applicants who comply with the following additional specific conditions will be eligible for admission as full members. Associate and full members may refer to themselves as such in their offer documents, advertising and other published material. Only full members are entitled to use the Association's logo.

5. **Demonstrate that the franchise network has developed over time with a proven trading and franchising record**. Provide a record of franchise openings, withdrawals and disputes (which required external intervention to resolve) together with evidence of the profitability of individual units and of the network as a whole sustained over a period of 24 months.

Franchise operations which form part of a larger group or company will be required to submit evidence concerning the franchised network, on a confidential basis if necessary, which is confirmed by a Director of the company as representing a true and fair picture of the franchised network. Additionally, such franchised operations will be required to provide a statement from the holding company or group confirming its intention to maintain the franchised operation for at least the forthcoming year.

Overseas franchisors franchising directly into the UK, and the master licensees of overseas franchisors, are eligible to apply for associate or full membership in respect of their UK operation. Additionally, overseas franchisors seeking only to operate through a master franchisee are eligible to apply for 'overseas membership'. To gain admission their overseas operation must comply with the general conditions of membership and the specific conditions applicable to a full member (excepting any terms of the BFA's Code of Ethical Conduct which would not be recognized by an association of similar standing in the country of origin). The BFA form of application for membership is contained in Appendix B.

The BFA now has 88 full members and 33 associate members whose business classifications are set out in Chapter 5 (pp. 45–7). The BFA also has an affiliate listing membership which permits those who provide services to franchisors to associate themselves with the BFA. The affiliates include solicitors, accountants, exhibition agencies, media and communications, surveyors, bankers, patent and trademark agents, insurance brokers, development agency and franchise consultants. The origins of the 88 members break down in the following way: 12 have clear origins in the USA and operate in the UK either directly, as subsidiaries or as master licensees; 5 have origins in overseas countries other than the USA; and 71 were devised and developed in the UK. Applying the same approach to the associate members, 1 has a clear origin in the USA and operates in the UK under master licence, and 32 were devised and developed in the UK. The trend towards the development of franchises in the UK is highlighted by these figures. One can expect this trend to continue, although many USA franchisors who have set their sights on overseas expansion see the UK as a target. There is also likely to be a greater movement of franchise systems within Europe than has so far been evident. Already there are signs that UK companies are establishing operations in continental Europe.

The BFA was originally promoted to achieve two objectives: to provide franchising with a collective voice and to perform the normal functions of a trade association; and to counteract the adverse publicity which franchising had attracted. The way in which the founder members sought to achieve these objectives are reflected in the BFA's main objectives, which are contained in the Association's Memorandum of Association. It will be noted that these objectives incorporate the definition of franchising commented on in Chapter 1. The objectives for which the Association is established are the following.

1. To promote, protect and further the interests of franchisors, that is, those who in the course of their business grant a contractual licence (a franchise) to another party (the franchisee) which:
    (a) permits or requires the franchisee to carry on during the period of the franchise a particular business under or using a specific name belonging to or associated with the franchisor; and
    (b) entitles the franchisor to exercise continuing control during the

period of the franchise over the manner in which the franchisee carries on the business which is the subject of the franchise; and

(c) obliges the franchisor to provide the franchisee with assistance in carrying on the business which is the subject of the franchise (in relation to the organization of the franchisee's business, the training of staff, merchandising, management or otherwise); and

(d) requires the franchisee periodically during the period of the franchise to pay to the franchisor sums of money in consideration for the franchise or for goods or services provided by the franchisor to the franchisee; and

(e) is not a transaction between a holding company and its subsidiary (as defined in section 154 of the Companies Act 1948) or between subsidiaries of the same holding company or between an individual and a company controlled by him.

2. Without prejudice to the generality of subclause (1):

(a) to formulate and to establish or to adopt a code or codes of proper business conduct for franchisors and to promote and to secure their compliance with the same and with high standards of business conduct generally;

(b) to consider and to advise and decide upon and generally to deal with all questions and problems connected with or concerning franchises and the carrying on of business by means of the same; and to promote acceptance of and compliance with such advice and decisions;

(c) to promote trust and confidence in the franchises granted by members of the Association;

(d) to inform and to educate in relation to franchises and on all matters concerning the same;

(e) to promote and secure co-operative action on the part of franchisors in advancing their common interests;

(f) to promote business usages and activities likely to increase the efficiency and economy of the carrying on of business by means of franchises.

The Association publishes a leaflet which describes its purposes, objectives and the means by which it proposes to achieve them. The purpose of the Association is to secure:

- the recognition and regulation of franchising in the UK;

- the recognition of the BFA in the UK and internationally as the single authoritative, self-regulating and representative body for UK franchising;

- the development and recognition of franchising within the European Community in partnership with European National Franchise Associations.

The objectives of the Association and the means by which it proposes to achieve them are set out as follows.

Self-regulation

	Objectives	Means
Standards	To protect the interests of franchisors and franchisees by developing and agreeing minimum verifiable standards for the structure and conduct of franchised businesses appropriate for the maintenance of graded categories of membership of the BFA.	Establish a Membership Committee to review and apply consistent, graded, and verifiable membership, affiliation, and exhibition entry criteria, and to establish appeals, complaints and disciplinary procedures recognized as objective and equitable by both the BFA and by appellants.
Best practice	To contribute to the development of best practice within franchising and to the guidance available to prospective franchisees, by developing a consensus within the franchising community on best practice which reflects the industry's varieties of sector and scale.	Consultation with the franchising community so as to secure editorial agreement on, and production of, a new series of booklets, *Guidelines to Best Practice*, to be published under the BFA's name and covering, in particular, the selection, engagement, management and support of franchisees by franchisors and supporting organizations.

| Liaison with government | To secure a substantial influence on the consideration by governments of legislation affecting franchising and the recognition by governments of the BFA as the self-regulating body for franchising in the UK by establishing links with UK, EC and international legislators, parliamentarians and their advisors. | (a) United Kingdom Support the all-party group of Members of Parliament on franchise development, and secure the understanding and active involvement in franchising of officials of the DTI, OFT and DOE. (b) EEC Help develop the European Franchise Federation as a body representing a European consensus amongst franchisors and establish links with appropriate EEC officials. (c) International Work with the IFA to ensure that UK and European views are properly represented internationally. |

Recognition

| Prospective franchisors and franchisees | To represent the business opportunities offered by franchising to prospective franchisors in industry and commerce, and to prospective franchisees. | The publication and promotion of information packs, the continued development of franchise exhibitions, the publication of a professional presentation pack for speakers on franchising and the role of the BFA, and the development of access routes to franchise ownership for high potential entrants on conventional career paths. |

BFA members and affiliates	To win for franchising and the BFA the active involvement and support of BFA members and affiliates.	(a) BFA members Develop the BFA's Newsletter, convention and other functions and offer a range of insurance and other services secured through the Association's purchasing and promotional potential. (b) Professional advisors Encourage the development and involvement of the BFA's affiliate group through consultative meetings and by engaging their expertise and resources on the Association's work.
The media	To secure appropriate and informed coverage for franchising by the national, local, and trade press and by national and local television and radio.	Develop and publish case studies, commissioned articles, 'facts and figures' summary, and other information to be represented to the media by the BFA, individual franchisors and professional advisors.

Development

Training services	Further the adoption of franchising and the BFA's standards of good practice by promoting and offering directly or through other agencies, training and development services, including government-sponsored programmes, for franchisors and franchisees (prospective and existing).	Design and introduce a range of training and development programmes for franchisors and their staff, on a commercial basis, and secure the support of government departments and agencies in funding the development and introduction of pre-entry training for prospective franchisees on evaluating a franchise proposition.
Research	To further the development and understanding of franchising by promoting, undertaking and disseminating research on the financing, performance, markets, staffing, profitability and control of franchised systems and units.	Form an advisory group of senior Business Educators to establish regional 'Centres of Excellence' to undertake research on franchising and introduce educational and qualification opportunities in it.
Contact services	To add value to membership of the BFA, by expanding and maintaining the opportunities for contact between members.	Develop the BFA's regional groups, conferences and seminars providing opportunities for the discussion of matters of mutual interest.

At the time of writing, the BFA is introducing new codes of procedure and conduct and strengthening its complaints and disciplinary procedures to ensure that its self-regulating functions are effective. The text of the procedure and recommendations which are contained in Appendix B have been agreed by the BFA members and adopted by the BFA Council. They should be effective by the date of publication of this book but since full implementation will require formal changes to the BFA's articles of association at an appropriate time the current status should be verified with the BFA if necessary.

Since its formation the BFA has become established as a recognized voice of franchising by the government and media. It has attracted to its membership most of the leading companies operating in franchising and many companies who are entering the field look to the BFA for guidance. The BFA also receives many enquiries from prospective franchisees who are seeking guidance. The BFA sells basic information packs to both prospective franchisors and prospective franchisees. The BFA office receives more than 10,000 enquiries a year and many of these enquiries are from those seeking advice and assistance.

The BFA also runs an extensive educational programme headed by seminars which have catered for a range of interests. Their programmes have included:

- Prospective franchisees, and 'how to evaluate a franchise'
- Is a business franchisable?
- How to set up a franchise
- International franchising
- Courses in franchising
- Franchising seminars

The BFA is particularly anxious to continue a very full programme of educational activities because ultimately the more understanding there is the greater the likelihood that standards will be raised. The more prospective franchisees understand franchising, the less likely they are to be defrauded by those who cloak their activities with an unjustified façade of franchising.

The appointment by the City University Business School in London of a Professor of Franchising is a step in the right direction and will hopefully provide a local point of interest in educational activity. The Business School has established the first full-time research centre in franchising anywhere in the world. It is sponsored by the National Westminster Bank plc. The BFA is working with the City University Business School to establish a post-graduate diploma course in franchising.

One should not assume that the BFA's progress has all been achieved without problems. Some member companies have had their difficulties and withdrawn. Some disputes between franchisor members and individual franchisees have emerged and the BFA has assisted in the resolution of these disputes without the need for costly and lengthy litigation. It would be impossible to achieve the Utopian state in which all problems and difficulties would cease to exist. There will be BFA members who fail and there will be franchisees of BFA members who are disgruntled and dissatisfied. The strength of the BFA will be dependent upon:

- its skill in investigating applications for membership so as to ensure that no questionable franchisors are admitted;
- the observance by its members of the Code of Ethics, not merely in principle, but also in spirit;
- rigorous attention to warning signs about members which emerge from complaints and criticism;
- its ability to persuade members to change undesirable practices;
- the maintenance of its reputation so that membership is an achievement which enhances the status of the member.

In its 13 years of existence the BFA has made significant progress under the full-time directorship of Tony Jacobsen, ably assisted by his wife, Dr Christine Jacobsen. Their dedication to the BFA was a significant factor in its establishment and growth. On 1 January 1984 Tony Dutfield, who was Chairman of the BFA in 1983 in his capacity as representative of Wimpy International Ltd, succeeded Tony Jacobsen as Director of the BFA. Tony Dutfield retired in 1989 and was succeeded by Brian Smart as Director. Under his direction the BFA is now moving into a new phase of development; one expects that with its sound foundations it will continue to fulfil its objectives, particularly in the light of the changes which have been made to strengthen its evaluation and re-accreditation procedure.

Chapter 18

The Franchise Consultants' Association

There have been franchise consultants for many years who offer a wide range of services, which include:

- the evaluation of a business and its suitability for franchising;
- preparing the franchise package;
- assisting with the preparation of, or even writing, the franchisor's operational manual;
- marketing the packages and selling franchises;
- ongoing development advice; and
- advising franchisees about franchise opportunities.

The mere fact that someone calls himself a franchise consultant does not mean that he is qualified to offer that service. There are no formal qualifications as a franchise consultant; the best that such a person can offer is past practical experience in franchising. It was this factor which led to seven franchise consultants joining together in 1986 to form the Franchise Consultants' Association (FAC). In this chapter, following a discussion of the role of franchise consultants, the approach adopted by the FAC will be explained.

Other than this there is the Institute of Management Consultants, which establishes qualification criteria and requires members to abide by a strict code of ethical professional conduct. Even so, if one is dealing with a member of that Institute his credentials to offer specialized advice on franchising will have to be examined.

Assuming that one wishes to employ the services of a franchise consultant, what are the criteria by which they should be judged and what safeguards are there? There are four general headings:

1. Ethical standards.
2. Experience in franchising.
3. Verification of reputation.
4. Terms and scope of employment (including charges).

ETHICAL STANDARDS

Any person who is offering consultancy services must be able to approach the client in an objective way. He must place the client's interests first and should be able to advise a client not to proceed with what he proposes, even when it means that the consultant will thereby lose business. He must avoid obvious conflicts of interest between clients and his own duties. In the author's view it is unethical for a franchise consultant who is assisting franchisors in setting up their business to hold himself out as being able objectively to advise franchisees who wish to have assistance in evaluating a franchise. The strong temptation exists to direct such a person from his area of interest to a client of the consultant, especially if the consultant is part of his client's sales force.

The question also arises as to how far the consultant should properly become involved in the selling of franchises for a client. There are a number of considerations to be taken into account, and those which apply to an employee and are dealt with in Chapter 6 should be reviewed since they apply equally to the use of an outside consultant. While a consultant may be able to give the franchisor advice on franchise marketing and on selection of a franchisee he should not be employed to sell franchises; nor should he be paid by reference to the number of franchises sold or upon a sale taking place. He should be paid for the advice given and not because he has persuaded someone to sign up. The decision about the acceptability of a franchisee must rest with the franchisor and no one else, and it must be a decision taken with pressure based solely upon the suitability or otherwise of the applicant.

In advising clients, all ethical consultants should bear in mind the codes of ethics of the FCA and the BFA. Although not every franchisor will wish to join the BFA, the Code of Ethics is a guide to proper conduct by franchisors to which no bona fide reputable franchisor should object. Indeed, if a consultant were to set himself as a target the eventual qualification for membership of the BFA by all his clients, the standards of franchising would undoubtedly benefit.

EXPERIENCE IN FRANCHISING

If a person wishes to offer himself as an adviser on franchising to others, based upon the experience he has in the field, the quality of that experience is important. Ideally he should have been involved in an actual franchise operation and at a sufficiently high level of management to have had responsibility for the operation of the franchise. Someone who is employed in a franchise company at a supervised low level of management is not capable of showing the requisite experience of franchising. After all, if the consultant is holding himself out as competent and able to advise how to go about setting up marketing and operating a franchise, it is best if he can demonstrate that he has a level of achievement which justifies his claims. There are a few questions which can be posed under this heading:

1. What is the consultant's experience in the field of franchising?
2. Is it general, or is it limited to a specific aspect?
3. Does he have experience in the particular aspect on which advice is required? (e.g. marketing image; design; retailing; distribution; fast food; practical field experience; the contents of manuals).
4. Has he actually worked in a franchisor company other than in a consultancy capacity? What was his job? To what extent was he under supervision or direction?
5. Is he a member of any professional body? What are his qualifications?

VERIFICATION OF REPUTATION

It is advisable to verify that the consultant has actually held the position which he represents that he has held. If a consultant or anyone is dishonest, that dishonesty is usually not confined to limited areas; it will be broader. One should therefore check up on the consultant as much as possible. No reputable franchise consultant will object; on the contrary, he will be pleased and proud to demonstrate his track record. He will also be pleased that one is taking such care, since if everyone did, the business opportunities for the incompetent and less reputable consultant would diminish rapidly. Additionally, the following questions should be asked:

1. Can the consultant provide you with references? You should specify the classes of persons from whom you would like to see references (e.g. bankers, accountants or solicitors) concerning his financial position and reputation. Other references could come from persons known and established in franchising who know of his reputation and background by personal contact.

2. Can, and will, the consultant make arrangements for you to select from his past and present client list and speak to your own selection about their experience with the consultant?
3. If he offers his services as a salesman of franchises (and you wish to employ him for that purpose despite the views expressed in this book), can arrangements be made for you to speak to franchisees, of your choice, to whom he has sold franchisees and also to their franchisors?

TERMS AND SCOPE OF EMPLOYMENT (INCLUDING CHARGES)

It is the prospective franchisor or franchisee who must decide upon the role which he wishes the consultant to play. The fact that one employs a consultant does not mean that the consultant is able to run the business or advise on every aspect of the business. It is the adaption of the business to the franchise method of distribution about which advice is being given. The range of services which are usually offered is set out above and a decision has to be made about the extent of the involvement of the consultant. It would be sensible to have exploratory meetings with the consultant and agree on terms of reference for his role. One should not employ a consultant unless and until those terms are clearly defined in writing. Agreement should also be reached over the method of calculating fees to be charged. A lump sum for a specific task should be avoided. It is far better to be charged an agreed hourly rate when it is easier to control the expenditure and assess the value of the work. It may be sensible initially to set a specific task for the consultant and either develop the relationship further, if the relationship works, or if not, to terminate it.

The above considerations have been taken into account by the FCA, which has established careful criteria for membership qualification and has adopted a Code of Ethics which appears in Appendix C. The membership criteria are as follows.

1. Membership is only open to individuals of more than 27 years of age who are engaged in the practice of business format franchise consultancy, and applicants must satisfy the membership committee of their suitability for membership, based on the criteria here described.
2. Applicants at some stage have been engaged at a senior executive level for a minimum of 3 years within a successful, ethical business format franchising company and have had the direct responsibility for the construction, operation and development of the company's franchise system and network.

3. Applicants should have submitted a completed application form, together with written references testifying to the completion of successful consultancy assignments concerned with the construction, operation and development of business format franchise systems for three ethical franchisors of which at least two are members of the BFA.

4. Applicants should show proof of a valid professional indemnity insurance policy for their practice of a minimum value of £100,000, or such other amount as the association from time to time may determine.

5. Applicants should give an absolute undertaking that, in the event of their application being accepted, they will at all times conduct their business in accordance with the Code of Ethics of the Association and they accept and agree to abide by the terms and conditions of membership as set out in the Memorandum and Articles of Association.

The application form, apart from dealing with issues relating to the above criteria, also poses four important questions.

1. Have you ever been insolvent, declared bankrupt, or made an arrangement with your creditors? If so, please provide details.

2. Have you been a director of a company which has gone into liquidation, or had a receiver appointed in respect of the whole or part of its assets? If so, please provide details.

3. Has any franchise company in which you have been involved been engaged in litigation? If so, please provide details.

4. Have you been convicted by the courts for any offences, other than minor traffic violations? If so, please provide details.

The Code of Ethics places a continuing emphasis upon proper professional conduct:

- to put the client's interests first (paragraph 1);
- to be independent and objective (paragraph 2);
- to respect confidentiality (paragraph 3);
- to disclose or avoid potential conflicts of interest (paragraphs 4, 8(b) and 9);
- only to undertake assignments within the member's level of competence (paragraph 5);
- to encourage clients to conform to the BFA's Code of Ethics (paragraph 7);
- not to accept payment by results for selling franchises and not to

interfere with the franchisor's judgement of prospective franchisees (paragraphs 8(a) and 8(c)).

The FCA has a disciplinary procedure built into its Articles of Association so that it can enforce the observance by its members of standards and the ethical code.

Appendix A

The NatWest–BFA Annual Survey

In each year since 1986 a survey of franchising in the UK has been commissioned by the British Franchise Association and sponsored by National Westminster Bank plc. The survey has been conducted by Michael C. Power of Power Research Associates, who has kindly provided a summary in graphical form of the information revealed over the period 1986–90 in various categories which display the progress which has been made. These figures provide a useful illustration of the trends which have become apparent. They do not necessarily answer all the questions which one might have and it is not suggested by Michael Power, the BFA or NatWest Bank that they will.

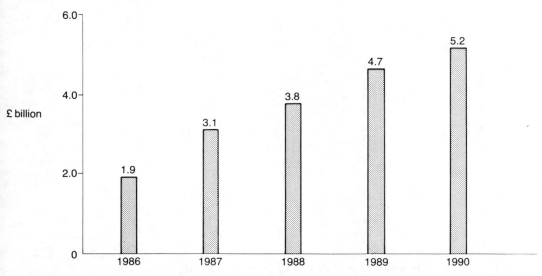

Figure A.1 *The aggregate sales by franchisors during the period 1986–90.*

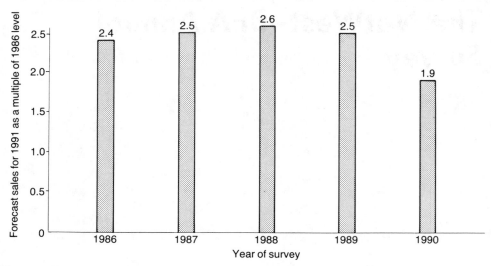

Figure A.2 *Forward forecasts. For example, in 1986 the forward forecast for 1991 suggested sales 2.4 times the 1986 level. In 1990 the forecast is less optimistic.*

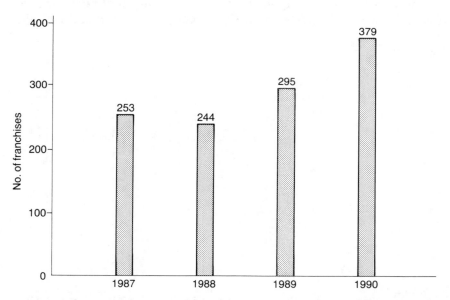

Figure A.3 *The growth in number of franchised systems identified as operating in the UK. No figure was available for 1986.*

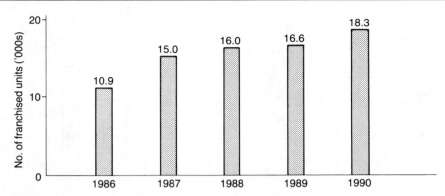

Figure A.4 *The growth in number of franchised units.*

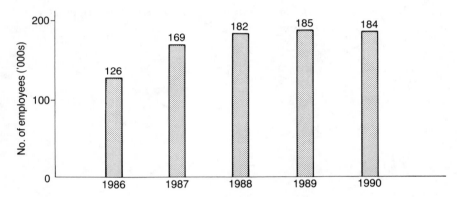

Figure A.5 *The number of employees in franchised units.*

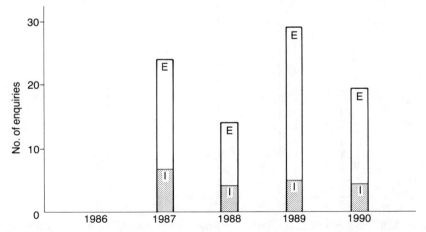

Figure A.6 *The number of enquiries received and prospective franchisees interviewed to result in the appointment of one franchisee. E, enquiries; I, interviews.*

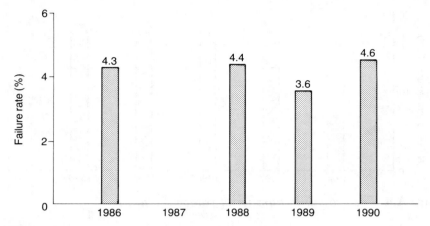

Figure A.7 *The number of individual unit failures by franchisees as a percentage of all units operating.*

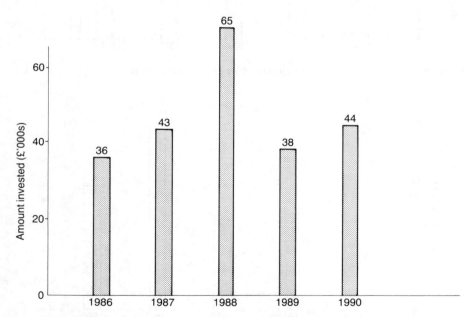

Figure A.8 *The average amount invested by franchisees to establish a franchised business. The exceptional 1988 figure may be affected by entry into the calculation of an unusual number of high-cost franchises set up during that year.*

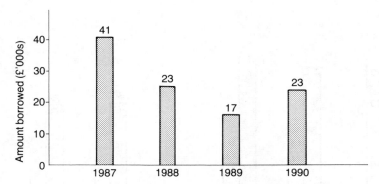

Figure A.9 *The average amount borrowed by franchisees to establish franchises. The rise in average cost in 1988 (see Figure A.8) is not matched by a rise in borrowings in 1988 or 1989, which is puzzling. The high level of average borrowing in 1987 compared with average initial outlay for that year is also somewhat puzzling. The figure for 1986 is not available.*

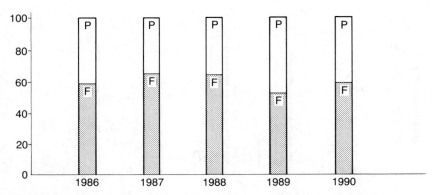

Figure A.10 *The percentage of full-time (F) employees compared with part-time (P) employees.*

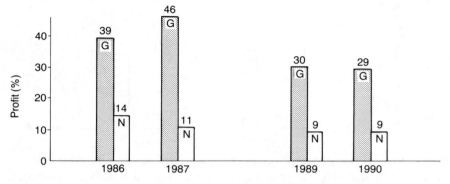

Figure A.11 *The levels of gross (G) and net (N) profits of franchisees expressed as percentages of gross sales.*

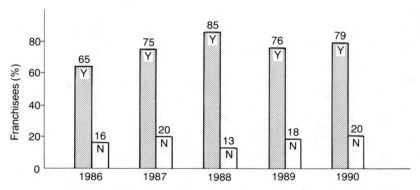

Figure A.12 *The percentage of franchisees reporting on the relationship with franchisors as being satisfactory. Y, yes; n, no.*

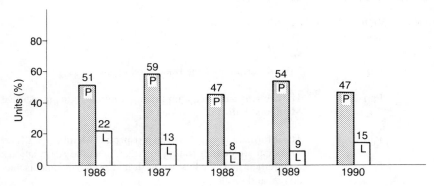

Figure A.13 *The percentage of units operating at highly/quite profitable (P) or not very/definitely not profitable (L) levels. The totals do not add up to 100% since there are some who fall between these two extremes. It should be remembered that the statistics do not reflect the development stage of franchisees who are experiencing losses while building their business.*

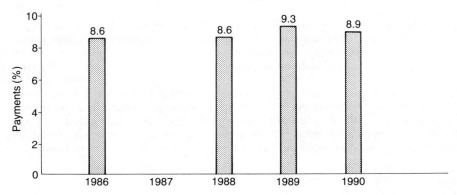

Figure A.14 *The payments to franchisors as a percentage of franchisee's sales. There are no figures for 1987.*

Appendix B

BFA: forms and Code of Ethics

APPLICATION FOR MEMBERSHIP

This Application Form has five parts :

Part 1.	Your description of the franchised business.
Part 2.	The declarations and commitments required by all prospective Members, Full and Associate.
Part 3.	The information required of all prospective Members, Full and Associate, in demonstrating that they meet the Association's requirement that their businesses should be viable, franchisable, ethical and disclosed.
Part 4.	The additional information required of prospective Full Members in demonstrating that their business has a proven trading and franchising record.
Part 5.	General Declaration.

For the purposes of Part 2 of this application you should also have received a document setting out the Codes and Procedures to which you are asked to give your commitment.

Please remember that for the purpose of Part 3 and, if it applies, Part 4, the onus is on you to provide the evidence which shows that you meet the Association's criteria. Please provide whatever information you feel is relevant.

You should have also received with this application form a copy of the Association's Purpose and Objectives. We hope this statement will be developed, as franchising develops, to meet the industry's changing needs. We hope also that you will want to play a part in the development of the Association and its work.

We would like therefore to welcome you to the Association as quickly as possible but we hope you will understand that our name and our purpose depend ultimately on the strength of our standards and the accreditation procedures that support them. Your accreditation may therefore take some time and may involve more than one exchange of correspondence between us. We hope you will bear with us during the course of these essential checks.

BRIAN SMART : EXECUTIVE DIRECTOR

APPLICATION FOR MEMBERSHIP

PART 1 : COMPANY INFORMATION

To be completed by all applicants

1. Registered Name of Applicant Company _____

2. UK Company Registration Number _____

3. Date Company Established/Incorporated _____

4. Name of Franchise (if different from 1 above) _____

5. Date of first use of the Name (if different from 3 above) _____

6. Names of Registered Directors :

Designation	Name	Date of Appointment
Chairman	_____	_____
Managing Director	_____	_____
_____	_____	_____
_____	_____	_____
_____	_____	_____
_____	_____	_____

7. Director Nominated as BFA Representative _____

8. Telephone Number _____ Fax Number _____

9. Address for Correspondence
    _____
    _____

10. Name of Parent or Holding Company _____

11. Names of Subsidiary Companies _____
    _____
    _____

12. Nature of Franchised Business _____
    _____
    _____

13. Do either your Parent, Holding or Subsidiary Companies
    act as a supplier to your business?　　Yes　　　No

14. Do any of your Directors have an interest in any
    company that acts as a supplier to your business?　　Yes　　　No

15. Have any of your Directors been convicted for theft
    or fraud, or been declared bankrupt or been a Director　　Yes　　　No
    of a company declared bankrupt?
    (If so, please enclose separately details of the convictions
    or declarations and any Certificates of Discharge.)

16. Did your company first operate through company　　Yes　　　No
    owned outlets?

17. If so, from what date?

18. Have you operated a company owned outlet as an
    arms length' pilot scheme for franchising?

19. If so, from what date (if different from 16)?

20. If not, on what date did you open the original franchised unit?

21. Number of company owned outlets operating at present

22. Number of company owned outlets achieving expected standard

23. Number of franchised outlets operating at present

24. Number of franchised outlets achieving expected standard

25. How many franchised units do you intend to open:

    in the next　　　　　　　　　in the next
    12 months?　　　　　　　　　5 years?

26. Please provide the following information (include name and address) : we will be
    seeking a reference from your Bankers.

    Bankers

    Accountants

    Auditors

    Solicitors

    Franchise Consultants (if any)

APPLICATION FOR MEMBERSHIP

PART 2 : DECLARATIONS & COMMITMENTS

This section invites you to give a commitment to procedures and codes which may be amended or developed by the Association. Such procedures and codes can only be amended or developed after full consultation with Members, Full and Associate, who, if they do not wish to continue the necessary commitments, will be afforded every opportunity to withdraw from the Association without penalty or disclosure of any kind.

To be completed by all applicants

1. The information provided in and with this application is, to the best of our knowledge, an accurate, full and fair representation of our business.

2. We agree to be bound by the Association's complaints, disputes, conciliation and arbitration procedures and any amendments thereto agreed by the Association.

3. We agree to be bound by the Association's disciplinary and appeals procedures, and to comply with any notices or instructions issued under those procedures and any amendments thereto agreed by the Association.

4. We agree to comply with Association's requirements and conditions for annual re-accreditation and any amendments thereto agreed by the Association.

5. We agree to comply with the Association's Code of Ethical Conduct and any amendments thereto agreed by the Association.

6. We agree to abide by the Advertising Standards Authority's Code of Advertising Practice.

7. We agree that we will not sell, offer for sale, or distribute any product or render any service, or promote the sale or distribution thereof, under any representation or condition (including the use of the name of a 'celebrity') which has the tendency, capacity or effect of misleading or deceiving purchasers or prospective purchasers.

8. We agree that we will not imitate the trademark, trade name, corporate identity, slogan, or other mark or indentification of another franchisor in any manner or form that would have the tendency or capacity to mislead or deceive.

9. We agree to use our best endeavours to adopt best practice in franchising as agreed and published by the Association from time to time.

10. We agree to notify the Association at the earliest possible opportunity of any material change in ownership, direction, financing, or operation of our business.

11. We agree to comply with the Association's request for copies of non-confidential information to be held by the Association, in the case of offer documents and franchise agreements, to be open to inspection by our appointed franchisees.

12. We agree to provide authorised full-time officials of the Association access to but not copies of confidential information reasonably required in accrediting or re-accrediting our company to membership but only on the basis that the conditions of employment of those full-time officials require them to maintain the confidentiality of the information to themselves alone subject on breach to their summary dismissal.

13. We agree to pass on all of our obligations as members of the Association to any Master Franchisee, Sub-Franchisee, Area Franchisee or equivalent licensee that we might appoint.

Signed _____

For and on behalf of _____

Position held _____

Date _____

This section must be signed by the Chairman or Managing Director of the company making the application.

APPLICATION FOR MEMBERSHIP

PART 3 : DEMONSTRATIONS

To be completed by all applicants

1. **VIABILITY**

   You must enclose with this application form evidence that your business is capable of selling its products or service at a profit that will support a franchised network.

   The submission of two years' trading accounts together with your audited accounts for the same period showing a business already securing, or capable of meeting a business plan to establish, a well financed and stable operation, would ordinarily be counted as sufficient evidence.

   Please list here the documents you are enclosing to demonstrate that your business is viable:

   _____

   _____

   _____

   _____

2. **FRANCHISABLE**

   You must enclose with with your application form evidence that you can successfully franchise your operation.

   The submission of the business plan for 12 months' trading and the audited accounts for either an arms length company owned pilot franchise, or a fully fledged franchise which show a trading performance at least in line with the business plan will be one part of the evidence ordinarily required here. You will also be expected to demonstrate that you have developed an operating system which enables you to pass on your "know-how" at arms length. You might do this by submitting details of, or providing access to, a copy of your operational manual and by setting out details of the training programme for franchisees.

   Please list here the documents (in addition to those provided in demonstrating viability) that you are submitting (or are prepared to give access to - marked "access only") to show franchisability.

   _____

   _____

   _____

   _____

   Please also summarise overleaf the costs you incur, on average, prior to, and including opening of, a franchised outlet.

cont/d.........

£

* Training and manual   _____

* Initial marketing operation including launch   _____

* Goods, material and equipment, if applicable   _____

* Other items - please specify   _____

Please summarise your support to franchisees ie management, technical and training resources

_____

_____

_____

3.   **ETHICAL**

The primary evidence required to show that your business has an ethical foundation is a copy of the franchise agreement currently in use. **Please provide a copy of that agreement with this application.**

We will seek references on your business from a small sample of any franchisees you already have. **Please also include a full list of their names, trading addresses, and the date of acquiring the franchise.**

4.   **DISCLOSED**

You will need to submit with this application copies of all the documents, brochures and particularly financial projections you give to prospective franchisees in advance of their signing a franchise agreement.

Please ensure you enclose copies of your offer documents.   £
Please also summarise below the information presented therein :
Cost of Franchise Package to Franchisee   _____

Initial franchise fee   _____

Franchisee's total investment (including working capital)   _____

Management service (or royalty) charge   _____

Advertising or Marketing levy   _____

Average period to establish franchise on a satisfactory basis   _____

Estimated period for franchisee to recover initial investment   _____

If you feel able to provide all the information requested in this Part 3 (and you have completed Parts 1 and 2) you are eligible for Associate Membership. As an Associate you will be able to refer to yourself as such (in a prescribed format) on your published material. You will also be eligible for the other services and discounts the Association offers.

If you also feel able to provide the evidence required under Part 4 (following) you will be eligible for Full Membership. If not please complete the general application and declaration (Part 5) at the end of this application.

APPLICATION FOR MEMBERSHIP

PART 4 : FULL MEMBERSHIP

To be completed by Full Member applicants

1. A PROVEN TRADING RECORD

You need to provide financial records to show that your franchised network is stable and profitable both for you and your franchisees. Your own audited accounts showing acceptable financial trends over an extended period will be required. We will also need to agree with you a selection of your franchisees from whom we will need to obtain trading accounts. These will be treated confidentially and in the knowledge that franchisees have an obligation to "husband" their accounts.

Please list here the series of your audited accounts enclosed with this application:

_____

_____

_____

_____

Please also provide with this application a complete list of your current franchisees (as also required under Part 3) and nominate below two franchisees from whom trading accounts can be obtained or in respect of which you are able to enclose or submit accounts (we will choose a further small selection of franchisees which we will ask you to approach for trading accounts).

(i)
_____

(ii)
_____

2. A PROVEN FRANCHISING RECORD

Please provide the following details, in confidence, covering at least two full reporting years:

	Current Year (Months)	Last Year	Year Before
(a) Franchise Starts			
(b) Franchise Failures (forced)			
(c) Franchise Withdrawals (voluntary)			
(d) Franchise Resales from (b)			
(e) Franchise Resales from (c)			
(f) Franchise disputes *			

* Only those disputes which have required intervention (through your solicitor, the franchisee's solicitor, or the Association's conciliation or arbitration schemes should be recorded).

If you have been able to provide the evidence requested in this Part 4 you are eligible for Full Membership of the Association. As a Full Member you will be able to use the Association's logo on your published material. You will also be eligible to vote at the Annual and Special General Meetings, to stand for election to the Association's Council, and to receive all services and discounts which the Association offers.

Please also complete the general declaration (Part 5) at the end of this application.

APPLICATION FOR MEMBERSHIP

PART 5 : GENERAL APPLICATION AND DECLARATION

To be completed by all Applicants

We, the applicant company declare, to the best of our knowledge and belief, that the franchise system we offer is based on sound business principles and provides a viable and ethical business opportunity for the franchisee and a genuine end-product or service for the consumer. It is our belief that the systems we operate, satisfactorily protect both the franchisee and the consumer and, accordingly, we hereby apply for membership of the British Franchise Association.

Signed _____

For and on behalf of _____

Position held _____

Date _____

The Form shall be signed by the Chairman or Managing Director of the company making the application.

CONCLUSION

Thank you for taking the time and trouble to complete this application form. Please do not forget to enclose the documents you have listed, and we have specified, in Parts 3 and 4. We appreciate the complexity of our Membership requirements but we hope you understand that it is essential in protecting the Association's name and standing - without which you would have little reason to join us.

CONSULTATIVE DOCUMENT

COMPLAINTS, DISCIPLINARY AND ASSOCIATED PROCEDURES

SUMMARY OF MAIN RECOMMENDATIONS

1. Individual disputes should be settled <u>before</u> any action is taken to judge more general questions of breaches of Membership criteria.

2. Members' obligations to use their best endeavour to resolve individual disputes should be given particular scrutiny as part of annual re-accreditation.

3. A formal conciliation scheme operating at arms-length from the Association should be introduced as a prior alternative or addition to the existing Arbitration Scheme.

4. All resolved individual disputes should be reviewed by the Membership Committee for possible breaches of Membership criteria.

5. The Membership Committee should be empowered to take disciplinary action (including precautionary action in cases of alleged serious breaches) with full Council acting as the Appeal body.

6. Disciplinary and precautionary action should include the option (not the requirement) to ask for the suspension of franchisee recruitment.

7. Where disciplinary action (but <u>not</u> precautionary action) is taken by way of suspension of franchisee recruitment, suspension of Association Membership, dismissal from membership, or otherwise, the Association should publish a notice (after appeal or a set period for appeal) setting out the company concerned and the disciplinary action taken.

3

CONSULTATIVE DOCUMENT

COMPLAINTS, DISCIPLINARY AND ASSOCIATED PROCEDURES

COMMENTARY ON MAIN CHANGES

PRIORITY FOR INDIVIDUAL DISPUTES

1.　The majority of claims of breaches of Membership criteria are associated with an individual dispute. Where the facts concerning that individual case are disputed it would be inappropriate to decide a general question of a breach of Membership criteria which was itself dependent on those facts before they had been established through the conclusion of the individual case. Thus, such individual disputes must be settled <u>first</u> in order to establish the facts on which the general question of breach is to be judged.

2.　The Membership Committee would remain free to consider the question of a breach of Membership Conditions where either:

(a)　the facts determining the breach were undisputed; or

(b)　the complainant gave a binding undertaking not to pursue any individual dispute based on the same facts.

BEST ENDEAVOURS TO RESOLVE INDIVIDUAL DISPUTES

3.　The Association's new Code of Ethical Conduct says that Members :

"should resolve complaints, grievances and disputes with good faith and goodwill through fair and reasonable direct communication and negotiation".

Complainants to the Association have sometimes suggested that franchisors have deliberately avoided conciliation or arbitration in the knowledge that the complainant cannot afford to pursue the matter through the courts.

4

4. The membership Committee therefore propose that, on Members' annual re-accreditation, they should give particular attention to the reasons why any dispute remains unresolved. If the Franchisor cannot show "best endeavour" in seeking to resolve the dispute, or adequate cause for declining arbitration, then the Membership Committee would be empowered but not obliged, to decline re-accreditation.

CONCILIATION

5. At the present time the Association's Officers seek to bring complainant and Member into "direct communication and negotiation" through repeated exchanges of correspondence. Some cases are thereby resolved quickly. The majority lead in the end to an invitation to go to arbitration which is ordinarily declined by one side or the other. The gap between attempts to resolve disputes through correspondence and the formal and legally binding Arbitration Scheme is too large. A voluntary conciliation scheme is therefore proposed involving the establishment of a panel of Full Members trained in conciliation.

6. The panel would need to be sufficiently broad to offer for each dispute a conciliator who would have no commercial interest in the dispute or its outcome. It is for that reason that it is not envisaged that Affiliates would be included. The conciliation process can end only in a mutual agreement between the parties which they have themselves reached (i.e. it is non-judgemental), or in failure to resolve the dispute. The only obligation on the parties in dispute might be to lodge a deposit with the Association to meet the conciliator's necessary expenses.

REVIEW OF BREACHES

7. The resolution of an individual dispute should not be the end of the matter, it is no guarantee that the complainant has not been "bought off" and could disguise conduct which continues to be contrary to membership criteria and which will thus, in the end, prove to be a millstone around the neck of franchising as a whole. The Membership Committee therefore proposes to review settled individual disputes as well as unresolved disputes (paragraph 4).

5

AUTHORITY FOR DISCIPLINARY ACTION AND APPEALS

8.　The Association's existing arrangements provide for the Council (or a Committee of the Council) to take disciplinary action, appeals being made to an extraordinary general meeting of Members. The latter provision is unlikely to lead to objective judgement and could easily lead to extended and possibly public lobbying.

9.　It is therefore proposed that the Council stand as the appeal body for decisions taken by the Membership Committee on their own authority. Any such appeals and the Council's consideration of them could be reported to the AGM.

10.　The subjects of complaints would have an automatic right of representation to a meeting of the Membership Committee considering for decision their case, and the right of Appeal to Council including similar rights of representation. Complainants dissatisfied with the Membership Committee's conclusions would have the right of appeal and representation to Council.

THE NATURE OF DISCIPLINARY ACTION

11.　The Association may already suspend or dismiss its Members but such action or the threat of it has only limited force over time and in promoting change. The essence of the Association's influence lies in the impact it can have on the public perception of a business.

12.　The Membership Committee therefore proposes to publish any adverse disciplinary conclusions it reaches so that the general public and other organisations dealing also with the general public in respect of that company may make their own decisions with adequate information. Although formal agreements between the Association and such organisations have been considered, they are unlikely to be realised within current legislation on the restraint of trade.

13.　Clearly Members must have confidence that the Membership Committee will discharge its responsibilities with due care, including the proposed power to seek suspension of franchisee recruitment for a fixed period both as a precautionary measure (in advance of a conclusion on a complaint of "serious" misconduct) and as a disciplinary measure in itself. The fourth part of this Consultative Document therefore sets out the steps leading up to disciplinary review (Annex A), the process of disciplinary review and the range of disciplinary conclusions (Annex B) and the categories of misconduct which relate to the disciplinary measures envisaged (Annex C).

6

COMPLAINTS, CONCILIATION AND ARBITRATION   ANNEX A

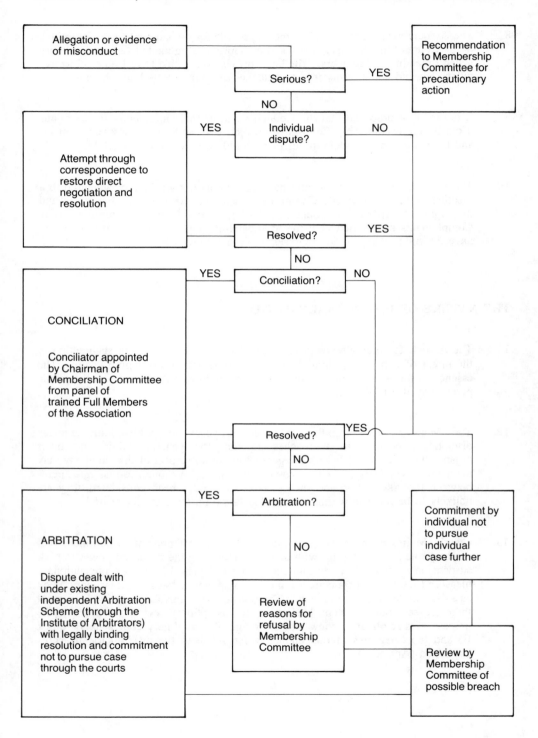

DISCIPLINARY AND APPEALS PROCEDURE

ANNEX B

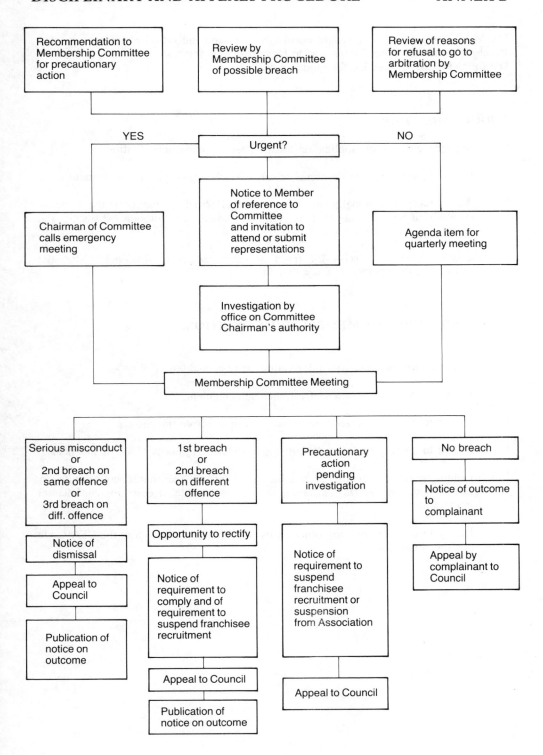

DISCIPLINARY OFFENCES   ANNEX C

The Membership Committee would decide in each case individually whether or not a breach of membership conditions was to be regarded as serious.
The following list is intended for guidance.

SERIOUS MISCONDUCT

*   Misrepresentation on application for membership or re-accreditation.

*   Failure to comply with the terms of any disciplinary or precautionary notice.

*   Action taken intentionally to, and with the effect of, jeopardising the name or standing of another member or affiliate outwith or without exhausting the disciplinary procedure.

*   Conviction of a Director for fraud or other serious professional misconduct concerning the operation of the Franchise.

OTHER BREACHES OF MEMBERSHIP CONDITIONS

*   Failure to disclose material information on re-accreditation.

*   Failure to honour the terms of a franchise agreement.

*   Failure to disclose material information to prospective franchisees.

*   Failure to comply with the Advertising Standards Authority Code of Practice.

*   Failure to comply within reasonable time and on reasonable notice with an Association request for information, or reasonable access to confidential information.

*   Failure to comply with any other terms of membership including the BFA Code of Ethical Conduct.

PRECAUTIONARY CIRCUMSTANCES

*   Failure to notify the Association of any major changes in the standing of Directors, the financial standing of the company, the circumstances of its franchisees, or the company's trading performance.

*   Evidence of insolvency.

*   Evidence of excessive franchise failures and/or withdrawals and/or sales.

*   Reasonable grounds for investigating serious misconduct.

NB : It would be open at any stage of the Complaints and Disputes procedure for the Director to recommend for the agreement of the Membership Committee Chairman, that a complaint or investigation was frivolous and should be discontinued.

ISSUE NO. 2
January 1991

BRITISH FRANCHISE ASSOCIATION

CODE

OF

ETHICAL CONDUCT

This *Code of Ethical Conduct* in franchising takes as its foundation the Code developed by the European Franchise Federation. In adopting the Code, the Federation recognised that national requirements may necessitate certain other clauses or provisions and delegated responsibility for the presentation and implementation of the Code in their own country to individual member National Franchise Associations.

The following *Extension and Interpretation* has been adopted by the British Franchise Association, and agreed by the European Franchise Federation, for the application of the *European Code of Ethics for Franchising* as presented herein by the British Franchise Association, within the United Kingdom of Great Britain and Northern Ireland.

BRITISH FRANCHISE ASSOCIATION

CODE OF ETHICAL CONDUCT : EXTENSION AND INTERPRETATION

This *Extension and Interpretation* forms an integral part of the *Code of Ethical Conduct* adopted by the British Franchise Association and to which its members adhere.

APPLICATION

1.   This *Code of Ethical Conduct* forms part of the membership agreement between the British Franchise Association and its member companies. It does not form any part of the contractual agreement between franchisor and franchisee unless expressly stated to do so by the franchisor. Neither should anything in this Code be construed as limiting a Franchisor's right to sell or assign its interest in a franchised business.

CONFIDENTIALITY

2.   For the generality of this *Code of Ethical Conduct*, 'know-how' is taken as being as defined in the European Block exemption to Article 85 of the Treaty of Rome. However, for the purposes of Article 3.4 of the *European Code of Ethics* it is accepted that franchisors may impose non-competition and secrecy clauses to protect other information and systems where they may be reasonably regarded as material to the operation of the franchise.

CONTRACT LANGUAGE

3.   Article 5.2 of the *European Code of Ethics* reflects the requirement in certain European member states that franchise contracts be written in the language of that member state. The requirements of national and European law are pre-eminent but franchisors should seek to ensure that they offer to franchisees contracts in a language in which the franchisee is competent.

CONTRACT TERM

4.   In suggesting in Article 5.4 of the *European Code of Ethics* that the minimum term for a franchise contract should be the period necessary to amortize a franchisee's initial investment, it is recognised

     (a)   that franchise contracts are ordinarily offered for a uniform term within a network;

     (b)   that for a minority of the largest franchise opportunities amortizing the initial investment may not be a primary objective for the franchisee. In such cases the objective should be to adopt a contract period which reasonably balances the interests of the parties to the contract.

     (c)   that this section could be subject to national laws concerning the restraint of trade and may need to be met through renewal clauses.

CONTRACT RENEWAL

5.   The basis for contract renewal should take into account the length of the original term, the extent to which the contract empowers the franchisor to require investments from the franchisee for refurbishment or renovation, and the extent to which the franchisor may vary the terms of a contract on renewal. The overriding objective is to ensure that the franchisee has the opportunity to recover his initial and subsequent investments and to exploit the franchised business for as long as the contract persists.

ADOPTION

6.   This *Code of Ethical Conduct* comprising this *Extension and Interpretation* and the *European Code of Ethics for Franchising* was adopted by the British Franchise Association, replacing its previous *Code of Ethics* on 30th August 1990, subject to a transitional period for full compliance ending 31st December 1991. During the transitional period members of the Association are nonetheless required to comply at least with the *Code of Ethics* previously in force.

EUROPEAN CODE OF ETHICS FOR FRANCHISING

P R E F A C E

The European Franchise Federation, EFF, was constituted on 23rd September 1972.

Its members are national franchise associations or federations established in Europe.

The EFF also accepts affiliates, ie non European franchise associations or federations, and other professional persons, interested in or concerned with franchising. Affiliates have no voting rights and cannot be appointed officers of the EFF.

The objects of the EFF are, among others, the ongoing unbiased and scientific study of franchising in every respect, the co-ordination of its members' actions, the promotion of the franchise industry in general and of its members' interests in particular.

The EFF also comprises a Legal Committee, composed of two lawyers from each national member association or federation and highly qualified in franchise matters.

The EFF has, furthermore, installed a Franchise Arbitration Committee which is at the disposal of parties preferring to submit their disputes to the latter's determination.

The evolution and the ever growing importance of franchising in the EC economy as well as the EC Block Exemption Regulation for franchise agreements, entered into force on 1st February 1989, prompted the EFF to revise its existing *Code of Ethics*.

This *Code of Ethics* is meant to be a practical ensemble of essential provisions of fair behaviour for franchise practitioners in Europe, but not to replace possibly related national or EC law.

This *Code of Ethics* is the end-product of work carried out by the European Franchise Federation and its member associations (Austria, Belgium, Denmark, Germany, France, Italy, the Netherlands, Portugal and the United Kingdom) in conjunction with the Commission of the European Community. It shall replace the previous *European Code of Ethics* as well as all national and regional Codes existing at that time in Europe.

By subscribing to the EFF, its members accept the *European Code of Ethics* and undertake not to delete or amend it in any way. It is, however, recognised that national requirements may necessitate certain other clauses or provisions and, providing these do not conflict with or detract from the Code and are attached to the Code in a separate document, permission to do this will not be withheld by the EFF.

By adhering to the EFF its members commit themselves to impose on their own members the obligation to respect and apply the provisions of this *Code of Ethics for Franchising*.

1

EUROPEAN CODE OF ETHICS

FOR FRANCHISING

1. DEFINITION OF FRANCHISING

Franchising is a system of marketing goods and/or services and/or technology, which is based upon a close and ongoing collaboration between legally and financially separate and independent undertakings, the Franchisor and its Individual Franchisees, whereby the Franchisor grants its Individual Franchisees the right, and imposes the obligation, to conduct a business in accordance with the Franchisor's concept. The right entitles and compels the individual Franchisee, in exchange for a direct or indirect financial consideration, to use the Franchisor's trade name, and/or trade mark and/or service mark, know-how(*), business and technical methods, procedural system, and other industrial and/or intellectual property rights, supported by continuing provision of commercial and technical assistance, within the framework and for the term of a written franchise agreement, concluded between parties for this purpose.

(*) "Know-how" means a body of non patented practical information, resulting from experience and testing by the Franchisor, which is secret, substantial and identified;

-   "secret", means that the know-how, as a body or in the precise configuration and assembly of its components, is not generally known or easily accessible; it is not limited in the narrow sense that each individual component of the know-how should · be totally unknown or unobtainable outside the Franchisor's business;

-   "substantial" means that the know-how includes information which is of importance for the sale of goods or the provision of services to end users, and in particular for the presentation of goods for sale, the processing of goods in connection with the provision of services, methods of dealing with customers, and administration and financial management; the know-how must be useful for the Franchisee by being capable, at the date of conclusion of the agreement, of improving the competitive position of the Franchisee, in particular by improving the Franchisee's performance or helping it to enter a new market.

-   "identified" means that the know-how must be described in a sufficiently comprehensive manner so as to make it possible to verify that it fulfils the criteria of secrecy and substantiality; the description of the know-how can either be set out in the franchise agreement or in a separate document or recorded in any other appropriate form.

2

2. GUIDING PRINCIPLES

2.1   The Franchisor is the initiator of a franchise network, composed of itself and its Individual Franchisees, of which the Franchisor is the long-term guardian.

2.2   **The obligations of the Franchisor:**

The Franchisor shall

-    have operated a business concept with success, for a reasonable time and in at least one pilot unit before starting its franchise network;

-    be the owner, or have legal rights to the use, of its network's trade name, trade mark or other distinguishing identification;

-    shall provide the Individual Franchisee with initial training and continuing commercial and/or technical assistance during the entire life of the agreement.

2.3   **The obligations of the Individual Franchisee:**

The Individual Franchisee shall

-    devote its best endeavours to the growth of the franchise business and to the maintenance of the common identity and reputation of the franchise network;

-    supply the Franchisor with verifiable operating data to facilitate the determination of performance and the financial statements necessary for effective management guidance, and allow the Franchisor, and/or its agents, to have access to the individual Franchisee's premises and records at the Franchisor's request and at reasonable times;

-    not disclose to third parties the know-how provided by the franchisor, neither during nor after termination of the agreement;

2.4   **The ongoing obligations of both parties:**

Parties shall exercise fairness in their dealings with each other. The Franchisor shall give written notice to its Individual Franchisees of any contractual breach and, where appropriate, grant reasonable time to remedy default;

Parties should resolve complaints, grievances and disputes with good faith and goodwill through fair and reasonable direct communication and negotiation;

3

3. RECRUITMENT, ADVERTISING AND DISCLOSURE

3.1 Advertising for the recruitment of Individual Franchisees shall be free of ambiguity and misleading statements;

3.2 Any recruitment, advertising and publicity material, containing direct or indirect references to future possible results, figures or earnings to be expected by Individual Franchisees, should be objective and capable of verification;

3.3 In order to allow prospective Individual Franchisees to enter into any binding document with full knowledge, they shall be given a copy of the present *Code of Ethics* as well as full and accurate written disclosure of all information material to the franchise relationship, within a reasonable time prior to the execution of these binding documents;

3.4 If a Franchisor imposes a Pre-contract on a candidate Individual Franchisee, the following principles should be respected:

- prior to the signing of any pre-contract, the candidate Individual Franchisee should be given written information on its purpose and on any consideration he may be required to pay to the Franchisor to cover the latter's actual expenses, incurred during and with respect to the pre-contract phase; if the Franchise agreement is executed, the said consideration should be reimbursed by the Franchisor or set off against a possible entry fee to be paid by the Individual Franchisee;

- the Pre-contract shall define its term and include a termination clause;

- the Franchisor can impose non-competition and/or secrecy clauses to protect its know-how and identity.

4. SELECTION OF INDIVIDUAL FRANCHISEES

A Franchisor should select and accept as Individual Franchisees only those who, upon reasonable investigation, appear possess the basic skills, education, personal qualities and financial resources sufficient to carry on the franchised business.

5. THE FRANCHISE AGREEMENT

5.1 the Franchise agreement should comply with the National law, European community law and this *Code of Ethics.*

5.2 The agreement shall reflect the interests of the members of the franchised network in protecting the Franchisor's industrial and intellectual property rights and in maintaining the common identity and reputation of the franchised network. All agreements and all contractual arrangements in connection with the franchise relationship should be written in or translated by a sworn translator into the official language of the country the Individual Franchisee is established in, and signed agreements shall be given immediately to the Individual Franchisee.

5.3   The Franchise agreement shall set forth without ambiguity, the respective obligations and responsibilities of the parties and all other material terms of the relationship.

5.4   The essential minimum terms of the agreement shall be the following:

-     the rights granted to the Franchisor;

-     the rights granted to the Individual Franchisee;

-     the goods and/or services to be provided to the Individual Franchisee;

-     the obligations of the Franchisor;

-     the obligations of the Individual Franchisee;

-     the terms of payment by the Individual Franchisee;

-     the duration of the agreement which should be long enough to allow Individual Franchisees to amortize their initial franchise investments;

-     the basis for any renewal of the agreement;

-     the terms upon which the Individual Franchisee may sell or transfer the franchised business and the Franchisor's possible preemption rights in this respect;

-     provisions relevant to the use by the Individual Franchisee of the Franchisor's distinctive signs, trade name, trade mark, service mark, store sign, logo or other distinguishing identification;

-     the Franchisor's right to adapt the franchise system to new or changed methods;

-     provisions for termination of the agreement;

-     provisions for surrendering promptly upon termination of the franchise agreement any tangible and intangible property belonging to the Franchisor or other owner thereof.

6.   THE CODE OF ETHICS AND THE MASTER-FRANCHISE SYSTEM

This *Code of Ethics* shall apply to the relationship between the Franchisor and its Individual Franchisees and equally between the Master Franchisee and its Individual Franchisees.   It shall not apply to the relationship between the Franchisor and its Master-Franchisees.

Appendix C

Franchise Consultants' Association Code of Ethics

The Code of Ethics and professional conduct which all members of the Association agree to abide by requires each member:

1. To put the interests of his client above his own interests and to observe the highest standards of competence and integrity.
2. To adopt an independent and objective attitude towards his clients so as to ensure that advice given is based upon an impartial consideration of the facts of objectives.
3. To respect the confidentiality of all information received concerning a client's business and not to disclose or permit disclosure of any such information without the client's prior permission in writing.
4. To disclose to his clients or prospective clients any personal or financial interests or other material circumstances which might in any way influence his work for that client, in particular and without derogating from the generality of the foregoing:
   (a) any directorship or significant interest in any business which competes with the client;
   (b) any financial interest (or other benefit) in goods or services recommended by the consultant for use by the client;
   (c) any personal relationship with any individual in the client's employment;
   (d) the existence but not the name of any other current client of the consultant whose business may compete with the client's;
   (e) not to advise any franchisee or prospective franchisee in relation to the scheme or opportunity offered by any franchisor for whom the consultant has acted or whose business may compete with that of a client or former client of the consultant,

and to inform the client immediately of any change in or the coming into existence of any such circumstances as are referred to.

5. To accept only those assignments which he is qualified and competent to undertake.

6. To provide clients with a written proposal of the terms of reference, including fees or fee basis for any assignment.

7. To encourage each client to conduct his business in such a manner as complies with the Code of Ethics of the British Franchise Association whether or not such client is a member of that association.

8. In relation to the marketing and sale of franchises:
   (a) not to accept payment based upon the achievement of sales of franchises;
   (b) not to offer advice to prospective franchisees where he is advising a franchisor in relation to the marketing and sale of a franchise where any conflict of interest may arise; and
   (c) to offer advice and assistance to any franchisor in connection with his sales and marketing efforts but not in any way to interfere with the final judgement of his client as to whether or not to accept a prospective franchisee into his network.

9. To refrain from inviting an employee of a client to consider alternative employment (an advertisement in the media is not considered to be an invitation to any particular person).

10. To abide by any decisions made by the Association as to the scope and meaning of the Code.

Appendix D

The Chartered Institute of Arbitrators British Franchise Association Arbitration Scheme

RULES (1987 EDITION)

These Rules provide an inexpensive and informal method of resolving disputes between franchisors and franchisees which the parties cannot resolve amicably between themselves. The Rules will apply to arbitrations commenced under the Scheme after 1 May 1987.

INTRODUCTION

1. In these Rules:
   (i) 'The Institute' shall mean the Chartered Institute of Arbitrators of 75 Cannon Street, London EC4N 5BH.
   (ii) 'The BFA' shall mean the British Franchise Association of 75a Bell Street, Henley on Thames, Oxon. RG9 2BD.
   (iii) 'The Arbitrator' shall mean a sole and independent arbitrator appointed by the President or Vice-President of the Institute in an arbitration under this Scheme.
   (iv) 'The Franchisor' shall mean a company, firm or person who is the franchisor in respect of any agreement under which a dispute arises and is referred to arbitration under this Scheme.
   (v) 'The Franchisee' shall mean a company, firm or person who is the franchisee in respect of any agreement under which a dispute arises and is referred to arbitration under this Scheme.
   (vi) 'The costs of the arbitration' shall mean the total of the Arbitrator's fee and expenses, the Institute's administrative

costs, and the cost of any independent examination under Rule 8(iv).

(vii) 'Costs in the reference' shall mean legal or other costs incurred by a party in connection with an arbitration under this scheme.

2. The Franchisee may apply for arbitration under this Scheme as an alternative to court action. He must decide at the outset whether to use this Scheme or to seek his remedy through the Courts. If he uses this Scheme he will not be able to start again with court action, because awards made under the Scheme are final and binding on the parties.

3. (i) Application for arbitration must be made on the prescribed application form which may be obtained from the BFA.

(ii) A deposit of £150 is payable by each party when an application for arbitration is submitted. These deposits may be refunded or may be applied in whole or in part towards defraying the costs of the arbitration, at the discretion of the Arbitrator.

4. (i) The application form should be completed by the Franchisee and returned to the BFA with the Franchisee's deposit.

(ii) The BFA will then refer the application form to the Franchisor, to be completed and returned to the BFA with the Franchisor's deposit.

(iii) The Franchisor's agreement to arbitration is necessary for the application to proceed. The BFA will encourage the Franchisor to agree, but he is not obliged to do so. If the Franchisor does not agree to arbitration, he is required to inform the BFA accordingly. The Franchisee's deposit will be returned and he may seek his remedy through the Courts.

INSTITUTION OR ARBITRATION PROCEEDINGS

5. Provided the application form has been signed by both parties and is accompanied by the appropriate deposits, it will be forwarded to the Institute by the BFA with the deposits.

6. The arbitration commences for the purposes of these Rules when the Institute despatches to the parties written notice of acceptance of the application. The notice sent to the party making the claim will be accompanied by a claim form.

PROCEDURE

7. General
    Subject to any directions issued by the Arbitrator the procedure will
    be as follows:

    (i)   The Franchisee is required, within 28 days of receipt of the
          claim form, to send the completed form, together with any
          supporting documents in duplicate, to the Institute. The
          Franchisee is also required to notify the Institute at this stage if
          he requests an attended hearing. (The Franchisee may not,
          without the consent of the Institute, claim any amount greater
          than specified on the application for arbitration.)

    (ii) A copy of the claim documents will be sent by the Institute to
          the Franchisor who is required, within 28 days of receipt of the
          documents, to send to the Institute his written defence to the
          claim together with any supporting documents in duplicate.
          (The Franchisor may include with his defence a counterclaim in
          respect of any balance of payment alleged to be due on the
          contract between the parties, or in respect of any other matter
          notified to the Franchisee before the Franchisee applied for
          arbitration.)

    (iii) A copy of the defence documents will be sent by the Institute to
          the Franchisee, who is entitled to send to the Institute any
          written comments which he wishes to make on the defence
          documents within 14 days of their receipt. Such comments
          should be in duplicate. They must be restricted to points arising
          from the Franchisors' defence, and may not introduce any new
          matters or points of claim.

    (iv) The President or a Vice-President of the Institute, at such stage
          of the proceedings as the Institute considers appropriate, will
          appoint the Arbitrator, taking into account the nature of the
          dispute and the location of the Franchisee's trading premises.
          The Institute will notify the parties of the Arbitrator's
          appointment.

    (v)   The Arbitrator may in his discretion call the parties to an
          attended hearing, and shall do so if the Franchisee has so
          requested in accordance with Rule 7(i). Subject to that, the
          Arbitrator will make his award with reference to the documents
          submitted by the parties.

    (vi) The Arbitrator will send his award to the Institute for
          publication. Unless the parties otherwise agree the Arbitrator's
          reasons will be set out or referred to in his award.

(vii) The Institute will notify the parties when it has received the award from the Arbitrator, and will also notify the Franchisor of any costs of the arbitration payable under Rule 11. On payment of such costs, the Institute will publish the award by sending copies to each of the parties. In normal circumstances the Institute will also send a copy to the BFA.

(viii) After publication of the award the Institute will return the Franchisee's deposit in whole or in part if so directed by the Arbitrator.

(ix) Unless directed otherwise in the award, within 21 days of despatch by the Institute to the parties of the copy award, payment shall be made of any monies directed by the award to be paid by one party to the other. Such payment shall be made by the party liable direct to the party entitled, and not through the Institute.

(x) If either party has sent original documents in support of its case to the Institute that party may within six weeks of publication of the award request the return of those documents. Subject to that, case papers will be retained by the Institute and may in due course be disposed of in accordance with the Institute's policies from time to time.

8. Supplementary

(i) Attended hearings shall be conducted in private at a place to be notified to the parties by the Institute on behalf of the Arbitrator, who shall use his best endeavours to take into account the convenience of the parties. The parties may attend a hearing in person or be represented by an employee (but not a person employed to give legal advice) unless the Arbitrator agrees they may be legally represented.

(ii) The Arbitrator may, through the Institute, request the provision of any further documents/information which he considers would assist him in his decision. If the documents/information are not supplied to the Institute within such time as it prescribes, the Arbitrator will proceed with the reference on the basis of the documents already before him.

(iii) Where in the opinion of the Arbitrator it is desirable, he may make an examination of the subject matter of the dispute without holding an attended hearing. The parties shall afford the Arbitrator all necessary assistance and facilities for the conduct of this examination.

(iv) Where, in the opinion of the Arbitrator, it is desirable that independent examination of the subject matter of the dispute be made, an independent examiner will be appointed by the Institute to make such examination and a written report thereon. The parties shall afford the examiner all necessary assistance and facilities for the conduct of this examination and copies of his report shall be sent by the Institute to the parties who will then be given 14 days in which to comment thereon.

(v) If the Franchisee does not furnish his claim within the time allowed and does not remedy his default within 14 days after despatch to him by the Institute of notice of that default, he will be treated as having abandoned his claim. The arbitration will not proceed and the Franchisee's deposit will be returned less the Institute's administrative costs to date. The Franchisor's deposit will be returned in full.

(vi) If the Franchisor does not furnish his defence within the time allowed and does not remedy his default within 14 days after despatch to him by the Institute of notice of that default, the Arbitrator will be appointed and subject to any directions he may give the dispute may be decided by him by reference to the documents submitted by the Franchisee.

(vii) If a party fails to attend or be represented at an attended hearing the Arbitrator shall either make an award *ex parte*, or, if he so decides, adjourn the hearing for such time as he considers reasonable and serve notice on the party failing to attend that the matter will be dealt with *ex parte* at the adjourned hearing.

COSTS

9. The Franchisor shall be responsible for the costs of the arbitration less any amount which the Arbitrator may order the Franchisee to pay but the Franchisor shall in any event be responsible for not less than two-thirds of the costs of the arbitration. Where the arbitration is conducted on the basis of documents only, the Arbitrator will not order the Franchisee to pay a contribution to the costs of the arbitration in excess of £150 unless he considers the application by the Franchisee to have been frivolous or vexatious. In the case of an attended hearing, if the costs of the arbitration exceed £300 the Arbitrator may order the Franchisee to pay part of such excess in addition to the sum of £150 (or more if he considers the application frivolous or vexatious).

10. The Arbitrator may order the Franchisor to pay some or all of the Franchisee's costs in the reference and may order the Franchisee to pay up to one-third of the Franchisor's costs in the reference.

11. The Franchisor agrees to pay to the Institute within 14 days of notice from the Institute of receipt of the award and of the amount of the costs of the arbitration, a total sum equal to the costs of the arbitration less the amount of any deposits ordered to be utilized towards payment of the fees and expenses. This is without prejudice to any right which the Franchisor may have to recover from the Franchisee a contribution to the costs of the arbitration or the Franchisor's costs in the reference, ordered in the Arbitrator's award to be paid by the Franchisee.

MISCELLANEOUS

12. The arbitration shall be conducted in accordance with the law of England.

13. The Institute reserves the right to appoint a substitute Arbitrator if the Arbitrator originally appointed dies or is incapacitated or is for any reason unable to deal expeditiously with the dispute. The parties shall be notified of any substitution.

14. Awards made under the Scheme are final and binding on 9 the parties. Subject to the right of a party to request the Institute to draw the Arbitrator's attention to any accidental slip or omission which he has power to correct, neither the Institute nor the Arbitrator can enter into correspondence regarding awards made under the Scheme.

15 Rights of application or appeal (if any) to the Courts are as under the relevant Arbitration Acts provided that the special costs provisions of the Scheme shall not apply to any such application or appeal.

16. Neither the Institute nor the Arbitrator shall be liable to any party for any act or omission in connection with any arbitration conducted under these Rules save that the Arbitrator (but not the Institute) shall be liable for any conscious or deliberate wrongdoing on his own part.

The Chartered Institute of Arbitrators
International Arbitration Centre
75 Cannon Street
London EC4N 5BH
Telephone: 071–236 8761
Telex: 893466 CIARB G

THE CHARTERED INSTITUTE OF ARBITRATORS
BRITISH FRANCHISE ASSOCIATION ARBITRATION SCHEME

APPLICATION FOR ARBITRATION

To: The Chartered Institute of Arbitrators
    (to be submitted through the British Franchise Association)

1. . . . . Franchisee

  of . . . . Phone: . . . .

                         and

  . . . . Franchisor

  of . . . . Phone: . . . .

Hereby apply to the Chartered Institute of Arbitrators for the following dispute to be referred to arbitration under the Rules of the British Franchise Association Arbitration Scheme for the time being in force for determination by an arbitrator for that purpose by the Institute.

2. The dispute has arisen in connection with the following:

  . . . .

  . . . .

  . . . .

  . . . .

(NOTE: Only an outline is required here to enable the dispute to be identified by the parties. The Franchisee will be asked to submit his specific claim in detail as soon as the arbitration request has been accepted by the Institute.)

3. We, the parties to this application, are each in possession of the current (1987) Rules of the Scheme. We agree to be bound by these Rules (or any amendment thereof for the time being in force that may be notified to us) and by the Award of the arbitrator appointed to determine the dispute.

4. A cheque for the sum of £150* in respect of the Franchisee's deposit, and a cheque for the same amount in respect of the Franchisor's deposit are enclosed.

   We agree to the disposal of these deposits in accordance with the Rules of the Scheme.

   Signed .... Date ....
          (Franchisee)

   Signed .... Date ....
          (Franchisor)

   * Cheques should be in favour of:
     'The Chartered Institute of Arbitrators'

Index

Notes BFA is used as an abbreviation for British Franchise Association. 'f' or 't' after page numbers denote figure or table respectively.